ARMAGEDDON

ALSO BY DICK MORRIS

Bum Rap on American Cities

Behind the Oval Office

The New Prince

vote.com

Power Plays

ALSO BY DICK MORRIS AND EILEEN McGANN

Off with Their Heads

Rewriting History

Because He Could

Condi v. Hillary

Outrage

Fleeced

Catastrophe

2010: Take Back America

Revolt

Screwed

Here Come the Black Helicopters

Power Grab

ARMAGEDDON

How Trump Can Beat Hillary

DICK MORRIS

EILEEN McGANN

Humanix Books
www.humanixbooks.com

Armageddon

Copyright © 2016 by Humanix Books
All rights reserved
Humanix Books, P.O. Box 20989, West Palm Beach, FL 33416, USA
www.humanixbooks.com | info@humanixbooks.com

Library of Congress Cataloging-in-Publication Data

Names: Morris, Dick, author. | McGann, Eileen, author.
Title: Armageddon : How Trump Can Beat Hillary / Dick Morris, Eileen McGann.
Description: West Palm Beach, FL : Humanix Books, 2016.
Identifiers: LCCN 2016003143 (print) | LCCN 2016013325 (ebook) | ISBN 9781630060589 (hardback) | ISBN 9781630060596 (e-book) | ISBN 9781630060596 (E-Book)
Subjects: LCSH: Presidents—United States—Election, 2016. | Republican Party (U.S. : 1854–) | United States—Politics and government—2009– | BISAC: POLITICAL SCIENCE / Government / Executive Branch. | POLITICAL SCIENCE / Political Process / Leadership.
Classification: LCC JK526 2016 .M67 2016 (print) | LCC JK526 2016 (ebook) | DDC 324.973/0932—dc23
LC record available at http://lccn.loc.gov/2016003143

Cover Photo: Visions of America, LLC / Alamy, FEE9ME, FEEBAG

Interior Design: Scribe, Inc.

Humanix Books is a division of Humanix Publishing, LLC. Its trademark, consisting of the words "Humanix" is registered in the Patent and Trademark Office and in other countries.

ISBN: 978-1-63006-058-9 (Hardcover)
ISBN: 978-1-63006-059-6 (E-book)

Printed in the United States of America
10 9 8 7 6 5

Contents

Preface

ARMAGEDDON:

a: the site or time of a final and conclusive battle between the forces of good and evil

b: the battle taking place at Armageddon

c: a vast decisive conflict or confrontation

THE ULTIMATE BATTLE TO save America lies straight ahead of us: it's an American Armageddon, the final crusade to defeat Hillary Clinton.

Donald Trump is the Republican warrior who will lead the charge. Trump is a fearless and formidable candidate whose brash, straight-talking anti-Washington message resonated with voters and catapulted him to the Republican nomination.

And he can go all the way to the White House. He can beat Hillary Clinton. He can triumph at Armageddon and save America.

Trump is a natural, the polar opposite of the ultimate insider and highly choreographed Hillary Clinton. Relying on his own impeccable instincts, he never needed political consultants to tell him what to do or what to say. He never needed to poll test issues or talking points to figure out where he should stand. He is the master of his own style and his own message. And that message is that America can be great again—in so many ways. It worked because he fervently believed it and so did the voters. A Pew Foundation survey in mid April 2016 found that 57% of America want "America First" and support solving our own problems before helping other countries. Trump tapped into that growing national feeling and championed what Americans believe in.

There has been a dramatic shift in American politics that was manifested in 2016. The debates and the primaries in both parties demonstrated vividly that the major fault line in our politics is not that which separates the Right from Left, but that which divides insiders from outsiders. The assumptions, outlook, policies, and proposals that emanate from Washington, DC, are routinely suspect and are almost totally at variance with those that animate the rest of the country. This sweeping unity against the establishment created the perfect storm for the Trump candidacy. Voters are in wholesale rebellion against Washington, DC, and the leaders of both parties. They don't trust them, they don't like them, and they want them out.

This phenomenon was seen in smaller Armageddons in the primaries of both parties. Along with Trump, insurgents Sanders, and Cruz challenged the dynastic establishment candidates, Clinton and Bush. The Republican voters actually succeeded in upending their ruling class and embraced change by choosing Trump. But not the Democrats. When the voices of change within the Democratic Party implored it to adopt new directions and turn away from a corrupt recycling of the past, the Empire would not permit it, smashing the insurgency beneath the bludgeons of money and power— and, instead, choosing the ultimate tired establishment candidate,

Hillary Clinton. The Democrats opted for same old, same old Washington retread.

But Donald Trump embodied the change that voters have demanded and heralded a new age in our politics. In a field of immensely talented candidates, he surged to the top. Rather than take advantage of his enormous wealth and widespread contacts throughout the business and corporate worlds, he financed his own campaign and actually spent less than his rivals by capitalizing on the unique power of his message to win. Its never been done before.

Trump intuitively grasped that Americans were tired of ideological debates. They demanded a change from Obama's radical policies, but had no wish to go back to the purely conservative agendas of either George W. Bush or even Ronald Reagan.

Often criticized by his opponents for straying from a strictly conservative viewpoint, Trump realized that voters wanted an American message—a candidate who would put America first and who would see to it that America won. And that's what he did.

On trade, immigration, jobs, the economy and a host of issues, Trump carved out a platform that embraced nationalism as it transcended ideology.

If Donald Trump has a precedent in our politics, it is not Ronald Reagan—it is Dwight Eisenhower. Building on a brilliant record of success outside the political system, Ike overturned the choice of the ideologues in his own party—who had favored Senator Bob Taft of Ohio—and then consigned to history the liberal Democratic programs of FDR and Truman. He staked out a different set of priorities—job growth, American economic dominance, reluctance to get involved in foreign wars, a balanced budget, and an emphasis on rebuilding America's infrastructure to make way for decades of economic growth.

Sound familiar? Those are the exact priorities of Donald Trump. His pragmatic, get-it-done approach will sharply contrast with the straitjacketed liberal dogma of Hillary Clinton and will appeal to Americans of every ideological stripe. Eisenhower was a historic commander and Donald Trump is an innovative CEO. Both had clear visions for America and refused to be mired in endless process, committees, or commissions.

Unlike Hillary, and like Ike, Trump escapes distracting details and focuses on objectives—the big picture—using talented people around him to map out the path to achieving them. He will get things done.

While Hillary will try to govern by achieving consensus among the special interest groups who have bought and paid for her and her party. Trump will barge forward, ignoring their self-interested pleadings, and act for the best interest of the country.

If he wins, Trump will be the first candidate in modern political history who takes office without being beholden to any major donors or corporate puppeteers. The Washington insiders do not understand him, cannot control him, and fear his advent. And because of that, they attack him.

Some say Trump is ill-informed. He's not. We've spent many hours with him, discussing a range of complex issues. His knowledge is uncanny, particularly for someone who has never served in government. He has a laser-like ability to distill complicated issues into a profound message. But he sees things differently—and more clearly—than those promoting the status quo. That's his strength.

Since his campaign began last June, he's repeatedly confounded the insular political and media establishment as he coalesced voters in every state—without a campaign apparatus, without a PAC, without campaign fundraising, and without the backing of the Republican elite.

The mainstream media refused to take him seriously and sometimes even ridiculed him, but the voters didn't. He inspired them. They quickly understood what the chattering class—those journalists and political consultants who consider themselves to be the self-appointed arbiters of who should be elected—could not comprehend. Those near-sighted insiders eagerly awaited Trump's implosion. They were still waiting when it was all over.

In fact, it wasn't until the very moment that Trump clinched the nomination after winning Indiana, *The New York Times*, for example, refused to credit the possibility that Trump would be the eventual nominee. But after eleven months of churning out anti-Trump stories that belittled his ability to succeed and discounted the dramatic inroads he was making, the *Times* looked in the rear view mirror and finally noticed that they had missed the signals all along that Donald Trump would win the Republican nomination.

In August 2015, Nate Silver, the numbers guru, had assessed Trump's chances of winning the nomination at only 0–20%. But on the day after Trump triumphed in Indiana, Silver suddenly saw the light and wrote: "We basically got the Republican race wrong."

They sure did.

And so did the rest of the political establishment. They didn't recognize the allure of Donald Trump and his no-nonsense message that emotionally connected him to grassroots voters who were sick of career politicians. Why didn't they get it? Because he wasn't one of the insider regulars who they feel so comfortable supporting. And so they didn't notice that he was changing the very nature of political campaigns in America.

Trump debunked the Washington consensus, taking it apart, piece by piece. The conventional wisdom had assured us that trade deals were good for America. Free trade was just what Adam Smith had in mind. The danger was protectionism and isolationism. Bill Clinton sold us trade deals with China and the North American Free Trade Agreement (NAFTA), Republicans lined up for free trade deals with Peru, Chile, and Colombia, and then Obama brought in the Trans-Pacific Partnership (TPP), to continue the consensus.

But Donald Trump ripped them all apart as bad deals negotiated by "political hacks" and "losers."

"We don't have our best and our brightest negotiating for us," he thundered. "China is killing us. Mexico is killing us. Japan is is killing us. Everybody is beating us."[1] Voters found it refreshing to hear this unparalleled and irreverent critique that mirrored their own thinking.

Meanwhile, on the Democratic side, Bernie Sanders was also shattering the establishment's consensus. Even as Trump attacked trade deals as bad for the American worker, Sanders ripped them as corporate welfare and hit hard at companies that outsource their manufacturing. From the Left and from the Right, a common agenda emerged: Against one-sided trade deals, opposed to Wall Street bailouts, and in favor of limits on the surveillance powers of the National Security Agency (NSA).

The two primaries will leave in their wake a new set of issues, a new consensus for change in American politics. In Trump, we have a candidate committed to these new ideas that are struggling to emerge in opposition to the old establishment wisdom and its epitome, Hillary Rodham Clinton.

Trump has sounded a new call in our politics: To put America first. He sweeps aside a politics based on ideology and demands that our programs and policies be rooted in advancing and improving the lives of our citizens. Like Voltaire's Candide, we are so fed up with ideology that we have all concluded that we must cultivate *our* garden first and foremost.

This book explores how to use this new issue consensus to defeat Hillary and elect an apostle of change.

And Trump can do it.

Is he a flawless candidate? Of course not. There is no such thing, His candor and rhetoric have definitely caused problems. When he called for building a wall on the Mexican border and halting Muslim immigration he outraged people inside and outside the U.S. Former Mexican president Vicente Fox—a former client of Dick's—used coarse and vulgar language to describe Trump's proposal for the Mexicans paying for his fence. Trump tweeted a demand for an apology. Months later, on the day after Trump became the nominee, Fox apologized and invited him to come to Mexico and discuss the problems. Most likely, Trump will meet with Fox and other Mexican leaders and come up with an acceptable plan. That's how he operates.

He's insulted his opponents. But, once they're no longer a threat, he speaks highly of many of them.

Trump's aggressive, bare knuckle style is something new to Washington insiders. But to put it in context, think about this story about the difference between Washington and New York told to us by Bob Crandall when he was President and Chairman of American Airlines.

"New York is tough but it's not mean," he said. "Washington is mean but it's not tough." Bob explained: "In New York, they'll fight you for every dime, insult you, disparage your motives. But, afterwards, once the deal is done, they'll go out to dinner with you and expect to have a pleasant evening. In Washington, they won't be tough negotiators. They'll give you whatever you want to your face and then, as you leave, shoot you in the back—just because it is so much fun to see you die."

Trump will undoubtedly offend people again. His free wheeling style, his spontaneity, and his strong opinions probably make that inevitable. It hasn't cost him many votes and his supporters either agree with him on some of his more controversial statements or will vote for him even if they don't. And, sometimes, like in the case of Vicente Fox, his targets ultimately agree with him.

But he's learning to moderate some of his more extreme comments and he's a quick study. He's a tremendously talented and unique candidate who has captured America and can seriously challenge Hillary Clinton.

But even with such a talented candidate, we need a go-for-the-jugular strategy to defeat her.

That's what this book is about.

Armageddon is here.

Introduction

On January 20, 2017, at precisely noon, our worst nightmare may, unfortunately, come true. Because at that moment, as the president-elect places a hand on the Bible to swear the oath of office before the chief justice, a smiling Hillary Clinton may be sworn in as the 45th president of the United States.

President Hillary Rodham Clinton.

Think about it. She could be our commander-in-chief in less than a year. We cannot let that happen. We've got to stop her. And Donald Trump, more than anyone else, can do that. He can win in November and save America from a Hillary presidency, save us from the ruination of America as we know it. Because we know all too well what a Hillary Clinton presidency would look like: four long years of another bizarre Clinton administration, featuring the Clintons' signature style of endless drama, interminable scandals, constant lies, blatant cronyism and corruption, incessant conflicts of interest, nepotism, pathological secrecy, hatred of the press, his and her enemies lists, misuse of government power, inherent paranoia, macho stubbornness, arrogant contempt for the rule of law, nutty gurus, and thirst for war. Those will be the disastrous and unavoidable hallmarks of a Hillary regime.

But there's even more to brace ourselves for: The inmates will be running the asylum. Just imagine Bill Clinton, Chelsea Clinton, Tony Rodham, Roger Clinton, Hillary guru Sidney Blumenthal (along with input from his anti-Semitic son, Max), the wacky David Brock, Huma Abedin, Terry McAuliffe, and all of Hillary's favorite Wall Street hedge fund guys crawling around the White House and determining our national policies. That's what we'll be seeing: Hillary's unqualified and greedy cronies and her money-grubbing family members running our country, ruining our country, as they frantically pad their pockets.

And coupled with that, there will be a resumption and expansion of the corrupt institutional intertwining of the Clinton Foundation and its donors with every government policy imaginable. Hillary did an outstanding job in rewarding the foundation's foreign and corporate donors with State Department largesse. But there's so much more to grab.

Think about the billions in energy contracts, grants from the Commerce Department or the Agriculture Department, and the myriad stores of other government money just waiting for the Clinton pirates. They've been thinking about it and undoubtedly have a long list and will be ready to pounce on day one.

For years, journalists have been discussing "Clinton fatigue." Nowhere is that exhaustion more evident than in the past year. After revelation after revelation about the corruption at the Clinton Foundation and the cozy relationship between its corporate and foreign government donors and the Clinton State Department, we're drained. The corruption is so vast, so pervasive, so complicated that we can't keep up with it. But remember, Bill and Hillary had no problem keeping track of the complexities of their vast unscrupulous activities.

After 55,000 Clinton e-mails were released and we've listened to her endless implausible explanations, we're worn out. We're suffering from advanced Clinton fatigue. We're becoming immune to the Clintons' conduct. It's too overwhelming. That's understandable, but that's exactly what they want us to do—just forget about it. After Hillary's negative publicity after her "dead broke" comment, Bill Clinton commented that it was lucky to be happening so far ahead of the election. He was counting on the memory fading. But we can't afford to do that. If we do, it will simply enable them to continue their corrupt conduct and embolden them to go even further.

That's why Donald Trump is the perfect opponent for Hillary. He's tough, he's audacious, and he's focused. He's not at all intimidated by the Clintons or their slimy investigators. In fact, it's just the opposite: the Clintons fear Trump's attacks and know that he won't hesitate to bring up anything—from corruption issues to Bill Clinton's women. Look at how effortlessly Trump injected the issue of Bill Clinton's womanizing into the campaign. The media had been silent on Bill's women for more than a decade. All that changed when Hillary accused Trump of being a sexist. The move backfired and gave Hillary a very clear idea of how Trump would unhesitatingly— and effectively—use her vulnerabilities against her. Within minutes of her comments, Trump countered by claiming Hillary was married to a sex abuser: "She's got one of the great women abusers of all time sitting in her house, waiting for her to come home for dinner."[1] Suddenly the mainstream media was loudly discussing Bill's dalliances. At the same time, a number of the women who had accused Bill of hitting on them came forward, including one who had made an accusation of rape. Even *The New York Times* and *The Washington Post* were suddenly covering Trump's comments about Bill Clinton's sordid history. How did Hillary react to Trump's dragging Bill's sex life into the campaign? Well, Bill and Hillary were suddenly very quiet about Donald Trump. No more barbs about Trump. So we know what to expect and so should Hillary: Donald Trump will never back away from a daily barrage of statements aimed at exposing Hillary's history or corruption and incompetence and Bill's history of sexual abuse and misconduct. Stay tuned.

Trump understands what's at stake if she wins.

If Hillary makes it to the White House, her misuse of government agencies to achieve her goals will be widespread. For those who were incensed by the illegal targeting of conservative groups by Obama's IRS, expect more of the same, just on a much larger scale. Hillary Clinton will heartily embrace any scheme that targets her enemies and weakens the Citizens United decision. The Clintons love to zero in on their enemies: investigating and targeting those who cause personal and political problems for them. They take no prisoners. Over the years, they've created their own private FBI, the detectives who find dirt on their political opponents, personal critics, and, especially, on Bill's women. We named them the Clinton's "Secret Police" in our columns in 1997. And they've been successful. Consider this: Every one of the women who accused Bill Clinton of sexual abuse while he was in the White House was eventually audited by the IRS. What a coincidence!

It seems that someone was watching out for Bill. Taylor Branch's audio diaries of his contemporaneous interviews of Bill Clinton in the White House revealed that Bill offered information about Paula Jones on October 2, 1997, just two weeks after Paula Jones and her husband received the audit notice. According to Branch, "Clinton said 'I didn't have anything to do with it, and I know nobody around here had to do with her getting audited by the IRS.'" (Of course not!) "'But,' he said, 'independently, it stands to some reason, she doesn't have any visible means of support and is always traveling around and driving a new car, no job, so forth.'"[2] It stand to reason? Hmmm. Wonder where Bill got that information about someone he claimed to know nothing about? From his private investigators, maybe? Yes, definitely. Terry Lenzner, head of the IGI Group recalled in his memoir that he "was hired by Clinton's defense lawyers to look into Mrs. Jones background . . ." using public documents, especially as it related to her "economic situation and sources of income."[3] So what public documents would tell them what Paula Jones's income was? Tax records and employee records are not public documents. Bank records are certainly not public documents. So how did they find out that Paula Jones was not regularly employed? (and how did they miss that her husband was employed and making $37,000 a year?) Did the IRS help out? And, speaking of the IRS, was it really ever the practice of the IRS to audit people because they get new cars? That's definitely a new criteria for an audit—undoubtedly a special one for women who cause trouble for a president. It's obvious that two things were going on here: first, someone was trying to dig up dirt on Paula Jones and, second, someone then got that information to the right folks at the IRS and an audit was initiated. How convenient that it was right in the middle of litigation by Jones against the President. In fact, Jones received notice of the audit several days after she refused a settlement offer from Clinton. But how would the sitting President know what was going on inside the IRS? Maybe he had a friend there. The IRS Commissioner at the time is still in the Clinton circle. Margaret Richardson, now sits on the Board of Directors of the front company headed by Hillary's conniving brother, Tony Rodham, Gulf Coast Funds Management, LLC, which tries to get visas for wealthy Chinese after they "invest" in their firm. And, no surprise, Gulf Coast was alleged to have tried to use political power to get the visas. (See more about this in Chapter 1, Section on Nepotism.)

So look for more of the same. The only thing that will be different in *this* Clinton White House is that all of Hillary's notorious personality traits and appalling instincts—the very ones we've seen on display all too often as First Lady, senator, and secretary of state—will intensify as she is emboldened by the unfathomable hubris that will animate her as soon as she assumes her status as president of the United States and leader of the free world: arguably, the most powerful and important person in the world. Nothing will stop her.

And she will definitely feel that power in every bone of her body and exercise it effortlessly and ruthlessly. Her audacity will know no boundaries. Watch. Because once Hillary is safely ensconced on her Oval Office throne—the one that she believes she was destined to occupy—all bets are off. The real Hillary will suddenly reemerge. And that is not a pretty picture.

But it gets even worse. Combine her unmistakable character flaws with her zealous commitment to four more years of Obama's unconstitutional, overreaching, anti-American, prointernational, socialist policies that will annihilate the core of America, and you get a feel for exactly what a Hillary administration would be like. It would be one we might never recover from.

Hillary's first act would be to throw open our borders and change America's demographics so drastically that we become a welfare-dependent third-world country, and she would be guaranteed a second term with the help of the new citizens. The federal tax balance would tip even further, permanently decreasing the number of people paying income taxes while permanently increasing the number of people dependent on government entitlements—the tax eaters. It's inevitable. If elected, Hillary Clinton will sink us further into the same death spiral of soaring taxes and expanding welfare that has doomed welfare states from Greece to Detroit. And President Hillary would flex her muscles to show the world just how tough she is, and start a war to prove it.

The prospect of a Hillary Clinton presidency is bad enough. But to confront it after eight years of steady erosion of our freedoms, economic liberty, incomes, national prestige, rule of law, and fiscal integrity, would be cataclysmic. We can't let it happen. That's why the 2016 presidential election is truly America's Armageddon—the ultimate and decisive battle between us and those who have no regard for our Constitution and who are determined to deform our system of checks and balances. These are the same forces that want to institutionalize the excesses of the Obama administration and grant him the equivalent of a third term. But we've had enough of him in his two destructive terms, haven't we?

Here's the problem: He won't really go away if Hillary is elected because his harebrained policies will happily live on in Hillary's priorities. In a few short months, Hillary Clinton could be sitting in the Oval Office following the Obama playbook he will carefully leave behind for her. That's one big reason why the thought of a Hillary presidency is a frightening one—so frightening, in fact, that it becomes nothing less than a virtual call to arms, a summons to join the ultimate crusade to save America and stop Hillary Clinton.

This is a contest with one overarching goal: to defeat Hillary Clinton and send her back to Chappaqua on a one-way train, once and for all. We can do it. We have to act. We have a candidate who can win and who can expose her for what she is. This battle is truly our last chance to save the America we love.

The battle lines are clearly drawn. On the one side are those who want to see America flourish as a free market economy that minimizes government intrusion in our lives and our economy. On the other side, the Hillary side, are the forces that embrace Obama's ideal of a huge, expensive federal government that becomes more and more involved in every aspect of our private lives and our businesses and intrusively regulates everything from what we say to what we eat to how we make a living and run our businesses. The ultimate nanny state with Nanny Hillary in charge.

The stakes couldn't be higher; the choices couldn't be more stark. Those of us who value our liberty and our history understand that Hillary Clinton must be stopped from using the Oval Office and the power of the presidency to systematically destroy the very essence of our culture, our values, and our way of life. Because that's what she intends to do.

Make no mistake about it: if Hillary Clinton is elected president, she will embrace and advance the Obama worldview, which means the end of the America we know and love, the end of our sovereign democracy, and the transformation of our political system to a European modal of social welfare. Look at Europe to see how Obama's social model of welfare dependency doesn't work. Look at Greece. Look at Detroit. That's where Hillary is headed.

A Hillary presidency would be a triumphant and audacious expansion of Obama's destructive economic and social programs, his failed foreign policies, his unconstitutional power grabs, and his divisive leadership. That's what we have to look forward to. And it would be an expansion from which we might never recover. Once our borders are open and our demographics are changed, there's no going back. A vote for Hillary Clinton will be a vote for more of Obama and a vote for a very different America—an ultimately unrecognizable America. An America we don't want, can't afford, and must defeat. We can do that. We still have a chance to defeat Hillary, to close the door on Obama. But time is running out.

So How Do We Stop Her?

This book is a manual on how the Republicans can resoundingly beat Hillary Clinton and win the 2016 election. It's a radical blueprint for winning that battle in an effective but unorthodox way. We have to stop playing by the old ground rules. We can't rely on tired strategies that worked in the past. They're obsolete and won't work anymore.

Barack Obama has changed America in such fundamental ways that we now need to revise our game plan and adapt to those elemental alterations in our body politic. We used to be one united country whose politics were dominated by an overriding consensus, but Obama has divided us into two armed camps glaring at each other across a no-man's land. Obama has all but eliminated the swing voter. You are either part of Obama's coalition—at its core a demographic grouping—or you are against him. If you are born black or Latino, if you are a single mother, LGBT, or under 35, you are part of the Obama Party. And now he seeks to make it the Hillary Party.

For 20 years, our politics have revolved around the pursuit of the swing voters. But it won't work today. There aren't enough of them. They've become an endangered species. Once our GOP candidates obsessively pursued moderate Republicans and conservative

Democrats, chasing down every last one and tempering their views to appeal to the center, but we cannot do that anymore. Instead, we have to win the same way Obama won: by drawing clear distinctions between the candidates and the issues, embracing what Reagan called "bold colors, not pale pastels."

In this election, the bold colors are the urgent issues that are important to voters from both ends of the spectrum—the Progressives on the Left and the Conservatives on the Right. Surprisingly, they have a lot in common. After all, they both live in the same country. Anyone who looks around will inevitably come to the conclusion that our economy is broken and that we are in trouble. The Left and the Right both see the rapacious Wall Street bonus boys draining our wealth. They both decry trade deals that close our factories and throw our people out of work. The Left and the Right are worried about the government's intrusive surveillance. Both ends of the political spectrum agree that our schools are failing. So some of the highest priority issues for both the Left and the Right are the same.

Ralph Nader made the case for this potential affinity between the emerging political insurgencies from the Left and the Right in his most recent book, *Unstoppable: The Emerging Left-Right Alliance to Dismantle the Corporate State*. Although Ralph Nader may be an unexpected source for conservative political strategy, his prescient point is that the real enemy of those on the Left and the Right who want dramatic change are not each other but the political and corporate establishment. As the change agents on the Left and the Right realize the potential of uniting against their common enemy, in what Nader calls "converging," the potential for new voters expands.

So how do we beat Hillary? First, the tactics: The heavy stakes in this election require us to fight like a boxer, using both hands to deliver powerful jabs that cripple our opponent and, at the same time, provide a strong defense. So we need to develop a right jab and a left hook.

We need to use the right jab to deliver powerful jabs that rock Hillary and resonate with our party base. But we also need the left hook to come around alongside the right jab to appeal to the Sanders voters and knock Hillary out. The right jab will pound out our core issues: the fight against terrorism, the need to restrict immigration, the importance of freeing our economy of taxes and regulations that stymie economic growth, and the urgent need to preserve private health care. Those are the issues that will drive our base to the polls. And Donald Trump is the one who will be able to bring back those who have stayed home in the past, numbed by cynicism into apathy.

But we need to battle with our left hook, too, to enlist our friends who supported Bernie Sanders in a common struggle to hold Wall Street accountable, end crony capitalism and corporate welfare, revise and junk one-sided trade deals that throw workers out of their jobs, and limit intrusive government surveillance of honest, good people. Most of the Sanders vote shares more than just ideology in common. They detest Hillary. These voters distrust her and see her as an essentially dishonest and as an opportunistic liar who will say anything to get elected and then do as she pleases. And Donald Trump will repeatedly reiterate the reasons for the rampant distrust of Hillary that she cannot conceivably overcome.

In an April 6, 2016, McClatchy/Marist survey, one-quarter of the respondents said they would never vote for Hillary in November. That's a lot of potential voters to join our cause. Throughout the campaign, Donald Trump offered a critique of the multiple trade agreements that Hillary has supported that fits perfectly into Sanders's criticism of income inequality. It is these deals, the Left and the Right know, that are driving down the middle class. We can unite with the Left in explaining how trade agreements that benefit the business establishments of both parties simultaneously impoverish American workers.

We also need to appeal to workers to split with their party dogma in favor of amnesty for illegal immigrants. In the elite Manhattan living rooms, the wealthy and those who Peggy Noonan calls the "protected" can talk about how we are a nation of immigrants, but the blue-collar mechanic who struggles with stagnant wages knows that it is competition from illegal immigrants who are willing to work for almost nothing that binds him to a third-world level of compensation.

Those establishment liberals who dwell in the "bicoastal" global economy may rail against the old "trickle down" theory, but the insurgents on the Left and the Right grasp that quantitative easing (QE), flooding Wall Street banks with cash, is the ultimate in trickle-down economics. The Trump and Sanders voters all realized that when the Federal Reserve showered Wall Street banks with $3.7 trillion in cash, they were simply paying off their friends and feathering the nests to which they would flock when their government service ends. There was never a real chance that the money would filter down to small businesses struggling to stay afloat.

The Left insurgents also know that there are only two candidates who rejected Wall Street money because they did not want to be beholden to them: Bernie Sanders and Donald Trump. Sanders will be gone, but his message about Hillary Clinton remains: Hillary is the darling of Wall Street, and those huge contributions come with a very long string attached. Donald Trump will continue that line of attack, pounding the message every day. And it will work. Because voters know that the candidate who has received the most direct campaign contributions from Wall Street folks is Hillary Clinton—in addition to more than $15 million they gave to her PACs.[4] They get it that these donations were on top of the $3 million in Wall Street speaking fees in the first two years since she left office. And then there's Bill's $8 million from the big Wall Street banks.[5] So there's lots of room for common ground. Let's find it and make it work to our advantage.

It's important to remember that Hillary Clinton is a deeply flawed candidate. And no one recognizes that like Donald Trump. Scandal follows her everywhere because she is corrupt and dishonest, and she believes, understandably, that she can get away with anything. After all, up until now, she has done just that. Like political acrobats, Hillary and Bill have successfully dodged scandal after scandal ever since they entered public life. Not because they were innocent, but because a variety of circumstances made it impossible to prove *beyond a reasonable doubt* that they were guilty. After all, sometimes guilt or innocence hangs on what the definition of "is" is.

But we forget that almost every single scandal in the Bill Clinton White House was caused by Hillary: Travelgate, Whitewater, Filegate, her amazing windfall in the commodities futures market, the Health Care Task Force's illegal secrecy, the household furniture and gifts taken from the White House to Chappaqua, Vince Foster's suicide, Webb Hubbell's disgrace—all Hillary scandals. Even many of the problems with Bill's women were seriously exacerbated by Hillary. When Paula Jones, who accused him of making sexual overtures, offered to settle her suit for no money, no apology, and no admission by Bill, Hillary wouldn't let him take the deal. Why not? Because Paula wanted Bill to say that he sent a trooper to invite her to his room. Even though the invitation could have been innocuous, Hillary was determined not to give credibility to an article in the right-wing *Spectator Magazine* that accused Bill of using troopers to arrange his illicit dates.

Bill, cowed, followed Hillary dictates, and the Jones suit went on and on. Ultimately, it led to his perjury, the revelation of the Lewinsky affair, his impeachment, his criminal misdemeanor conviction, his disbarment, and his disgrace. It also cost the Clintons almost $1 million. But Hillary was spared the embarrassment of an implication that Bill had cheated on her. The Clinton White House pardon scandal was largely Bill's doing, but Hillary played a role there too. The FALN, a Puerto Rican terrorist group that bombed the Capital and Fraunces Tavern, killing four civilians, never even asked for a pardon of any sort and suddenly saw their sentences commuted.

Why? Because Hillary needed the Latino support for her New York senate race. Likewise, a Hasidic group successfully lobbied Hillary to get her husband to pardon key leaders in their community. He did— after she arranged a meeting with President Clinton for their supporters. And then, of course, her brothers were paid huge sums of money to lobby the president to pardon their jailed clients, including one of the biggest crack dealers in the country. Again, Bill bowed to Hillary's wishes. Just as once all roads led to Rome, so all scandals lead to Hillary. And after the White House years, the scandals continued. Hillary's and Bill's speaking fees, the Benghazi cover-up, and her use of a private e-mail server all riveted our attention.

For decades, people have wondered about the Clinton marriage. Dick believes that it was a real romance that gradually became a marriage of convenience by two business partners. But who knew that it would become a RICO, a virtual racketeering organization? Bill ran around like a bag man collecting a staggering $221,139,516 in speaking and consulting fees that he deposited in his joint bank account with Hillary, while his wife, the secretary of state, reciprocated by doing favors for foreign governments. Do the Russians want to own 20% of the US uranium supply? Does the dictator of Kazakhstan want international approval? Does Dubai want to attract foreign investment? No problem. Just invite Bill to give a speech and, presto, you have Hillary's State Department working 24/7 for you—and even organizing an event at the State Department for the top 100 CEOs in America to meet the business community in the U.A.E.

What are friends for?

Bill and Hillary seem to have gotten away with it all. But did they? The constant drumbeat of scandal, caused by their addiction to skating right up to the line, has left a deep legacy of distrust and dislike by American voters. Hillary trumpets the fact that after all of the investigations, she has never actually been convicted of anything, or even indicted. But as Mark White, former governor of Texas, once told Dick about his predecessor John Connally, he "taught us all the difference between not guilty and innocent." So have Bill and Hillary. If Hillary escapes indictment after the FBI investigation of her misuse of her e-mail at the State Department, will she learn her lesson, draw in her horns, and walk the straight and narrow? If you ask, you don't know Hillary.

The threat and fear of punishment is intended to deter the offender from repeating the prohibited conduct. But in Hillary's case, evading the punishment, once again, will have the opposite effect—it will embolden her. It will be the final vindication of her lifelong certainty that the rules don't apply to her, that by having a thick skin and, perhaps, no superego, she can make it through anything. The famous quote from Shakespeare's Hamlet, "Conscience doth make cowards of us all," has nothing to do with Hillary. Hillary is animated by a deep sense of entitlement. She feels herself to be so superior in morality to mere mortals that rules and laws don't bother her. They're for other people.

When Dick called Hillary in 1997 to report that he had heard that Special Prosecutor Kenneth Starr was near to indicting her, she responded, "He wouldn't dare!" And she believes that. She's different; she's special. Nobody would dare try to make her accountable for her conduct. If she dodges another bullet, she will definitely know that she can get away with anything. Meanwhile, her credibility has taken a big hit. A Quinnipiac poll in the summer of 2015 found that 61% of the respondents felt that Hillary was not "honest and trustworthy," while only 34% felt she was.

Hillary even lied about lying! Asked by CBS reporter Scott Pelley whether she always tells the truth to the American people, she pondered the question. "Mmmhmmm." Finally she offered a strange response. It was not a yes or no. Instead, she said that she "does her best to level with the American people." What the heck does that mean? You are either honest with people or not. There's no such thing as doing your best to be honest. It was vintage Hillary. You could almost see her brain whirling and her paranoia overtaking her. Does he have something on me? Is he going to trick me and get me to say yes, when he has proof of a lie? Time to play it safe and block any opportunity, so she left it with doing her best to be honest.

Message for Hillary: Your best isn't good enough.

When asked to explain why nearly two-thirds of Americans find her to be dishonest and untrustworthy, Hillary says it has nothing to do with her and routinely blames it on the Republicans. Her rationale is that the Republicans have told such horrible lies about her for so long, that voters believe them. Let's hope so. But despite her decades of scandal, she is not in jail or even on her way. So will these attacks matter? Damn right they will. Each hit has taken a chunk out of her armor and made her more vulnerable and less believable. "Mmmhmmm."

Donald Trump will exploit the rampant distrust of Hillary every single day. He's already calling her "Hillary the Crook." This pet name evokes the worst of Hillary and we'll be hearing it from now until November. It's like a Rorschach test—each time Trump says it, every voter can conjure up the meaning for themselves. (And there's so much to choose from!)

The Democratic Party's Civil War

The nomination contest between Hillary Clinton and Bernie Sanders has been nothing less than a civil war, splitting the Democratic Party and publicly shattering its unity. Even as Hillary closes in on the nomination, the party's grassroots is in full revolt against the establishment, embodied by Hillary Clinton. The privilege, entitlement, and corruption that she and Bill have manifested by taking $153 million in speaking fees from major special interests makes her the epitome of corruption, the poster child for the establishment.

The outing of the covert and illicit liaison between the Democratic Party and Wall Street has dramatically shattered the faith of the average Democratic activist in their party's leaders. Hilary Clinton's millions in speakers fees from Wall Street and her refusal to release the transcripts of her speeches to Goldman Sachs have fueled the anger of the Sanders voters, who rightfully connect the dots and see the quid pro quos that are lurking out there—and still due.

This discord in the Democratic Party has not been merely a personal repudiation of Hillary Clinton; it challenges the very essence of the Democratic Party and what it claims to stand for. The grass roots are fed up. A revolt is in progress. Even as Hillary proceeds to do battle with us in November, the rifts that have surrounded her party are not about to heal by themselves. The Sanders voters are not going away. Hillary's futile attempts to scare the party's base with lurid warnings about the evil Republicans won't be enough to bring them back into the fold. Remember what happened in 1968 when the Democratic Party was last ripped apart by its young college activists challenging the leadership. Back then, it was the students protesting the war in Vietnam. Led by Bobby Kennedy and Eugene McCarthy, they attacked President Lyndon Johnson and the party's candidate, Hubert Humphrey. The establishment won. But the kids stayed home and Richard Nixon won the election. That's what may be happening here. All the king's horses and all the king's men cannot put the Democratic Party together again.

But the Democratic civil war holds opportunity for us in November only if we exploit it—only if the Republicans stand on the same ground as Bernie Sanders did in the primaries. We must pick up where he left off in his critique of Hillary and the sell-outs who comprise her party's leadership.

Count on Donald Trump to do that.

Hillary Would be Obama's Third Term

The 22nd Amendment to the Constitution limits presidents to two terms. But history is full of men who reached their eighth year in the White House and sought to install their favored successor to extend their power for four more. Andrew Jackson had Van Buren. Theodore Roosevelt had Taft. FDR had Truman. Reagan had Bush. Now Obama seeks to have a figurative third term through Hillary.

She may not have been his first choice. Rumor has it that he would rather his successor were to be his VP, Joe Biden. But Hillary will do. Whatever the personal friction between Bill and Barack, Hillary can be counted on to follow Obama's agenda faithfully. To the letter. So the question is: Are we about to grant Obama a third term? We have a moral duty to protect America from that future, to protect our families from that future. Let's do it together.

We've already seen what eight years of Obama has done to us at home as well as to our standing in the world. Four more years would permanently expand Obama's massive assaults on our national psyche, our national culture, and our national reputation. It has to end. November 8, 2016, will be our Armageddon, our last battle to stop Obama, to stop Clinton, and to stop the advent of socialism. Our last battle to save America. If we don't change the power structure by throwing the Democrats out of the White House in November, we are unquestionably doomed to Obama's third term.

We've seen a preview of what to expect in the future. Already, Hillary Clinton has grabbed on to every last one of Obama's catastrophic policies and, in most cases, suggests expanding them. They're two peas in a dangerous pod. Even during the Democratic primary, Obama has shown his preference for Hillary and brazenly commented on an FBI investigation that he admits he knows nothing about, but dismisses to help Hillary. It's a mutually beneficial political deal. He supports her and she agrees to protect his legacy. That won't be a big problem for Hillary because she sincerely embraces Obama's warped vision. Let's get rid of them both.

We need you to enlist and join the ultimate battle, the war to stop Hillary Clinton once and for all. Yes, we're all weary. The battles of the past eight years of the Obama presidency have sapped our strength. But we are not dead, not by a long shot. As the poet John Dryden wrote, "I am sore wounded, but not slain. I will lay me down and bleed a while and then rise to fight again." We have bled for eight years as we have been bludgeoned by Obama's actions that will be expanded by an emboldened Hillary Clinton. But now it's time to rise up to fight again. And this time, we have to win. We will win.

It's Our Last Chance

This election truly our last chance—and we must take it.

It is our last chance to stop Obama and Hillary from so permanently changing America that it will be impossible to restore the ideals that we have cherished all of our lives. 2016 will be our last, and decisive, battle in the struggle against the socialist uniformity, collective anti-individualism, executive usurpation, and political corruption that will unquestionably be the hallmark of a Hillary Clinton presidency. If we win, we can rebound and return to what we once were before Obama and Clinton. If we lose, we will be condemned to a traumatic loss of our historical freedoms and constitutional protections.

Donald Trump can stop that. We have to help him do it.

If Hillary wins, we can expect cataclysmic changes to voting rights. November 8, 2016, may well be our last chance to cast votes in an election where our votes are not drowned out by those of millions of illegal immigrants. First, Hillary will grant them amnesty, then citizenship, and then she will use their votes to stuff the ballot box and let her party govern in perpetuity. That's what immigration "reform" is all about—loading up Democratic Party votes by generating a massive pool of new voters beholden to the Democrats.

This election will be our last chance to vote to curb the myriad of welfare payments that are sucking our nation dry. Obama and Clinton want to transform America into a European model of social welfare in which a majority of citizens receive government support and see no problem in taxing the minority who pay for the entitlements. Taxes are paid by fewer and fewer people each year—only 45% last year—at the same time that entitlements are drawn by more and more. We have to stop this. This election is our very last chance to stop the insanity. If we can't, we are bound to go the way of Detroit or Greece.

It is also our last chance to stand up against ISIS and terrorism before the cancer metastasizes and spreads throughout the West. Before we see terrorists, disguised as refugees, flock to our soil and wreak their havoc and mayhem directly on our families, we must defeat Hillary. Because she wants to let them in and will not admit that there is no way to "vet" migrant immigrants from Syria and Libya. Why does she want them? Because surveys show that 80% of Muslims vote Democrat.

We can count on Donald Trump to carry that banner and stop her plans to change America.

It is definitely our last chance to prevent a new crime wave from sweeping our land, animated by those who will be released from prison by so-called sentencing "reform." It's not reform; it's appeasing Democratic Party constituents who have disproportionately high numbers of arrests in their family. Our police will be helpless to stop them, checkmated by the Black Lives Matter movement so dear to Hillary.

Likewise, it is our last chance to preserve our private health care system. With Obamacare failing, the Left will move on to its real goal: socialized medicine. If insurance companies cannot make a profit in the jerry-rigged Obamacare system, the Left will cut them out and go to a single-payer government-controlled system.

Beating Hillary Clinton will be our last chance to keep the Second Amendment in force. If we lose, Hillary Clinton will bind us hand-and-foot to international gun control treaties that override our inherent constitutional protections and the established laws of our land. These treaties, rarely submitted to Congress for review and approval, nevertheless impose registration requirements on our citizens and will ultimately result in the confiscation of privately owned firearms. Hillary supported these UN treaties when she was secretary of state and she will promote them as president. One more good reason to stop her.

Hillary's subservience to Chinese American business interests and her addiction to their campaign donations and speaking fees will lead her to surrender our entire economy to Beijing. With Beijing finding willing allies in the corrupt establishments of both parties, it will proceed to extinguish all American manufacturing and finish the job it started when Bill Clinton misguidedly let the Chinese into the World Trade Organization in 2000, causing a massive loss of American jobs.

Defeating Hillary will be our last chance to eliminate the crony capitalism that is the trademark of her career. Her coziness with Goldman Sachs, Boeing, Corning, GE, and so many others in return for campaign contributions has led her to put their interests well ahead of those of the American worker or our people. But it is our civil liberties that will face the sharpest curtailment. Through a combination of federal regulation and the decisions of a newly compliant Supreme Court, the Second Amendment will become a nullity. The NSA will run amok and will increasingly be used as a tool of domestic oppression.

Can you imagine if the woman who sent private detectives all over the country to track down, investigate, and intimidate all the women with whom her husband was involved got power over the FBI, CIA, IRS, NSA, DOD, and FCC? The extent of her use of government agencies to blackmail and besmirch political opponents is mind boggling—and terrifying—to contemplate.

Finally, defeating Hillary is our last chance to preserve our constitutional system of checks and balances. If we lose, she will replace conservative Supreme Court Justices with rubber stamps jurists who will OK the unprecedented executive seizure of power that has been the hallmark of the Obama presidency. This will only embolden a President Hillary. The Obama executive orders will all be enforced, and unfavored industries, such as coal, will, pardon the pun, bite the dust. She will use environmental enforcement to regulate every aspect of our lives as smart meters monitor our every move, even within our own homes.

And she will get us into wars. A hawk by nature, Hillary will perpetually feel pressure to show strength as the first woman president. Faced with options of diplomacy or force, she will wilt under charges of weakness and will opt for military action every time. The woman who backed both wars in Iraq, the war in Afghanistan, the war in Libya, and intervention in Syria will get us into more wars to prove her toughness—by shedding our blood. She can't stop; she won't stop. But Donald Trump can stop her.

Armageddon is here. We have our work cut out for us—and we can do it. We must do it. America is well worth it. Let the fight begin.

CHAPTER 1

A Dozen Reasons Hillary Clinton Should Not Be President

Reason One: She Demonstrated Her Inability to Be Commander in Chief at Benghazi

Hillary HAD ALL THE warning in the world that things were brewing in Benghazi. But she did nothing. In fact, she cut the security at the consulate. Few candidates for president have the chance to show how they would handle a crisis of the sort that arises in most administrations. Hillary had the chance in 2012 and showed up wanting.

· March 28: Ambassador Gene Cretz cabled Clinton requesting additional security in Benghazi.

· April 10: An explosive device was thrown at a convoy traveling in Benghazi carrying United Nations envoy Ian Martin.[1]

- April 19: Cretz got a reply acknowledging his request, but was told that we were going to scale back our security, not enhance it.

- May 22: A rocket-propelled grenade (RPG) hit the Benghazi offices of the Red Cross.[2] Terrorists attacked the Red Cross in Benghazi. That should have been a warning.

- May 30: The State Department turned down the request from Ambassador Cretz for security aircraft.

- June 6: An improvised explosive device detonated just outside the Benghazi consulate compound.[3]

- June 11: An RPG hit a convoy carrying the British ambassador in Benghazi. The United Kingdom left the city for good.[4]

- June 15: Charlene Lamb, on Hillary's staff, said the security team contract to protect Benghazi would not be renewed.

- June 22: Ambassador Chris Stevens warned State that extremist groups were operating in the open in Benghazi carrying out terror attacks and said he was a target.

If a president ignored warnings of this sort and frequency, he would be excoriated as a failed commander in chief. In fact, Hillary set up the State Department bureaucracy in such a way that she would not be annoyed by such matters as requests for additional security. She testified before Congress that none of the approximately 600 requests for extra personnel in Libya and Benghazi alone ever reached her desk.[5]

In the run-up to the Benghazi attack on September 11, 2012, the Defense Department offered to increase the security at the compound in Benghazi. But Ambassador Stevens pointed out that Defense Department personnel, unlike the State Department counterparts, would not have diplomatic immunity, so he turned down their offer. He was, naturally, worried that if Defense personnel had to shoot, they could be prosecuted in a Libyan court, while State personnel would be shielded. But Hillary's State Department never came through with the additional guards he requested.

The dreadfully eloquent film *13 Hours* recounts the desperation of a handful of US troops trying to defend the CIA compound against an attack by hundreds of organized terrorists armed with mortars. As *Fox News* reported, when the attack in Benghazi unfolded, "a high-ranking Pentagon official urgently messaged Secretary of State Hillary Clinton's top deputies to offer military help, according to an e-mail obtained by Judicial Watch." *Fox News* noted that "the revelation appears to contradict testimony Defense Secretary Leon Panetta gave lawmakers in 2013, when he said there was no time to get forces to the scene in Libya."[6]

Actually, Panetta's chief of staff Jeremy Bash was actively trying to get troops to Benghazi. He wrote to one of Hillary's deputies: "I just tried you on the phone but you were all in with S [apparent reference to then Secretary of State Hillary Clinton]. After consulting with General Dempsey, General Ham, and the Joint Staff, we have identified the forces that could move to Benghazi. They are spinning up as we speak."[7] But no forces were sent. Why not? Hillary and Obama were more concerned with limiting the footprint of the operation so that it would not be so high profile that it would contradict their campaign narrative that al-Qaeda was on the ropes after bin Laden was killed. Because additional reinforcements were not sent, four Americans, including Ambassador Chris Stevens, died.

Symptomatic of Hillary's isolation is the unfortunate fact that Ambassador Stevens did not have Hillary's e-mail address, so he could not figuratively have made the 3:00 a.m. phone call that Hillary's ads say only someone of her experience would know how to handle. Then the lying started. Anxious not to alarm the country and let people figure out that al-Qaeda was far from dead even after bin Laden was slain, the president and his secretary of state conspired to lie to the American people about the attack, describing it as a demonstration against a film criticizing the Prophet Mohammed gone awry.

Hillary not only lied to us, but she fabricated the tale of the movie demonstration and repeated it to the grieving families of the victims. Several of them reported that Hillary promised them that they would get the person who made the anti-Muslim video. The public Hillary released a statement at 10:00 p.m., as the attack was still in progress, blaming the movie for the attack. But one hour later, the private Hillary sent an e-mail to her daughter, Chelsea, saying that "two officers were killed today in Benghazi by an al-Qaeda-like group."[8]

The next day, the public Hillary kept up the lie that the attack was a demonstration gone violent. But as she did, she was telling the truth to the Egyptian prime minister in a telephone call. The notes of the call indicate that she made no mention of the anti-Muslim Internet video that she publicly claimed triggered the demonstration, but described the situation in Libya as a "terrorist attack."[9] Confronted by her lie, Hillary retreated from her bland assertion that the attack stemmed from a demonstration to say that it was a possibility but that, at the moment of the attack, the "fog of war" prevented American officials from determining the truth.[10]

It was no fog of war. Fog of war is a description usually used by commanders who, on the battlefield, cannot see through the smoke and the fire to what is going on beneath. Mistakes made because of these conditions are often attributed to the "fog of war." Used in a political context, we are not dealing with the romantic notion of the fog of war. Instead, Hillary's and Obama's lies were a smokescreen designed to conceal the facts from the American people. What a wonderful qualification to find in a presidential candidate.

Despite a lengthy Congressional hearing on Benghazi, Hillary has never really been held to account. The revelations of her inaction and concealment have come in such dribs and drabs that we have never really had the full story. Leave it to Donald Trump to set it in perspective. One can only imagine how the Donald will rip her apart in a debate raking her over the coals for her lies and duplicity.

Reason Two: She Is a Compulsive, Pathological, and Serial Liar Who Cannot Be Trusted to Tell the Truth to the American People

Hillary has always believed that she can put something over on us, that she can lie with impunity and get away with it. And for a long time, that's exactly what she's done. But those days are over. We're on to her now. And Donald Trump is on to her, too, and he will relentlessly point out each and every one of her lies.

That doesn't mean she's stopped trying. Not at all. It seems that she really can't help herself. Because, for Hillary, lying is routine. It comes naturally—like breathing. For the last 40 years, she's been embellishing her credentials and experience, covering up corrupt conduct, erasing unflattering incidents, confirming Bill's false statements, disseminating disinformation about her enemies and Bill's women, distorting the truth about her conduct in office, and making up self-congratulatory fake stories about herself. She just can't stop.

But her lies have finally caught up with her. By any measurement, an overwhelming majority of American voters recognize that Hillary doesn't tell the truth and can't be trusted. They simply don't believe what she has to say. Every major poll conducted over the last year has shown an increase in the number of people who think she is dishonest. And they are unambiguous about it.

A Quinnipiac poll in late August 2015 asked respondents to describe Hillary Clinton in a single word. The results were brutal. The most frequently mentioned answer was "liar," followed by similar words like dishonest, untrustworthy, crook, untruthful, deceitful, crooked, sneaky, and devious.[11] That is an amazing indictment of her credibility and her overall image.

Take a look at the list of the words selected to describe Hillary along with the number of people, out of a sample of 1,000 Americans, who chose the particular word:

LIAR	178
DISHONEST	123
UNTRUSTWORTHY	93
CROOK	21
UNTRUTHFUL	19
CRIMINAL	18
DECEITFUL	18
E-MAIL	14
BENGHAZI	12
CORRUPT	12
CROOKED	11
MURDERER	9
BITCH	9
PHONY	8
CHEAT	7
DECEPTIVE	7
SNEAKY	7
THIEF	6
DEVIOUS	5
UNQUALIFIED	5

Those voters sure know whom they are dealing with.

In addition to the negative image, the cynicism about her has reached historic levels. Two later polls in December 2015 by Quinnipiac and *ABC News* found that only a little more than a third of the voters believe that Hillary is "honest and trustworthy." That's stunning: 59% of the voters don't believe that she is genuine. And why should they? She's been caught in so many lies that nothing she says is believable anymore. Years ago, voters and the press accepted what she said at face value, but now her claims are routinely challenged because so much of what she says is just pure fiction.

Whether reacting to Benghazi or covering up her use of a private server, she lies out of a well-honed instinct for self-preservation.

Essentially, she has escaped indictment by lying, sometimes under oath.

- She lied about being instrumental in the Travel Office firings.

- She lied about being the attorney for a fraudulent real estate transaction in Arkansas connected with Whitewater.

- She lied about how she transformed a $1,000 investment into a $100,000 windfall through insider trading on the commodities market.

- She lied about Benghazi.

- And she lied about why she created a secret e-mail server and when she said that she never sent or received classified material on her private e-mail server at the State Department.

Her standard lie, especially when confronted with evidence of Bill's inappropriate behavior, is to say "it never happened." That's the world according to Hillary—if she says it never happened, it goes away. Dick can attest to this lie from a personal experience. During Bill's 1992 run for president, a reporter from the *Los Angeles Times* appeared at the door to our home and asked about a physical altercation between Dick and Bill Clinton that had occurred in 1990 in the Arkansas Governor's Mansion. Dick called Hillary to tell her about it and discuss how to handle it. "Just tell them it never happened," she told him. "We'll deny it on our end." When Dick told her that he could not do that because he had already told another political consultant about it right after it happened—and that this consultant was likely the source, she wasn't at all worried. "Deny it. It'll be your word against his."

The story was, of course, absolutely true. And Hillary had been right in the middle of it—literally. During a contentious late night meeting in May of 1990, Bill, furious, spewed out a stream of verbal abuse aimed at Dick. Finally, after a particularly obnoxious exchange, Dick stood up and started to walk out the front door. Bill immediately ran after him, tackling him and throwing him onto the foyer floor.

As Dick was struggling to get up, Bill raised his fist and leaned down to strike Dick. Hillary ran in, screaming at Bill: "Stop it, Bill! Think about what you are doing! Stop it!" She grabbed his arm and he moved away. As Dick got up and stormed out, Hillary followed him and asked him to walk around the grounds, apologizing profusely and telling him, "He only does this to people he loves." Think about that line. Was it supposed to be a compliment? Sounds like a lot more.

Without Dick to confirm the story, it went away for a while. But months later, when the story finally came out, Hillary asked Dick to at least modulate his description of what had happened, leaving out the physical assault. She never gives up. And then, years later in 1997 when Dick eventually wrote about it, Bill read the galleys and asked Dick if he could just say that he tripped. Dick wouldn't.

That's how the Clintons solve embarrassing problems. Pretend they never happened. Swear that it never happened, if you have to. They would have handled the Monica Lewinsky scandal that way except for DNA on a blue dress. That was a big issue for the Clintons, obviously. But so many of Hillary's lies are gratuitous. The obvious question is this: Why does such an accomplished and successful woman who has been First Lady, a US senator, and secretary of state find it necessary to lie so often about herself and her record? Why does she do this?

An analysis of her most well-known lies indicates that a lot of them are exaggerations of her background and experiences that are carefully designed to make her look better. Others are devices for feigning camaraderie and identification with the audience. Her constant lying suggests an underlying problem with self-esteem, which seems surprising in a woman of her position and her verbal confidence. But what else could account for her recurring aggrandizement of her achievements and her obsessive need to create an inflated image of herself?

We know that her mother believed that she could do anything and would be a great success. But her father was apparently a social misfit and an emotionally withholding critic who could not ever acknowledge his daughter's academic successes, attributing stellar grades to attending a school with low academic standards. So Hillary clearly got a mixed message at home.

Author Gail Sheehy once told us of visiting the Rodham home and meeting Hillary's parents. She described Hugh Rodham as "crude" and "controlling." In one telling—and sad—story, Hillary's mother's told Sheehy that it was embarrassing to attend her high school graduation ceremony and sit with the other parents when Hillary won most of the awards. Embarrassing? How weird is that? Just about every other parent would be thrilled. But not the Rodhams. That's the mixed message of Hillary's upbringing.

So it's certainly possible that her early parental put-downs and her father's constant lack of approval took a toll. The way we present ourselves in everyday life is not always indicative of the insecurities lurking in our inner psyche. Hillary is not charismatic but her circumstances are. They create a temporary aura of glamour. Her arrivals at an event are always dramatic, not because of any personal magnetism, but because of the unusual optics with which she surrounds herself.

First, a Secret Service motorcade of large black bulletproof cars drives into the venue. The bustle begins immediately. Agents with earphones jump out of the cars and surround her as she makes her way inside. A coterie of fawning aides carry her bag, books, and notes, and make sure that the stage is exactly as she demanded down to the size of the chair and pillow and the temperature of her drinking water (room temperature, not too cold), and don't forget the Diet Dr. Pepper!

Photographers and TV cameras line the entranceway and corridors, flashing multiple lights as a sea of microphones is lifted toward her. Crowds of onlookers try to snap photos from their phones. It's usually a friendly crowd, generally handpicked, that gives her a roaring welcome. Only Donald Trump puts on a better show.

But once she takes the podium, the theatrics are gone and the bland midwestern twang takes over and dampens the earlier excitement. Unlike Bill Clinton, Hillary can't energize and dazzle an audience. She doesn't have the preternatural talent that Bill demonstrates when he works a room. Scanning a space, he effortlessly makes eye contact, smiling, shaking hands, and enjoying the moment. As he looks around, he instinctively identifies those people who don't like him. He can feel it. And for the next hour, he will turn on the charm until they do. He's involved, engaged, and the audience is in rapt attention. He's a pro. He instinctively understands their collective mood. He is there to persuade, convince, listen, and make friends. While Hillary reads from the teleprompter and bobs her head up and down, he's unplugged. She leaves at the exact appointed time, using the Secret Service as a barrier to separate herself from the hoi-polloi. Bill wings it and connects with everyone in the place, lingering to shake the last hand.

In public, Bill is the opposite of Hillary. She is stiff, remote, and focused on her prepared script. She's on a schedule, and each event is something to get through. Since she can't succeed in wooing a crowd like Bill does, she tries another ploy. She lies to try to imitate the empathy that naturally flows from Bill. She carefully manufactures a story about herself that will likely resonate with her audience and create at least a temporary connection with them. She appropriates something about their collective experience that suggests that she is just like them.

Let's catalog her lies.

MEMORIES OF PAINFUL DISCRIMINATION IN MIDDLE SCHOOL

While she was First Lady, Hillary spoke at a 1997 race-relations forum for teenagers in Massachusetts. In an attempt to empathize and identify with the young victims of racial prejudice, she made up a heartbreaking tale. She desperately wanted to connect with the young people, but it was hard to use personal examples from her own upbringing. Growing up in an upper-class Chicago suburb, attending elite schools, being married to a president, Hillary couldn't easily make the case that she was a victim of the same racism that they had experienced. So she simply made up a story.

According to Hillary, she recalled the "pain" of a "childhood encounter" that helped her understand the injury suffered by racial prejudice. During a junior high school soccer game, on a cold day, she claimed that an "ethnic" goalie told her, "I wish people like you would freeze." Stunned, Hillary asked the goalie how she could feel that way when she didn't even know her. "I don't have to know you to know that I hate you," the goalie purportedly replied.[12] Wow! How harsh! That must have been horrible for poor young Hillary. People hating her? What could that possibly mean?

As we've written earlier, it's a touching story, but it's highly unlikely that it ever happened. It's just another example of Hillary making up a story from whole cloth to try and show that she's just like her audience. Hillary was in middle school in 1959–1961. There were virtually no girls' middle school soccer teams in existence in the entire United States at the time. It was not until well after the passage of Title IX in 1972 that schools were required to provide girls equal athletic opportunities. Even then, it took a long time before there was a proliferation of soccer teams available to girls. The athletic director of the Maine South High School in Park Ridge, Illinois—a 34-year veteran of the school—confirmed to us in 2003 that there were no girls' soccer teams there in the 1960s. In fact, even in 1972, there were only 28 schools in the United States with girls' soccer teams. But Hillary undoubtedly attended Chelsea's school soccer games in the 1990s and learned the lingo and knew of the popularity of girls' soccer teams. So she imagined a story and delivered it with a straight face. This haunting and unforgettable incident didn't make it into Hillary's memoirs—for good reason—it never happened. Nothing to remember.

HILLARY'S PANDERING PRETENSES: WHAT SHE'S LEARNED FROM HER IMMIGRANT GRANDPARENTS WHO WEREN'T IMMIGRANTS

She was at it again in this year's campaign, twisting the truth to make herself seem just like her audience so that they would identify with her and like her. This time it was immigrant families that she wanted to pander to. She tried to illustrate that her family was the epitome of the American melting pot, with all of her grandparents coming to the United State as immigrants to seek a better life.

At a campaign stop before a business roundtable in Iowa, Hillary spun a story about her four immigrant grandparents, suggesting there would be lots of immigrant stories like hers in the room. But it turns out that three of those four "immigrant" grandparents she cited were actually born in America. Her immigrant grandparent story just wasn't true. Hillary's maternal grandparents were born in Illinois, where she grew up, and her paternal grandmother was born in Pennsylvania.

She was caught by the sleuths at *Breitbart*, who checked census records. When confronted, she claimed that she got mixed up and thought that her three grandparents were actually immigrants because they talked about the "immigrant experience." Well, her maternal grandfather (who wasn't an immigrant) died in the year she was born, so he wasn't telling her any stories about his immigrant experience. And she knew her maternal grandmother very well and had to know she wasn't an immigrant. Same with her paternal grandmother. *Hint*: They were born in America and had no accent.

Hey, Hillary, haven't you ever heard of ancestry.com? You can build your family tree there. You would easily see that. You won't have to look through the Ellis Island documents, though, because they don't exist for your family. Why make up such an unnecessary story? Hillary does that to make the discussion more personal and to connect her to today's immigrants, an important constituency of the Democratic Party. How great to be an immigrant success story!

Here's the narrative: Four grandparents came here from Europe. One worked in the lace mills and now, guess what? One of their grandchildren is running for president of the United States. It's a nice story, but it's not true. But she wanted to be just one of the folks, so she told a new story.

"PRIVATE HILLARY" TRIED TO JOIN THE MARINES

Then there was her absurd claim that she had unsuccessfully tried to join the Marines—both the reserves and active duty—in Arkansas in 1975, shortly before she married Bill Clinton. That story made its first appearance in 1994 when she gave a speech to a group of women in the military in Washington. She repeated the tale in early 2016.

Clearly, Hillary had no military experience in common with the women. In fact, if anything, her background was downright hostile to the military. Ron Kessler, author of *First Family Detail,* wrote of the animosity Hillary engendered in the Secret Service. "Hillary didn't like the military aides wearing their uniforms around the White House," one former agent remembers. "She asked if they would wear business suits instead. The uniform's a sign of pride, and they're proud to wear their uniform. I know that the military was actually really offended by it."[13] But never mind her personal preferences; she needed a hook to appeal to the military women. So she made up a story designed to show her empathy for them as well as to subtly suggest that they shared joint values of patriotism and service to our country. She reported that she was turned down by the Marines because of her eyesight and her age. According to Hillary, that rejection led her to "look for another way to serve my country."[14] Yet, she never filled out an application and never took any physical. She doesn't recall to whom she spoke.

Her implication that the Marine Corps was not interested in women or discriminated against them at the time was simply not true. According to the Women Marines Association, women first joined the Marines in 1918. There were 2,700 women in the Corps during the Vietnam War and over 1,000 women were deployed during Operation Desert Storm. In 1967, the first woman was assigned to a combat zone—in Vietnam. And of course the Judge Advocate General's Corps

(JAG) was actively recruiting women at the time Hillary dreamt that she went to the Marines. They were looking for women. It was Hillary who wasn't looking for them.

Maureen Dowd of the *New York Times* didn't buy the story of Hillary's military sisterhood when she initially unveiled it. Dubbing her "Private Hillary," Dowd pointed out why the story didn't add up. She was right. Think about Hillary's background. What is the likelihood that she would choose to join the military? Zero. She was part of the student antiwar movement at Yale, a passion she shared with Bill. When George McGovern ran on an antiwar platform, she moved to Austin, Texas to work on his campaign. Was she really going to join the military three years later and leave her soon-to-be new husband behind? The *Washington Post* fact checker reviewed her story, and two more "Pinochios" were added to her growing collection.

SHE WAS NAMED AFTER SIR EDMUND HILLARY

Hillary even tried to concoct a romantic association for her name, claiming to have been named after Sir Edmund Hillary, the first person to climb Mt. Everest. She apparently told the lie to Bill, who faithfully recounted it in his own autobiography. But when her own book came out, it was missing, raising suspicions about its veracity. These suspicions stemmed from the obvious fact that Sir Edmund was an unknown beekeeper in 1947 when Hillary Rodham was born. He rocketed to world fame when he climbed Everest in 1953. Hillary claimed that her mother told her that she had named her after Sir Edmund, making the point that both the mountain climber and her daughter spelled the name with two Ls. When the lie was exposed, Hillary had her campaign simply issue a press release in 2008 noting that she was not named after Sir Edmund. We expect that she'll have a lot of new press releases coming up.

SHE WAS INSTRUMENTAL IN THE IRISH PEACE PROCESS

As she ran for president in 2008, Hillary was desperate to establish her foreign policy bona fides. Her First Lady ceremonial ribbon cutting wouldn't cut it. So Hillary claimed that she was "instrumental"[15] to the Irish peace process, a claim that brought immediate criticism from some of the diplomats who were actually involved in the process. According to Hillary's own memoirs, it seems that Hillary's involvement in Ireland was simply to attend a meeting of women from Ireland and Northern Ireland where they presented her with a teapot. She also lit a Christmas tree at Belfast City Hall and read letters from Catholic and Protestant children hoping for peace. And she spoke to a group of women from the North and South in Dublin. That's it. That's her idea of a foreign policy achievement and ending a war that lasted more than 75 years. Lord Trimble, who shared the Nobel Peace Prize for his tireless work to end the troubles in Ireland, publicly disagreed with Mrs. Clinton's own characterization of her leadership in the peace process, calling it "a wee bit silly" for Mrs. Clinton to claim an important role. He said, "I don't want to rain on the thing for her but being a cheerleader for something is slightly different from being a principal player."[16]

If anyone would have firsthand knowledge of the then First Lady's role, it would be the chief negotiator for the United States, former Senator George Mitchell. But in his book *Making Peace,* the senator's only mention of Hillary is that she and the president "were warmly received in London, cheered in Belfast, and embraced in Dublin. Huge crowds met them with rousing enthusiasm. The president rose to the occasion."[17] Nothing further about Hillary. Bertie Ahearn, the Irish prime minister at the time, described her role to *The New York Times,* "She was the first lady of the United States, not a party leader in Northern Ireland . . . No one would expect her to get into the nitty-gritty of the process."[18] Even Bill Clinton must have forgotten Hillary's seminal role, because he didn't include it in his memoir. Of all of the principals involved in the peace process, only one mentions the name Hillary Clinton. That was Jonathan Powell, then chief of staff to UK prime minister Tony Blair, made only a passing reference to Hillary in his depiction of the peace talks in his book *Great Hatred, Little Room: Making Peace in Northern Ireland.* It seems that Powell mistook a Secret Service officer assigned to Hillary for a friend and boldly asked for a kiss. That's the only way that Hillary was mentioned by anyone writing about the peace process first hand.

But years later, as she began her campaign for president, Hillary was inducted into the "Irish Hall of Fame" **in recognition of her role in the Irish Peace process.** Yes, looking back, some of Bill's cronies and Hillary supporters actually arranged for this dubious award. What Hillary's role was never really came out. It couldn't because it never existed. It wasn't either the Irish government or the principals in the peace process who arranged the prestigious award from an Irish magazine. It was cronies of Bill's who promoted the Clinton Foundation with international businesses and who coincidently were awarded lucrative business opportunities in Haiti and elsewhere. Several of them were big whigs at Teneco, where big business, foreign governments, and the Clinton Foundation all help each other out. None of these folks had anything whatsoever to do with the peace process.

HILLARY LANDED UNDER SNIPER FIRE IN BOSNIA

In a foreign policy speech on Iraq on March 17, 2008, Hillary recounted how she had "landed under sniper fire" during a trip to Tuzla, Bosnia, in March of 1996. She said, "I remember landing under sniper fire. There was supposed to be some kind of a greeting ceremony at the airport, but instead we just ran with our heads down to get into the vehicles to get to our base."[19] What guts! What an experience! But it never happened. In fact, when Hillary's jet touched down she was greeted by a young girl who presented her with a poem. No snipers. So why the lie? Again, to create the charisma and experience that she lacks. Hillary wanted to show how important her role was as First Lady. The fact is the only snipers she has ever faced are political critics.

Hillary's had dozens of other lies: There was her famous claim that she and Bill were "dead broke" when they left the White House, despite having an income of over $10 million. She hides everything but pretends to be so open. Hillary once said that she is "the most transparent person in public life." She's right. So transparent that we can see right through her!

In the ultimate insult, Hillary even lies about lying! Pressed at a Nevada town hall in early 2016 about whether she is truthful to the American people, she answered: "I do my best to level with the American people."[20] She does her best to tell the truth? What does that mean? It means that she will tell the truth when there is no better option.

Note to Hillary: Donald Trump will be watching. Be careful with your tales.

Reason Three: She Will Get Us into a War

Would President Hillary Clinton tack to the left, as Obama has, on economic and social policy or move more to the center as Bill did? We don't know. But on foreign policy, there can be little doubt that Hillary Clinton is much more likely to get us into a war. Perhaps because she is a woman eager to cast herself in the mode of Margaret Thatcher; she has been hawkish ever since she launched her independent political career as a senator from New York in 2000.

She took office in January 2001, just eight months before her adopted state of New York was devastated by the horrific terror attacks of 9/11. Eager to prove herself worthy of being trusted to be the senator from a state in which she had never lived, she postured herself as a hawk during her tenure in the Senate. When time came to choose committee assignments, for example, she broke with the pattern of liberal Democrats and opted to join the Senate Armed Services Committee. And when President Bush sought congressional approval for the war in Iraq, she joined 29 of the 50 Democrats in voting for the use of force, putting her squarely on the hawkish end of the Democratic policy spectrum.

Meanwhile, Donald Trump opposed the war in Iraq, predicting, accurately and depressingly, that it would land us in an open-ended commitment from which we would have great difficulty extracting ourselves. He also predicted that thousands of Americans would never be extracted but would perish in the war and that hundreds of billions would be squandered, not to disappear but to be included for years on end as part of our national debt.

Hillary went down the line supporting the war in Iraq and also voted for the Patriot Act and most of the appropriations to fund the war. She now says it was a mistake. In her 2014 book, *Hard Choices*, Hillary apologized. "I thought I had acted in good faith and made the best decision I could with the information I had. And I wasn't alone in getting it wrong. But I still got it wrong,"[21] she wrote. "Obviously, if we knew then what we know now, there wouldn't have been a vote. I certainly wouldn't have voted that way."[22] When the Iraq War bogged down in 2007, Senator John McCain (R-AZ) pushed for a "surge" in American forces to drive back the dissidents and establish control over the country. President Bush adopted the idea, but the Left fiercely opposed it. Supporters of the surge were surprised to see Clinton vote against it, in view of her earlier support for the war. But observers came to understand her switch in positions after Bush's and Obama's Defense Secretary, Bob Gates, quoted in his book a conversation between Hillary and Obama in the Oval Office shortly after she became secretary of state.

Gates wrote: "Hillary told the president that her opposition to the [2007] surge in Iraq had been political because she was facing him in the Iowa primary. . . . The president conceded vaguely that opposition to the Iraq surge had been political. To hear the two of them making these admissions, and in front of me, was as surprising as it was dismaying."[23] Once in office as secretary of state, she reverted to a warlike attitude as she aggressively pushed for US intervention in Libya and in Syria, involving us in one war and seeking to ensnare us in another. Hillary was determined to go to war over Libya. She fantasized that genocide was unfolding in the streets of Tripoli, with no evidence, and hyped demands for US intervention. Everyone agreed that Libyan dictator Muammar Gaddafi was a monster. He ordered the bombing of a night club frequented by US troops in Berlin and orchestrated the downing of Pan Am Flight 103 over Lockerbie, Scotland, killing 270 people in 1988.

Responding to the Berlin bombing, President Reagan ordered a devastating air strike against Gaddafi, killing his son. Chastened, the dictator began to pull in his horns and, when Saddam Hussein was toppled in Iraq by US forces, he saw the handwriting on the wall and gave up his ambitions to build weapons of mass destruction (WMD). He had been minding his manners ever since. But Hillary, fed by almost daily e-mails from her close aide Sydney Blumenthal warning about slaughter in the streets of Libya, was determined to have the United States intervene and depose Gaddafi. Blumenthal's interests in hyping the situation may have been financial. *The New Republic* reported that Blumenthal was pushing for armed intervention while he was "both employed by the Clinton Foundation and advising businessmen angling for contracts from the country's transitional government."[24]

On Hillary's part, she was worried about the political implications of ignoring genocide as she and Bill had done in Rwanda during the mass slaughter/genocide there in 1994. Widely criticized for their inactivity in the face of the death of millions, she was loath to risk being criticized for inaction again. Samantha Power, who served on the National Security staff as Senior Director for Multilateral Affairs and Human Rights, had studied Rwanda and was obsessed with the possibility of another genocide. She warned Hillary that a human tragedy might be unfolding. When Hillary told the Joint Chiefs of Staff of her concern over events on the ground in Libya, they dispatched their own intelligence officer to check things out and he reported that there was no genocide in progress.

Nor did Human Rights Watch, a nongovernmental organization (NGO) dedicated to battling genocide, find evidence suggesting an impending slaughter by the time NATO intervened: "Our assessment was that up until that point, the casualty figures— around 350 protesters killed by indiscriminate fire of government security forces—didn't rise to the level of indicating that a genocide or genocide-like mass atrocities were imminent."[25]

Nevertheless, Hillary pounded away at Obama and the national security staff to push for armed intervention in Libya to topple Gaddafi. In March of 2011, she told an interviewer, "Imagine we were sitting here and Benghazi had been overrun, a city of 700,000 people, and tens of thousands of people had been slaughtered, hundreds of thousands had fled. . . . The cries would be, 'Why did the United States not do anything?'"[26]

Under unrelenting pressure from Hillary, Obama agreed to participate in the NATO no-fly zone over Libya that led to Gaddafi's killing. *The Washington Post* called it "Hillary's War" and, after the dictator fell, the former secretary of state proudly paraphrased Julius Caesar, "We came, we saw, he died."[27] Is Julius Caesar to be the role model for the new president?

The fact is that the Libya invasion opened the door to Islamist terrorists, the very ones who killed US Ambassador Chris Stevens and three other Americans in Benghazi. Many of the weapons we supplied to the rebels in Libya ended up in ISIS hands during the ensuing years. The Libya invasion may yet lead to another ISIS-controlled state, all because Hillary wouldn't let well enough alone and insisted on sending in the cavalry.

Fortunately, Donald Trump is calling Hillary to task for her role in advocating intervention in Libya. In an interview with Chuck Todd on *Meet the Press*, he said: "If you look at Libya, look at what we did there—it's a mess—if you look at Saddam Hussein with Iraq, look at what we did there—it's a mess—it's going to be the same thing."

When Todd asked if the Middle East would be better if Gaddafi and Saddam were still in power, Trump answered "It's not even a contest, Chuck. It's not even a contest. Of course it would be [better]. You wouldn't have had your Benghazi situation which is one thing which was just a terrible situation. But, of course, nobody even knows what's going on over there. It's not even a country anymore."[28]

In Syria, Hillary clamored for American arming of the rebels against dictator Bashar al-Assad, but the White House resisted. Like much of the Arab Spring, the rebellion in Syria began as an effort by democratic forces to topple a horrific dictator who had slaughtered his own people by the hundreds of thousands. But the rebellion was soon co-opted by the extremist Islamist forces that ultimately formed the core of ISIS. Hillary was intent on finding "moderates" to arm, hoping that they would serve as a counterweight both to al-Assad and to the Islamists.

In her memoir, *Hard Choices*, Hillary writes that "wicked problems rarely have a right answer; in fact, part of what makes them wicked is that every option appears worse than the next. Increasingly that's how Syria appeared." Returning from an overseas trip, Hillary recounts how she became convinced that arming and training the rebels might strengthen their hand against al-Assad: "The risks of both action and inaction were high, [but] the president [Obama]'s inclination was to stay the present course and not take the significant further step of arming rebels. . . . No one likes to lose a debate, including me. But this was the president's call and I respected his deliberations and decision."[29] But eventually, Obama did decide to try to arm and train the Syrian "moderates" on a limited and secret basis. That proved to be a disastrous decision.

The *International Business Times* reported that "by the reckoning of experts and members of Congress from both parties, that strategy [of arming the moderates] appears in tatters. The moderates the United States bet on as the means of pressuring al-Assad have been routed by . . . ISIS."[30] The US-led strategy of airstrikes and arming Syrian moderates may have "actually hurt the moderate opposition," reported Robert S. Ford, former Obama administration ambassador to Syria. He said US intervention had led to retaliation by ISIS "against the moderate rebels, who were largely unprepared to deal with such attacks and fled."[31]

Leslie Gelb, an assistant secretary of state in the Carter administration and now a fellow at the Council on Foreign Relations, said the moderates in Syria "are not a viable fighting force. They couldn't win no matter how many arms we gave them. That has been the story war after war, I don't know why we have to learn this one lesson administration after administration. We learned this in Iraq."[32] Indeed, since many of the so-called moderates we armed in Syria ended up fighting for ISIS, we may well have armed our enemy by following Hillary's recommendations. But the question lingers: Why is Hillary so hawkish, voting for wars in Iraq, Libya, and Syria?

One theory is that she perceives it as a political need for a woman in politics to be a hawk. She may worry that people don't trust a woman to be commander in chief, and that her strong defense record is a reassurance. She may also be casting herself, consciously, in the mold of Margaret Thatcher and Golda Meir, two highly successful wartime leaders of their countries. Or it could be an offshoot of her own personality. Everyone who knows Hillary describes her as combative, stubborn, and fixedly determined to defend her views. She values courage above all and places great store in standing up for herself. She constantly repeats her mother's advice, given when she was four after a playmate hit her, to never back down. But in either case, one thing is most likely: if Hillary is elected, we will probably get into at least one war.

Donald Trump has understood from Day One that Hillary Clinton's vote on the war in Iraq and her hawkish record is a big negative. We can count on him to remind the voters about it over and over again.

Donald Trump is under no compulsion to show his macho qualities by wading into wars. He has been reluctant to back a no-fly zone in Syria and is demonstrating a maturity in restraint in the use of force we know will be absent in Hillary Clinton.

Reason Four: Hillary and the Muslim Brotherhood Are Perfect Together

Hillary's closest aide and current vice chairwoman of her 2016 campaign is Huma Abedin, who has strong connections to the

Muslim Brotherhood. Abedin, who *Vanity Fair* called "Hillary's Second Daughter,"[33] was born in Kalamazoo, Michigan to Pakistani and Indian immigrants and moved with her family to Jeddah, Saudi Arabia, where she spent her entire childhood until she entered George Washington University in the United States.

Huma and Hillary are joined at the hip. They began their relationship in 1996 while Huma was serving as a White House intern assigned to Hillary. In Mrs. Clinton's 2000 Senate campaign and during her subsequent tenure, Huma was Hillary's traveling chief of staff and body aide. But apart from Hillary, Huma Abedin and her family have a long history of involvement with Palestinian causes. In 1998, Huma served as assistant editor of the *Journal of Muslim Minority Affairs*. Five Republican congressmen charged that Huma's late father, and her mother and brother are connected to the Muslim Brotherhood.

Her mother, Saleha, "is a sociologist known for her strong advocacy of Sharia Law," according to *FrontPage Magazine*, and a member of the Muslim Sisterhood, the Brotherhood's sibling. Saleha is also a board member of the International Islamic Council for Da'wah and Relief. This pro-Hamas entity is part of the Union of Good, which the US government has formally designated as an "international terrorist organization."[34] *FrontPage Magazine* notes that "from 1996–2008, Huma worked at the Institute of Muslim Minority Affairs as the assistant editor of its in-house publication, the *Journal of Muslim Minority Affairs* (JMMA)." For seven years of her tenure, she worked with "al Qaeda-affiliated Abdullah Omar Naseef" at the JMMA.[35]

Trump has excoriated Huma, focusing particularly on her marriage to former Democratic Congressman Anthony Weiner who was involved in a sexting scandal. The candidate said "so now, think of it, Huma is getting classified secrets. She is married to Anthony Weiner, who is a perv. Now these are confidential documents and guess what happens to Anthony Weiner. A month ago he went to work for a public relations firm."[36]

Huma's presence has been quite influential in Hillary's and Obama's treatment of the Muslim Brotherhood, an organization labeled as terrorist by most Middle Eastern countries. The Brotherhood is considered a terrorist organization by the governments of Bahrain, Egypt, Russia, Syria, Saudi Arabia, and the United Arab Emirates. The Brotherhood's stated goal is to instill the Qur'an and Sunnah as the "sole reference point for . . . ordering the life of the Muslim family, individual, community . . . and state." Its mottos include, "Believers are but Brothers," "Islam is the Solution," and "Allah is our objective; the Qur'an is the Constitution; the Prophet is our leader; jihad is our way; death for the sake of Allah is our wish."[37]

The *National Review* lists the ways since Hillary Clinton's tenure at the State Department began that "the United States has aligned itself with the Muslim Brotherhood. . . . Our government

- reversed the policy against formal contacts with the Brotherhood;

- funded Hamas;

- continued funding Egypt even after the Brotherhood won the elections;

- dropped an investigation of Brotherhood organizations in the United States that were previously identified as co-conspirators in the case of the Holy Land Foundation financing Hamas;

- hosted Brotherhood delegations in the United States;

- issued a visa to a member of the Islamic Group (a designated terrorist organization) and hosted him in Washington because he is part of the Brotherhood's parliamentary coalition in Egypt;

- announced that Israel should go back to its indefensible 1967 borders;

- excluded Israel, the world's leading target of terrorism, from a counterterrorism forum in which the State Department sought to 'partner' with Islamist governments that do not regard attacks on Israel as terrorism; and

· pressured Egypt's pro-American military government to surrender power to the anti-American Muslim Brotherhood parliament and president just elected by Egypt's predominantly anti-American population."[38]

While Hillary was pushing Israel to stop building settlements on the West Bank and bought into Obama's line that their failure to do so was torpedoing the peace process, she worked hard to help the Muslim Brotherhood take over in neighboring Egypt.

In Egypt, the so-called Arab Spring erupted early in 2012, fanned by pro-democracy protests in Tunisia. Demonstrators took to the streets of Cairo demanding the ouster of dictator Hosni Mubarak, whose vicious but pro-Western regime had evoked howls of protest, forcibly put down for years.

The West was thrilled. Some alarmists worried that if Mubarak fell, the pro-Islamist Muslim Brotherhood might take over. But the Obama administration dismissed their concern and welcomed the end of Mubarak. As this former US ally struggled for traction in the streets, Hillary urged "a peaceful, orderly transition to a democratic regime" and called on Mubarak to respond to "the legitimate needs and grievances expressed by the Egyptian people and chart a new path."[39]

After Mubarak fell, the hopes and dreams of the Egyptian people for democracy were again crushed as the Muslim Brotherhood and its leader, Islamist Mohamed Morsi, took power. Domestically, Morsi cracked down on the secular elements who had tried to oust Mubarak and moved to restore Sharia Law. He was particularly vicious in his persecution of Egypt's Coptic Christians, the minority that comprises between a tenth and a quarter of Egypt's population.

Shortly after Morsi took office, a wave of violence gripped the Coptic community and their leader accused Morsi's government of "delinquency" and "misjudgments" for failing to prevent sectarian street-fighting. He noted that "this is the first time the main Coptic Orthodox Cathedral has been attacked in Egypt's history."[40] In foreign affairs, Morsi steered a course of cooperation with the Palestinian terrorists and appeared to all but junk the 1979 Camp David accords that brought peace to the Egyptian-Israeli relationship.

But Hillary was Morsi's biggest fan. On July 14, 2013, as millions of anti-Islamists demonstrated in Cairo against his regime, Hillary flew to see the embattled leader and lend him support. But the Egyptian Army, long a key force in their politics, wanted Morsi to go. As the threat of military intervention to unseat Morsi hovered over his presidency, Hillary declared that the United States "supports the full transition to civilian rule with all that entails." She demanded "the military's return to a purely national security role."[41]

Breitbart News reported that "the meeting itself sent a historic message. Seated in an ornate room in the presidential palace, Mrs. Clinton smiled for cameras and traded pleasantries with President Mohamed Morsi of the Muslim Brotherhood, an Islamist jailed more than once by the American-backed autocracy overthrown 18 months ago. She became the highest ranking United States official to meet Mr. Morsi since he was sworn in."[42]

Hillary's visit cemented what Morsi's wife called a "special relationship" between her husband and the secretary of state.[43] Of Mrs. Clinton, she said, "We have a long friendship of many years. We lived in the U.S. and my children learned there. This friendship increased further when my husband became the legitimate president of the country."[44]

Hillary's backing for Morsi was very significant. The United States gives Egypt almost $3 billion of foreign aid each year, the bulk of it aimed at subsidizing the country's military—a payoff given for their entry into the Camp David Accords which guaranteed peace between Egypt and Israel.

Huma Abedin was not the only hook the Muslim Brotherhood had into the secretary of state. She had another Islamic radical in her midst. As noted, Gehad el-Haddad, the son of Morsi's foreign affairs advisor, served as the Muslim Brotherhood's top English language communications official in Egypt. At the same time, he was employed by the Clinton Foundation, heading the Cairo office of the Clinton Climate Initiative. In April 2015, el-Haddad was sentenced to life in prison in Egypt for his work with the Muslim Brotherhood. With her top aide, Huma Abedin, an open sympathizer with the Muslim Brotherhood, and el-Haddad working for her foundation as he advised Egyptian president Morsi, we are right to ask Hillary, Which side are you on?

Reason Five: Which Hillary? She Flips, She Flops, and Then She Flips Again

It can be dizzying to watch the fast changing policy positions of Hillary Clinton. With no real convictions other than ambition, she changes her views with the rapidity and totality of a kaleidoscope. The only thing her shifting views have in common is that they are driven by her political needs at that moment. It is a wonder that anyone listens to her anymore. Her political views have a half-life of a few months . . . or until the wind changes. Here is just a sampling of some of the recent flip-flops. Just a sampling.

GAY MARRIAGE

As she began her solo political career in 2000, she announced in White Plains, New York that she opposed gay marriage: "Marriage has got historic, religious and moral content that goes back to the beginning of time, and I think a marriage is as a marriage has always been, between a man and a woman."[45] Indeed, Hillary supported her husband's decision to sign the now infamous (to the Left) Defense of Marriage Act, designed to make sure states without gay marriage did not have to give "full faith and credit" to gay marriages in other states.

In the 2008 campaign for president, she moved somewhat to the left as she turned to face a primary challenge from Barack Obama. At that time, during a debate sponsored by a gay-oriented television station, she was asked, "What is at the heart of your opposition to same-sex marriage?"[46] She bobbed and weaved, but let her opposition stand saying, "Well, I prefer to think of it as being very positive about civil unions. You know, it's a personal position. How we get to full equality is the debate we're having, and I am absolutely in favor of civil unions with full equality of benefits, rights, and privileges."[47]

By 2016, facing an all-out challenge from Vermont Socialist Bernie Sanders, she abandoned all reservations in a full-throated defense of gay marriage, saying, "LGBT [lesbian, gay, bisexual, and transgender] Americans are our colleagues, our teachers, our soldiers, our friends, our loved ones. And they are full and equal citizens, and they deserve the rights of citizenship. That includes marriage. That's why I support marriage for lesbian and gay couples. I support it personally and as a matter of policy and law, embedded in a broader effort to advance equality and opportunity for LGBT Americans and all Americans."[48]

FREE TRADE AGREEMENTS

The signature foreign policy achievement of the Clinton administration was the ratification, in 1993, of NAFTA, providing for free trade among the United States, Mexico, and Canada. In her memoir, *Living History*, published in 2003, Hillary strongly supported NAFTA: "Creating a free trade zone in North America—the largest free trade zone in the world—would expand U.S. exports, create jobs and ensure that our economy was reaping the benefits, not the burdens, of globalization. Although unpopular with labor unions, expanding trade opportunities was an important administration goal."[49]

But when the Bush administration extended NAFTA to Central America in CAFTA in 2006, she voted against it. As public attitudes toward NAFTA soured (See our Chapter Four on how badly we have done under NAFTA), she began to criticize the accord and called for a moratorium on trade deals: At a debate hosted by CNN in November 2007, Clinton said, "NAFTA was a mistake to the extent that it did not deliver on what we had hoped it would, and that's why I call for a trade timeout."[50]

But the mother of all trade flip-flops came in 2015, when Hillary Clinton opposed ratification of a trade deal *she* helped to negotiate and had strongly endorsed—the TPP. This trade deal, discussed later in this book, links the United States with Chile, Peru, Mexico, Canada, Japan, Vietnam, Malaysia, Singapore, Brunei, Australia, and New Zealand. Not only does it eliminate tariffs, but it also limits our flexibility to adopt food and other regulations in our own country.

Hillary loved TPP before she started to run for president. In 2012, she praised it to the skies during a visit to Australia: "So it's fair to say that our economies are entwined, and we need to keep upping our game both bilaterally and with partners across the region through agreements like the Trans-Pacific Partnership or TPP. Australia is a critical partner. This TPP sets the gold standard in trade agreements to open free, transparent, fair trade, the kind of environment that has the rule of law and a level playing field. And when negotiated, this agreement will cover 40 percent of the world's total trade and build in strong protections for workers and the environment."[51]

As secretary of state, Hillary positively gushed about the benefits of the TPP, calling it "exciting," "innovative," "ambitious," "groundbreaking," "cutting-edge," "high-quality," and "high-standard."[52] Her support for TPP was fanned by her top advisors who held top positions with banks such as Morgan Stanley and other institutions deeply interested in selling the deal for their own profit.

Morgan Stanley spent $4 million in 2013 and $4.8 million in 2014 lobbying for TPP. Morgan's former employees seeded the top ranks of Hillary's State Department staff. Thomas Nides, Morgan's chief operating and administrative officer, joined Hillary's State Department as deputy secretary of state for management, a post from which he could advocate TPP at key junctures. When he left State, he was rewarded for his service by returning to Morgan as the bank's vice president.[53]

Open Secrets reported that "Morgan Stanley's role in the Clinton orbit" goes beyond Nides, noting that "two prominent alumni of former President Bill Clinton's administration . . . serve on Morgan Stanley's board of directors: Erskine Bowles (its lead director) and Laura Tyson." Bowles served as Bill's Chief of Staff and Tyson was the chairman of his Council of Economic Advisors.[54]

Doubtless, Hillary expected to coast into the presidential race touting TPP as a major achievement of her tenure at the State Department. But enter Bernie Sanders, an inveterate opponent of the deal. Facing a challenge from the Left, she flipped and flopped and condemned TPP. Suddenly, it was not just short of the gold standard. It also fell short of her standards. Now, she told PBS, "I'm worried about currency manipulation not being part of the agreement . . . We've lost American jobs to the manipulations that countries, particularly in Asia, have engaged in."[55] (This from a former secretary of state who uttered not a peep when President Obama refused—several times—to certify China as a currency manipulator and invoke sanctions for doing so.) And, Hillary complained, drug companies may have gotten too much in TPP: "Pharmaceutical companies may have gotten more benefits and patients and consumers got fewer," she commented.[56]

But if businesses got too much, Hillary got a piece of it in her campaign contributions. *The Hill* reported that "Democratic presidential frontrunner Hillary Clinton has received more campaign cash from drug companies than any candidate in either party, even as she proudly declares the industry is one of her biggest enemies. Clinton accepted $164,315 in the first six months of the campaign from drug companies, far more than the rest of the 2016 field . . ."[57]

What would she do as president with TPP? Oh, that's easy. She'll make a few minor changes and declare it fixed. It will be the gold standard again.

SECOND AMENDMENT

Her positions on guns have oscillated back and forth with incredible speed and frequency. When she ran for the Senate from antigun

New York State, she backed a national registry for guns.* But when she ran for president and was seeking votes in rural Pennsylvania, Ohio, and Michigan—gun country—she was so pro-gun that Obama quipped that she seemed to want to be "Annie Oakley."[58] When Obama was quoted as saying that rural Pennsylvanians "cling to guns or religion," she countered with a strong defense of guns. Suddenly, she was Hillary the Hunter and opposed a national registry for firearms.

She even brought her father into it. "You know," she said, "my dad took me out behind the cottage that my grandfather built on a little lake called Lake Winola outside of Scranton and taught me how to shoot when I was a little girl. Some people now continue to teach their children and their grandchildren. It's part of culture. It's part of a way of life. People enjoy hunting and shooting because it's an important part of who they are, not because they are bitter." Hillary said that blanket federal rules weren't the answer.[59]

ILLEGAL IMMIGRANTS

In the 2008 presidential contest, Hillary distinguished herself as an opponent of illegal immigration, tangling with the rest of the Democratic field on the issue of driver's licenses for the undocumented. She said, "As president, I will not support driver's licenses for undocumented people and will press for comprehensive immigration reform that deals with all of the issues around illegal immigration, including border security and fixing our broken system."[60] But in 2016, she flip-flopped. Her spokesman told the *Huffington Post* that "Hillary supports state policies to provide driver's licenses to undocumented immigrants."[61]

As hundreds of thousands of children from Central America illegally sought to enter the United States over the porous Mexican border in the spring of 2014, Hillary wanted to send them back:

---

* Then, in 2015, she was back again as a gun control supporter, attacking Bernie Sanders for his votes against holding gun manufacturers and vendors liable for the damage their firearms do. What is her real position on guns? Read the polls.

"They should be sent back as soon as it can be determined who responsible adults in their families are," Clinton said. "There are concerns about whether all of them should be sent back, but I think all of them who can be should be reunited with their families. We have to send a clear message: Just because your child gets across the border, that doesn't mean the child gets to stay," Hillary declared. "So we don't want to send a message that is contrary to our laws, or will encourage more children to make that dangerous journey."[62]

But when the time actually came to start deporting the children, Hillary changed her position once again. Her campaign spokesperson said, "Hillary Clinton has real concerns about these reports [of deportations], especially as families are coming together during this holiday season." The campaign statement added, "She believes it is critical that everyone has a full and fair hearing, and that our country provides refuge to those that need it. And we should be guided by a spirit of humanity and generosity as we approach these issues."[63]

These are just a selection of Hillary Clinton flip-flops. On virtually every major issue, she has taken one side and then the other, always shading her position so as to give herself maximum political advantage.

Reason Six: She Is Corrupt . . . Always Immersed in Scandal

If Hillary is elected, she will take her place along with Warren G. Harding and Richard M. Nixon as one of the most corrupt presidents in our history.

Corruption with Hillary is a way of life. She justifies her corruption by a personal narrative that suggests that she eschewed big bucks on Wall Street as a major corporate lawyer to serve the public in Arkansas. The narrative is, of course, fanciful. She failed the Washington, DC, bar exam, foreclosing most of the lucrative opportunities, and was glad to go to Arkansas, the only bar she had passed.

From the very beginning of her public life, she has always been corrupt. It started in small ways.

CATTLE FUTURES INSIDER TRADING

In 1978, Hillary invested $1,000 in cattle futures contracts. The all time best investment ever made, Hillary walked away with $100,000 the very next year. Having no experience in the futures markets, Hillary was guided in her investment by James Blair, a friend who was outside counsel to Tyson Foods. The editor of the *Journal of Futures Markets* said in April 1994 that Hillary's gains in the cattle futures market were "like buying ice skates one day and entering the Olympics a day later."[64] Two economists from the University of North Florida and Auburn University calculated the odds of such winnings without outside fixing as 1 in 31 trillion.[65]

Blair and Tyson Foods were well compensated for their efforts on Hillary's behalf. Not only did Governor Clinton waive environmental standards to help Tyson's chicken industry in Arkansas, but as the *Wall Street Journal* reported, the firm also got special treatment in Washington after Clinton became president. The *Journal* wrote in 1994, "Over the past year, an Agriculture Department blitz against unsanitary slaughterhouse practices has bypassed Tyson's 66 plants altogether. The department also has sided with the Tyson-dominated Arkansas Poultry Federation in a court fight over a California labeling law. And while it has imposed a 'zero tolerance' fecal-matter policy on meatpackers, it has yet to do the same for poultry, despite high rates of salmonella and other bacteria on chicken and turkey."[66]

THE WHITE HOUSE TRAVEL OFFICE FIRINGS

Hillary's next close call with the law came when her husband fired the staff of the White House Travel Office shortly after taking office as president. The Travel Office, in charge of arranging presidential travel and lodgings, was staffed by career people and the Clintons wanted to put patronage employees in there instead.

Hillary was particularly anxious to steer travel business to her good friend Harry Thomason, who had produced many of the ads and videos during Bill's 1992 run for the presidency. *The Washington Post* describes how Harry "had contacted the Clintons on behalf of a Cincinnati-based aviation consulting firm in which he had a minority interest, seeking a piece of the White House travel business. Within six weeks, [White House] officials had launched an investigation into alleged financial mismanagement of the travel office, ultimately firing seven employees—who were later cleared of wrong doing."[67]

To cover their tracks and justify the dismissals, the Clinton people charged that Billy Dale, the head of the office, was guilty of misconduct.

After it turned out that Dale was not guilty of any impropriety, the special prosecutor interviewed Hillary to ask if she was the one who ordered the firing of Dale and his staff. Hillary lied (under oath) and said no. A memo surfaced from a top Clinton aide named Watkins contradicting Hillary's sworn testimony saying that the First Lady had ordered the firings and that "there would be hell to pay if we failed to take swift and decisive action in conformity with the First Lady's wishes."[68] The Watkins memo dramatically differed from Hillary's sworn statement that she did not order the dismissals. Why was she not indicted for perjury? Because the special prosecutor could not prove that she was in the chain of command, and her statement that the staff must be fired was merely an opinion, not an order. She was, after all, First Lady, not the president. Whew! A close one.

WHITEWATER: ALMOST INDICTED AGAIN

Jim McDougal, the head of the Madison Guaranty Savings and Loan Association, had been convicted of fraud and ordered to stop doing real estate deals with his bank's money. So he turned to Hillary's law partner Web Hubbell and arranged for Seth Ward, Web's father-in-law, to be a straw purchaser on a deal called both Castle Grande and

IDC (Industrial Development Commission), putting the loan and sale in his name. And he hired Hillary to do the legal work for this illegal deal.

The special prosecutor subpoenaed the law firm's billing records to determine if Hillary worked on the deal, but they had disappeared. When they finally surfaced two years later, they showed that she had, in fact, worked for 60 hours on IDC. But called before a grand jury, she denied doing any work for the "Castle Grande" project. Nobody asked her about an IDC deal.

Subsequently, Barbara Walters asked her about her denial of working on Castle Grande. She explained that she knew the project as "IDC" and did not know it was also called "Castle Grande." Nonsense. Everyone knew both names. Hillary lied again saying, "The billing records show I did not do work for Castle Grande. I did work for something called IDC, which was not related to Castle Grande."[69] Another lie. It was not only related, it was a synonym.

THE CLINTON FOUNDATION

The Clintons have their own language. The Clinton Library has no books. The Clinton Foundation makes no grants. Or at least very few.

The *New York Post* reported on April 26, 2015, that "the Clinton Foundation's finances are so messy that the nation's most influential charity watchdog put it on its 'watch list' of problematic nonprofits last month."[70] In 2013, the foundation took in more than $140 million in grants and pledges but gave only $9 million in grants for direct aid. The watchdog reported that the foundation spent most of its money on "administration, travel, and salaries and bonuses, and payouts going to family friends."[71]

The *New York Post* reported, "On its 2013 tax forms, the most recent available, the foundation claimed it spent $30 million on payroll and employee benefits; $8.7 million in rent and office expenses; $9.2 million on 'conferences, conventions and meetings'; $8 million on fundraising; and nearly $8.5 million on travel."[72] While the foundation does not pay any of the three Clintons directly, it does pay for their first class airfare. Some of the "administrative cost" finances more than 2,000 employees, including aid workers and health professionals around the world. But still, the Charity watchdog finds that its expenditures fall short of the 75% spent-on-foundation-mission that is the basic standard in the field.

Charity Navigator, an NGO, put the foundation on its watch list, which warns potential donors about investing in problematic charities. So the Clinton Foundation now joins the Rev. Al Sharpton's troubled National Action Network on the watch list. "It seems like the Clinton Foundation operates as a slush fund for the Clintons," said Bill Allison, a senior fellow at the Sunlight Foundation, a government watchdog group where progressive Democrat and Fordham Law professor Zephyr Teachout was once an organizing director.[73]

Responding to the negative Charity Navigator ratings, the Clinton Foundation made four years of tax returns available and a public memo describing its operations. The Navigator rescinded its watch list designation but still refused to rate the Clinton Foundation citing its "atypical business model" and noting that it could not be "accurately captured" by the group's rating methodology.[74]

Because the Clinton Foundation does not primarily exist to give out grants to do its work but rather directly employees the aid workers, the Navigator could not easily distinguish those employed to furnish aid to mankind from those only serving the Clintons. Was this the deliberate goal the Clintons had in organizing their foundation that way?

In July 2013, Eric Braverman, a friend of Chelsea Clinton from when they both worked at McKinsey & Company, took over as CEO of the Clinton Foundation. He took home nearly $275,000 in salary, benefits, and a housing allowance from the nonprofit for just five month's work in 2013, tax filings show. Less than a year later, his salary increased to $395,000, according to a report in Politico.[75]

Nine other executives received salaries over $100,000 in 2013, tax filings show. Recently, the foundation brought in former Health and Human Services Secretary Donna Shalala to help straighten out the mess. The former president of the University of Michigan and University of Miami is widely respected for her integrity but might be hobbled by health problems, having suffered a recent stroke.

But how the foundation spends its money is only a small part of the controversy it has generated. It's whom it gets its money from that is the real nub of its problems.

One of the most dangerous examples of this interplay between donations and favors concerned control of the world's uranium supply. The saga, spelled out in Peter Schweizer's landmark work *Clinton Cash,* involved Frank Giustra, a mining executive and a friend of Bill's and a member of the foundation's board. Giustra has pledged to donate $130 million.

It began when Giustra sold his mining company to Rosatom, a Russian firm seeking to acquire a dominant position over the world's uranium supply. Former President Clinton helped Giustra get a lucrative uranium mining deal with the nation of Kazakhstan. Giustra, in turn, helped arrange for Bill to be paid a half-million-dollar speaking fee. Giustra also arranged for Uranium One, a Russian-controlled company, to donate $2.35 million to the Clinton Foundation. Giustra personally donated $31.3 million to the foundation.

Kazakhstan, ruled by an iron-fisted tyrant named Nursultan Nazarbayev, is home to 20% of the world's uranium deposits. Giustra brought Bill Clinton there for a visit with Nazarbayev in 2005, during which Clinton praised the dictator for "opening up the social and political life of your country." Bill endorsed Nazarbayev's effort to become leader of the Organization for Security and Cooperation in Europe (OSCE) in 2009. The United States refused to follow up on Bill's lead and endorse him itself due to corruption and rights abuses, and he lost. But the real purpose of Bill's endorsement was achieved—Nazarbayev got a quote from a former American president that he can use to answer those who criticize him.

A day after President Clinton left Kazakhstan, its government signed a $450 million deal with Giustra's company that the *New York Times* reported propelled the company to becoming one of the world's leading uranium producers overnight.[76] Then the Russians moved in. In 2007, a South African company bought Giustra's company, and, in 2010, the Russian government-sponsored uranium company tried to buy the South African concern. But because the South African company, Uranium One, owned mining interests in the United States, the deal had to be approved by the US government Committee on Foreign Investment, a body that included Hillary Clinton, the secretary of state.

The stakes were high. Uranium One owned 20% of all uranium mined in the United States. Since we are not self-sufficient in that crucial metal, any deal that transfers ownership of our precious stockpiles requires government approval. And when the country getting control of a fifth of our uranium is Russia, the stakes are even higher.

On June 29, 2010, a few weeks after Russia sought to buy Uranium One, a Russian investment bank with ties to the Kremlin paid Bill (and therefore Hillary) $500,000 for a speech in Moscow. And in October 2010, the deal was approved by Hillary's committee. Stinks right? This cannot be dismissed as a partisan attack. Originally published by Peter Schweizer in his book *Clinton Cash*, the story was researched by *The New York Times*, a liberal organ. They subsequently ran it on page one. Schweizer's book is filled with conflict-of-interest stories like this one, but the uranium deal should draw particular fire as we run against Hillary. We can be thankful that no less a spokesman than Donald Trump will be attacking this loathsome deal.

E-MAILS

Regardless of the endless contradictory explanations that Hillary has given for her use of her private server, we know this: Hillary's sole purpose in keeping a secret server in her Chappaqua basement was to make sure that neither people in government nor those seeking her documents under the Freedom of Information Act would ever see them. Why? The most benign reason is her paranoia about secrecy. She never wants anyone to see anything. And, of course, she knew that she would run for president and wanted to make sure nothing transacted over e-mail would be a problem for her in the future. The more nefarious reason is that she wanted to transact business that could benefit her family financially. Transactions like helping the U.A.E. and the Saudis, who were the most generous benefactors to the Clinton Foundation and the Clinton bank accounts through speeches and other business arrangements.

We also know that Hillary knew all about the vulnerability of her unsecured Blackberry when she repeatedly refused a government issued one and insisted on using her own. In her own book *Hard Choices,* which chronicles her years as Secretary of State, Hillary describes the explicit warnings she received from State Department security officers to refrain from using her personal Blackberry in foreign countries. But Hillary's e-mails document how she and her top staff repeatedly flaunted that warning and, instead, used their cell phones all over the world.

In *Hard Choices,* Hillary recalled that:

"When we traveled to sensitive places, like Russia, we often received warnings from Department security officers to leave our Blackberrys, laptops, anything that communicated with the outside world—on the plane, with their batteries removed to prevent foreign intelligent services from compromising them. Even in friendly settings, we conducted business under strict security protections, taking care where and how we read secret material and used our technology."

She repeated that supposed protocol in a 2014 video released by the Daily Caller, claiming that she always had to leave cell phones on the plane because "they would get it . . . in a nanosecond."

So there's no question that she knew what she was supposed to do. She just chose to disregard it. E-mails show, that despite the acknowledged warnings, Hillary and her top aides routinely—and carelessly—used their Blackberrys all over the world.

In one strange e-mail, it appears that Kurt Campbell, Former Assistant Secretary of State for East Asian and Pacific Affairs, left his Blackberry in a car in Bejing and needed the Chinese to unlock the car and get it for him. Here's the exchange in an e-mail to Hillary from her personal assistant, Monica Hanley:

First, Hillary asks: "Any luck for Kurt?"

Then Hanley's response:

> "We see it in the car but the doors are locked and were waiting for the Chinese to bring the key. Agents and Caroline and I are waiting for the keys to come. Will e-mail you as soon as he has his berry."

Some security!

Hillary refused to use a government issued Blackberry, even though Eric Boswell, the Assistant Secretary of State for Diplomatic Security at the time, issued another strong warning about the dangers of using an unclassified Blackberry:

> **"I cannot stress too strongly, however, that any unclassified Blackberry is highly vulnerable in any setting to remotely and covertly monitoring conversations, retrieving e-mails, and exploiting calendars."**

But Hillary continued to use her unsecured Blackberry in Ireland, Paris, China, Russia, the U.K., Georgia, Estonia, Tanzania, and who knows where else.

Although Clinton denies that her Blackberry was ever hacked, *The Daily Caller* reported on a March 5, 2009 e-mail that suggests otherwise. The e-mail appears to be from Boswell, but is heavily redacted:

> "Her attention was drawn to the sentence that indicates that we (Diplomatic Security) have intelligence concerning this vulnerability during her recent trip to China."

So what was the intelligence they had regarding the vulnerability of Hillary's unsecured Blackberry?

Now Guccifer, the Romanian hacker who infiltrated Sid Blumenthal's e-mails to and from Hillary, has claimed that he hacked directly into Hillary's e-mails, too. In an odd turn of events, Guccifer was extradited by the Justice Department from a Romanian prison where he was serving a sentence for other hacking crimes. He has said that Hillary's server was easy to hack.

The timing of Guccifer's extradition on a charge of hacking into the e-mails of private citizens is odd. It's not exactly a priority case for the Justice Department. He was already in jail serving a seven-year term, and could not hack anything. And he was extradited for only 18 months. That's very odd. Because if he were to be tried and convicted, he might get a sentence of more than 18 months. So, is it possible that the FBI brought Guccifer to the U.S. to talk about Hillary's e-mails?

The FBI is still investigating Hillary's use of e-mails and has admitted that it is a criminal investigation. Hillary's top aides have been notified that the agency intends to question them—and Hillary too.

Each week brings new information on Hillary's use of a private e-mail server while she was secretary of state. And it seems that each revelation is coupled with Hillary's release of a new restatement of her position.

- When the server was first discovered in March 2015, Hillary originally insisted that no classified information was ever transmitted on her servers. (It's not illegal to have a private server; it is illegal to use it for classified information.)

- Then her story changed to insist that she never personally sent or received classified e-mails.

- Then, at least 104 e-mails were released by the State Department that were classified that Hillary wrote and sent herself.

- So then her story changed again to say that she never sent or received e-mails with "classification markings." This revision of her defense raised two questions that have not yet been answered satisfactorily:

1. On some of the e-mails, Hillary is caught directing her staff to remove the classification marking and to send the information to her as a "paperless" document. This would vitiate her defense that none of the docs were marked classified; and

2. Hillary, as secretary of state, is one of the few people who is charged with the duty of deciding what is classified and what is not. Many of her documents contained material that was obviously classified and, marked or not, she should have known it.

The State Department, in releasing Hillary's e-mails sent over her private server, redacted material from hundreds and even thousands of them. Each redaction is presumably of classified material, undermining further Hillary's claim not to have used the server for classified material.

At this writing, we have no idea how this scandal will end up. Some predict an indictment. Others suggest a special prosecutor will be appointed. Many fear that Attorney General Loretta Lynch will refuse to move against Hillary once she becomes the Democratic nominee. Then the question will be: What did the FBI investigators find and what did they recommend to Attorney General Lynch? Any way it comes down, the e-mail scandal will be devastating for Hillary. But for our purposes, the very fact that Hillary so wanted to guard her secrecy that she used a private server and engendered all this unnecessary controversy emphasizes Hillary's penchant for secrecy and paranoia and is, in itself, a pretty good reason not to elect her.

Reason Seven: Hillary Is Obsessively Secret and Paranoid

"Even paranoids can have enemies," said Henry Kissinger.[77] The former secretary of state probably wasn't directly referring to his successor, but it's not a bad fit. Hillary has far more than her share of enemies, critics, and partisan opponents. So do most politicians. The longer they have played the game, the more they attract. But the good ones handle it lightly. Like Reagan, they don't dwell on it and tend to laugh off the attacks.

Then there is the Nixon/Hillary sort who let their resentments fester and spread. They brood over slights and suspect everyone of being an enemy. Hillary's entire political career is one big example of how such paranoia can be one's own undoing. Like a Greek tragedy where the heroine is undone by her shortcomings and defects, Hillary's paranoia has gotten her into no end of trouble time after time after time.

Dick recalls from his own dealings with her how often she needed to be saved from her own paranoia. In August 1996, Dick and Eileen attended Bill Clinton's 60th birthday party. Typical of the Clintons, it was not a small intimate affair but a gigantic fundraiser at Radio City Music Hall in New York City to amass money for his reelection campaign. In the middle of Bill's speech, a group of gay demonstrators called Act Up stood in their seats and shouted at the president, demanding that he veto the Defense of Marriage Act and allocate more to AIDS research. The cops hurried over and removed them, with the president cautioning them, in his microphone, to be respectful and not to injure anyone and to respect their rights.

Hillary was not so tolerant a few days later when Dick met with her and the Convention Committee to finalize plans for the Democratic National Convention to be held three weeks hence. She was in a foul mood. "Were you at the birthday party?" she asked Dick, pointing her finger in his face.

"Yes, Hillary, Eileen and I both went," he answered.

"Where were you sitting? How much were your seats?" she asked. Briefly, Dick wondered if she was trying to figure out if he paid the $1,000 maximum.

When Dick told her he had, her real purpose in the interrogation emerged. "Did you see those gay demonstrators?"

"Yes," Dick replied. You couldn't miss them.

"Do you think they paid for their own seats?" she followed up.

"I don't know."

"Well I'm sure they didn't. Where would they get the thousand dollars each? They were planted there by the Republicans who paid their way so they would disrupt our birthday party," she said, her voice rising in intensity and volume, her face crunching into a hateful grimace.

She was off. "They're going to do that at our convention. They'll plant people in the galleys and get them to scream and yell and disrupt the convention during Bill's speech and mine." She continued: "I want to know who is in that [convention] hall. I want IDs, Social Security numbers, background checks on every single person in that hall."

Oh my God, Dick thought. *That would make a great story, having the FBI go around the country interviewing the friends, neighbors, business associates, and families of all our supporters and contributors. That would be great. Smile and nod your head*, he said to himself. *Don't challenge her when she's on her soapbox.* The next morning dawned bright and clear, and Dick found himself in the Oval Office meeting with the president. Dick told him of Hillary's thunderstorm the night before and prepared to make his case against her request. Dick never got the chance. "Don't worry," the president said. "She's on a tear on this. We're not going to do any of that shit." *Thank God he's president and not her*, Dick thought. Now she might be.

Here are some other stories of her paranoia and its destructive impact:

· The *Washington Post* demanded to see the family's tax returns and threatened to call for a special Whitewater prosecutor if they were not forthcoming. Hillary refused because, as noted, she did not want to reveal her winnings on the futures market until the statute of limitations on insider trading had lapsed. We got our prosecutor, eventually leading to impeachment.

- We've told the story of how Paula Jones offered to settle her lawsuit and Hillary wouldn't let her because it might lead to allegations that Bill used troopers to get women.

- We believe that Hillary demanded that the staff pull the FBI files on prominent Republicans—like Nixon with his enemies list. In any event, they all ended up in the White House being reviewed by a former bar bouncer Hillary had helped to hire.

- As noted later in the book, when Hillary insisted that her health care task force meet in secret with sealed records, she gave her program an inauspicious beginning from which it never recovered.

But there is no better example of the Greek tragedy than Hillary's e-mail scandal—a totally unnecessary precaution that ended up causing so many more problems for her than it prevented. Why doesn't this woman ever learn?

Reason Eight: Hillary Lives in a Bubble and Is Clueless About How People Live

Back during the Bush 41 presidency, we all laughed when the president had no idea what a supermarket bar code was. The rest of the country saw them every day, but Bush lived inside the White House cocoon and had actually never seen one. It was completely alien to him. It was just as funny to see Hillary having difficulty negotiating her way through a subway turnstile in New York City with her Metro Card, when she was pretending that she was just like other New Yorkers. But these amusing episodes raise an important question: Do we really want a president who has no idea what is going on in the real world? Because that's what we'll be getting if Hillary is elected.

She doesn't have a clue about the world outside of work and campaigning; it doesn't exist. For at least the past two and a half decades, she's relied on taxpayer-paid employees to take care of her every whim 24/7. She's a high-maintenance lady who has always required umpteen assistants to get her through the day, providing for everything from childcare for Chelsea to personal shopping. Nothing was ever too mundane to assign to government workers.

Hillary lives in a protected bubble, immune to the daily challenges that most of us encounter, unable to perform the simplest tasks on her own, and completely unfamiliar with the routine encounters of the "everyday Americans" she claims to represent. She lives a life of privilege and entitlement, but that very lifestyle makes her singularly isolated and unqualified to represent the voters who make up the other 99.9% of the economy and have nothing in common with her. She doesn't know them and she cannot empathize with them. After she left the White House, her circle of attendants followed her to the Senate, and then to the State Department. After that, her personal entourage moved on with her to the tax-exempt Clinton Foundation and/or her campaign, where they still loyally—and royally—serve her. If she's elected, they'll follow her back to the White House. Part of their job has been to keep the real world and the real people at bay. And, they've succeeded. Hillary is isolated from the real world and doesn't get how the rest of the world lives. In a recent debate, for example, Hillary was told a story by a worried woman whose family health care premiums had increased significantly under Obamacare, causing a serious hardship for her family. Hillary, still covered by government paid health insurance, suggested that the woman shop harder and keep checking the exchange for better rates.[78] That was her response. No criticism of Obamacare, no empathy for the woman's situation. Just shop better. Is there anyone besides Hillary who thinks that's the solution? Shop harder?

Hillary does not have the routine experiences that the rest of us do. Unlike most people, she hasn't driven a car for the last twenty-four years. She doesn't need to. Her lifetime Secret Service protection includes a car and driver and, of course, insurance and maintenance. No need to stand in line at the Department of Motor Vehicles like the rest of us. As frustrating as that experience may be, it's an equalizer. Everyone is the same. Take a number and wait. But Hillary doesn't ever have to wait. It's always taken care of for her by the innumerable civil servants and paid employees at her beck and call.

And we, the taxpayers, foot much of the bill. By the way, Bill has the same perk, so they have two free, perfectly maintained, chauffeured cars available to the family. Their twin black extra-large SUVs came in handy when Chelsea came home from the hospital after giving birth to Hillary's granddaughter, Charlotte. After the family photo op outside the hospital, Bill herded everyone to the awaiting government-paid, chauffeur-driven SUVs, and they all piled in and headed home. And of course the Clintons don't have to worry about burglar alarms and security at their DC and Chappaqua homes. Again, the Secret Service handles that, and we pay for it. And there's no issue of lost keys: the 24/7 guards make locking the doors unnecessary.

Hillary doesn't even shop for food or clothes. Her e-mails show that Huma Abedin, her longtime personal assistant in the White House, the Senate, the State Department, and her campaign, coordinates her wardrobe needs with a personal shopper at Bergdorf Goodman, the elite New York City department store. She also deals directly with expensive designers including the late Oscar de la Renta and Ralph Lauren. No need to cope with crowds in stores, or even shop online. It's all taken care of by the staff and, once again, we often paid for it. Hillary doesn't have to worry about what she should wear to each campaign event. Huma tells her what to wear. In one e-mail, she told her to wear a dark color, "maybe your new dark green suit."[79]

As for food, the State Department executive chief chef, hired by Hillary and paid by the taxpayers, often shopped and prepared food for her personal use. Hillary questioned whether she had actually paid the chef for his wonderful personal services, but no response was ever disclosed. Keep in mind that over 30,000 e-mails that Hillary unilaterally decided were personal were destroyed. So lots of what was personal but transpired at the State Department is not available. But we have enough to see how much of her personal business was executed by the government employees.

Hillary's usual response to criticism—"Everybody does it"—just doesn't work. Can you imagine Colin Powell e-mailing staff on a Sunday night to ask what time a TV show starts? Or James Baker asking his staff to arrange for some new suits or print out instructions for his new hair cut? Or Secretary of Defense Robert Gates taking directions from his staff on what color tie to wear? No, this is not the usual behavior of a high-level public official. It's the behavior of a pampered, self-involved, and probably lonesome person who knows no boundaries.

And it is pervasive. Hillary doesn't do grocery stores. Minor personal needs are taken care of by her staff (presumably her housekeeper takes care of larger food needs). When Hillary wanted skim milk, for example, she e-mailed one of her assistants on a Sunday night, asking her to buy it. She also asked her to remind her to bring more tea cups to the office. Her hair-dos even need some help from the office. She asked an employee to print out directions for how to make a "fish-tail bun." It's nice to have minions at your beck and call—especially when you don't have to pay for them.

The government employees also do heavy duty helping Hillary with her TV and entertainment needs. It seems that she couldn't figure out how to find a guide to television stations to look for her favorite shows. One Sunday night, she actually asked a State Department employee to tell her what time *The Good Wife* and *Parks and Recreation* came on. And she e-mailed another high-level employee to ask where she could watch *Homeland*. He tried to find the answer for her, but she didn't know the name of her cable provider. Do you get the picture?

There's always someone available to carry her bags. When she was carrying a lot of "stuff," in the limo ride from her home to the office, she e-mailed her staff to come down to the car and meet her. And then there's the weather. Rather than look out the window, she e-mailed her staff to ask, "What's the weather for today?" Staff were frequently asked to make sure she woke up at a certain time in the morning. That's what they're there for, aren't they? No need for alarms or wake-up calls.

Then there was her frequent need for technical assistance. We know from her e-mails that she isn't familiar with computers, faxing, Wi-Fi, and so on. And we know from our personal experience that she doesn't know how to type and doesn't use a computer at all—just an iPad and a phone. It's hard to believe, but according to her e-mails, she seriously had no idea what Wi-Fi was, whether she had it, or even how to check whether she did. Is she kidding? She repeatedly asked her staff for help with her fax machine—to no avail. She could not master it, despite repeated attempts to walk her through the process. And she did not have the ability to print any documents—personal or professional—so she directed staff to do so. And of course she often asked staff to bring her "berry" charger to her, wherever she was. So transportation, security, food, clothing, tech assistance, directions on TV shows, wake-up calls, and other mundane errands are all covered by free staff. It's a good life.

Her staff even kept tabs on where Bill Clinton was each night. Her daily schedule prepared by the State Department ended with "RON," meaning "rest of night." According to the schedules published in her e-mails, they were rarely together—usually reading:

RON	HRC	WASHINGTON
	WJC	CHAPPAQUA

The schedule would close with the weather report.

Hillary's years in the White House had prepared her for life outside the building. For special occasions like dinner parties at her home, for example, her 24 place settings of china is just perfect. Her pattern, Spode Stafford Flowers, is one of the most expensive china dinnerware patterns available and now retails for about $600 a place setting. But, of course, Hillary and Bill never paid for it. The china was a gift from many donors who were solicited on her behalf by her White House decorator to donate the place settings Hillary wanted. She had actually chosen thousands of dollars of high-end tableware and decorative objects items that she wanted and made a list. Like most brides today, she was registered at a store so that friends would know what she wanted. Hers was Borsheim's Fine Jewelry and Gifts.[80] It worked out quite well.

Except for the fact that she wasn't a bride. As they left the White House, the Clintons disclosed that they had received $190,000 worth of gifts, including $17,000 in silver flatware, $21,000 in china, $52,021 worth of furniture, $71,650 in artwork, and three carpets worth $12,282. Also included was $60,000 in glass sculptures by renowned artist Dale Chihuly.[81]

So their two multimillion-dollar houses were all set. And all of it was given as a reward for their public service. Don't you wish you had a benefactor like that? Both Donald Trump and Hillary Clinton live lives of privilege and luxury surrounded by solicitous staff who tend to their every need. But there's one key difference: Trump earned his own money to pay for his comfort. Hillary got hers as a government perk, a by-product of her so-called public service. And, unlike Hillary, Trump is always out and about with people. At Mar-a'Largo, Trump's Florida mansion and club, he is seen every weekend night during the season. Rather than hide away, like Hillary, he talks and listens to the guests, introduces his family, and enjoys himself. He plays golf, drives his car, and mingles with people. So, in every way imaginable, Hillary doesn't have a clue about life in the real world. She's the wrong choice for president.

Reason Nine: She Doesn't Know Anything about Our Biggest Problem—the Economy, Stupid

Aside from terrorism, most Americans cite the economy as our major national problem. And Hillary doesn't know much of anything about economics. In her long political career, she has grappled with any number of problems and issues: education reform, utility regulation, child care, equality for women, health care, human trafficking, terrorism, foreign affairs, and human rights. But she has never spoken out about any economic issue.

Not only is her record devoid of advocacy on the economy, she never introduced a bill in the Senate related to it or used her position as secretary of state to address it. She could have taken the lead in berating China for its currency manipulation or to warn its leaders against the gigantic financial bubble they have created that may yet plunge us into a global depression. But she didn't. She chose instead to lecture them on human rights and abortion. She might have shined at meetings of global leaders by taking the lead in pushing policies to counter the emerging worldwide recession and unemployment. But she didn't.

As First Lady, she left economic management to Bill and his advisors. As a candidate for president, she never spoke out about near-zero interest rates or the looming economic crash or the unsustainable housing bubble about to burst or the dangerous proliferation of subprime mortgages. She simply knows nothing about the economy and has no qualifications to lead us out of our stagnation and recession.

Bush-43, by contrast, had graduated from the Harvard Business School. Bill Clinton was well tutored on the economy, and Ronald Reagan's entire career was based on his economic views. But Hillary, like Obama before her, approaches the economy without any preparation or particular knowledge. The White House is a dangerous place to learn about our most important problem. Hillary's campaign rendition of her economic plan is little more than a repetition of Democratic Party dogma, doubtless drafted for her by others.

For example, her recipe for "boosting economic growth" includes "tax cuts to the middle class and small businesses." The last Democratic presidential candidate to urge a middle class tax cut was husband Bill who not only failed to deliver the promised cut, but actually sharply increased taxes. She also calls for "an infrastructure bank" that will spend $27.5 billion on "roads, bridges, public transit, rail, airports, the Internet, and water systems." If the trillion-dollar stimulus package proposed and passed by President Obama upon taking office did little or nothing to stimulate growth, how will Hillary's public works program do any better? And as a throw in, she says, without specificity, that she will fund "more scientific research."

Just in case her stimulus plans trigger any economic growth, she will see that it is extinguished by raising the minimum wage to $15, "increasing workers' benefits, expanding overtime, and encouraging businesses to share profits with employees." Her proposed hike in the capital gains tax, requiring investments to be held for six years in order to qualify for the current 20% rate, will make capital for new inventions and processes harder and harder to get, stymieing economic expansion. It is the program of an economic ignoramus, copied from boiler-plate language in every past Democratic platform. Her own campaign website boasts of her "economic priorities as Secretary of State." The list is pathetic and shows how little she focused on economic issues. The site says that she

- "lobbied for American companies in foreign countries" (She did, as long as they gave generously to the Clinton Foundation and invited Bill to speak for a six-figure fee.)

- "drafted the Trans-Pacific Partnership" (She now opposes it.)

- "pried open Chinese markets to U.S. companies" (She was so effective in doing so that our trade deficit with China now exceeds $500 billion annually.)

Some record!

Reason Ten: Hillary Is Governed by Gurus

Hillary is not a creative thinker. She is accustomed to getting her talking points from Bill or some other key advisor and going out there and fighting for them. She is an advocate in the purist sense of the term, not an innovator. So, for her entire political career, she has always been in the thrall of some political guru or other. Under her gurus' influence, she adopts their priorities and programs, often hook, line, and sinker.

If we elect Hillary as our president, we can't be sure who the guru who guides her will be. Every president has advisors upon whom he relies. But Hillary takes it to an obsessive degree. She hangs on his or her every word as a lodestar. Dick knows. He served as her guru from 1995 to 1996. Hillary listened to his every word. Bill told Dick in 1995, "She reads your memo every day and is doing just what you suggest."

In 1993, when Hillary took over the health care task force, she appointed Ira Magaziner, a protégé of former Labor Secretary Robert Reich, to direct its efforts. Magaziner sold Hillary on the total overhaul of the entire system that she ultimately recommended. She followed his advice so literally that the final, unwieldy product went down in flames.

During her 2008 run for the White House, she put Mark Penn in as her chief strategist, giving him much of the guru role Dick had occupied in Bill's 1996 campaign. Penn's advice was ultimately so bad that the rest of the staff revolted and forced Hillary to sideline him. Many blame Penn for her disastrous defeat by Obama.

As secretary of state, Sidney Blumenthal was her guru. The revelation of her numerous e-mails back and forth to Sidney demonstrate the degree of her dependence on his input. Hillary tried to hire Blumenthal to her State Department staff, but Obama blocked the appointment, so she got him consulting deals with the Clinton Foundation and her puppet front group, Media Matters. With a cunning mix of half-baked intelligence and sound political advice, Sydney held Hillary almost hypnotized. In electing Hillary, we don't know whom we are getting. We don't know who will fill the space in her mind reserved for gurus.

Reason Eleven: She Is Rigid and Stubborn

Nobody is as pig-headed as Hillary Clinton. Once she gets an idea in her mind or decides on a course of action, she will doggedly pursue it regardless of its obvious limitations and political cost. Her rigidity stands in contrast to her willingness to flip-flop on issues. When a new political season is upon her, with new demands and political needs, she unhesitatingly throws away her previous platform and takes whatever position will benefit her current needs. But on a tactical level, she is almost totally inflexible.

· She insisted on keeping the proceedings and records of her health care task force secret until a federal judge ordered them opened and fined the federal government $285,864 for the damage caused by Hillary's secrecy fetish. The harm to the program that the task force ultimately produced was immeasurable.

· Hillary insisted she had no role in firing the White House Travel Office Staff in 1993 despite extensive evidence—and staff memos—the proved otherwise. In the end, she was almost indicted for perjury for her stubbornness in swearing under oath that she was not involved. There was nothing illegal about the firings. The staff served at the president's pleasure. But Hillary didn't want her role out there in public. Her stubbornness almost led to her indictment.

· When the *Washington Post* asked for the Clintons' tax returns in 1993, she refused to let Bill release them because they contained evidence of her futures market winnings. Her stubbornness this time led to the appointment of a special prosecutor who dogged the Clintons during Bill's entire presidency.

· As noted, when Paula Jones sued the president for sexual harassment and was willing to drop her suit without requiring an admission of guilt or any money, Hillary refused to let Bill settle because Paula asked that he confirm that he sent a state trooper to fetch her. Hillary was afraid that this admission would reinforce a story that Bill used troopers to get women. Because Hillary wouldn't settle, the suit continued and eventually led to the Lewinsky scandal and impeachment.

· Hillary insisted on using a private server while secretary of state despite the virtual certainty that she would be challenged for doing so. She stubbornly claimed that she never handled classified material on the server even after over a thousand e-mails confirmed that she did. Her constantly changing stories of what she used the server for caused a massive erosion in public trust, but she stood her ground.

- While running against Bernie Sanders, she doggedly refused to release the texts of her speeches to Goldman Sachs that she delivered after leaving the State Department and for which she received six-figure fees. Her obstinate refusal gave Sanders a campaign issue he used to pummel her repeatedly.

Hillary sees flexibility as a sign of weakness and holds to her established position like Krazy Glue. Her macho insistence on never giving in denies her key tactical flexibility. Like German and Russian soldiers in World War II who were ordered to take "not one step back," Hillary's stubbornness denies her the ability to execute tactical retreats or even to maneuver.

Reason Twelve: Nepotism — the Clinton Family Money Grab

The practice of nepotism, giving special favors to family members and special friends, reached brand new levels in the Clinton White House. Every one of the Clinton siblings, Roger Clinton and Hugh and Tony Rodham, traded on their family names and were paid hundreds of thousands of dollars to secure presidential pardons. Even after Bill Clinton left office, Roger Clinton and Tony Rodham have continued to trade on the family name and relationships. And especially since Bill Clinton became the virtual ruler of Haiti and Hillary was viewed as a likely next president, great opportunities for the family have continued to pour in. And now even Chelsea has joined the nepotistic team.

CHELSEA CLINTON TRADES IN ON THE FAMILY NAME

Chelsea is out there now, campaigning hard for Mom, attacking Sanders and Trump, and even fanning speculation that she might become the third Clinton to launch her own political career. God help us. Chelsea Clinton has lived a life of privilege and entitlement, and her professional life has been entirely based on exploiting her family connections. Unlike the rest of the world, Chelsea has never had to look for a job. They've all been handed to her because her last name is Clinton, and not because of any special, or even not so special, talents. She's the Princess of Nepotism. Her first job was an entry-level position at McKinsey, where she certainly had to be viewed as an asset for attracting clients. Next, one of her mother's biggest donors hired her at Avenue Capital, where she didn't exactly wow the financial community. She left after three years, once she realized that she just "couldn't . . . care about money."[82]

How touching and insightful. No need to care about money when it's just handed to you. No need to worry about student loans when you have degrees from Stanford, Columbia, and Oxford (2), and you didn't need any student loans. No need to worry about money when your parents help your husband's career and their donors invest in his hedge fund, even though it's not too successful. No need to worry about housing when you live in a $10 million apartment in New York. No need to worry about a job when you're given one, regardless of your qualifications (or lack of them). Really, who needs money?

Certainly not Chelsea. After she left Wall Street, she pursued an academic career, once again, using her family contacts. In 2010, NYU president John Sexton, friend of Bill, appointed her as assistant vice provost of the Global Network University at NYU, bringing together Muslims and Jews in New York and around the globe. Not clear what her qualifications were, other than daughter of Bill and Hillary, when asked about this role, she told *Time Magazine* that she was passionate about "trying to really figure out what the right pedagogy should be in multifaith and interfaith education and leadership."[83] Sounds fascinating. And typical Chelsea Clinton blah-blah-blah-blah-blah.

In 2013, she allegedly cofounded and chaired the NYU multifaith "Of Many Institute for Multifaith Leadership." She insisted that her interfaith marriage to a Jewish husband qualified her for this position. Of course. When evidence of brutal treatment of workers and violations of basic human rights were lodged against NYU's construction workers at the new campus of the Global Network University in Abu Dhabi, Ms. Clinton was silent about the abuses to her new Muslim constituency. Could her silence be related to Bill's fees for speaking at NYU graduations or to his trip to Abu Dhabi to speak to the first graduating class of the Global Network University, where he never mentioned the controversy? That's not her department.

Chelsea's next job was as a Special Correspondent for NBC TV. That was a bust, but a lucrative one. She had a contract for $600,000 a year, although in 2014 she only appeared on four very boring segments, including an interview with the Geico Gecko. So bad was she on camera that she usually did only voice over segments with very little actual live time, if any, on camera. Even NBC realized how bad she was and dumped her, but not before she collected over $1.5 million. Apparently, Ms. Clinton received very special treatment at NBC. Agents hired by her parents basically came in and convinced the idiots at the network that she would be an asset. They were dead wrong. And she insisted on being treated like a prima donna. NBC staff were told not to approach her but to go through her producers. The few interviews she did were painful to watch. Chelsea is not a natural.

She was also reportedly paid $300,000 for sitting on the board of a Barry Diller's company. No telling what that's about. Barry and his wife, Diane von Furstenberg, are big fans and supporters of Bill and Hillary. It's lucrative and prestigious to have the Clinton last name.

Now Chelsea is vice chairman of the Clinton Foundation, another position where she seems to be in over her head. She has six staffers at her disposal. Bill only has five. And although scarcely an inspiring speaker, she goes out to speak on behalf of the foundation—at least five organizations have actually been so shameless in courting her parents that they paid to hear her speak. Hard to believe. One Florida charity even paid $75,000. Embarrassingly awkward in front of a microphone, even after years of practice, her speeches are littered with the same canned lines no matter who she is speaking to.

Apparently Chelsea's leadership and management talents are not really appreciated at the foundation. Since she has been involved, lots of folks have left, claiming she was "unpleasant" to deal with. Of course, she's had no management experience.

Chelsea also has no experience as an author. Yet the Clinton-friendly publishing house reached out to her to write a book about issues that are important to young adults. Anyway, she'll figure it out—with help from aides, ghosts, and so on. And once again, she'll trade on the Clinton name. That's what she does.

THE RODHAM AND CLINTON BROTHERS' CONSTANT QUEST TO GRAB BIG BUCKS

Tony Rodham Tries to Get Visas for Chinese Cyberspies

Hillary's ne'er-do-well brother, Tony Rodham, was implicated in a federal investigation about his efforts to obtain visas for two Chinese nationals linked to a company controlled by the Chinese Army after their applications and appeals were categorically denied by the government. Their Chinese employer, Huawei Technologies, then invested in a company ostensibly headed by Rodham to help them out. Nobody in the Clinton-Rodham family seemed to notice that this might be a big conflict of interest while his sister was Secretary of State. The brouhaha is all about the federal Immigrant Investor Program, also known as EB-5. The United States Citizenship and Immigration Services administers this program that offers foreign investors, mainly Chinese, a path to citizenship in return for a $500,000 cash investment that is used to create 10 US jobs.

The investments were supposed to help immigrant investors. But these were no ordinary investors—and no ordinary immigrants. No, Huawei Technologies had been caught pirating American technology and there have been serious national security concerns about their activities. Huawei has repeatedly tried to purchase stakes in American telephone and communications companies, only to be denied permission by the Foreign Investment Review Board on national security grounds because of suspected links to the Chinese military. We don't trust them. And we shouldn't. Equally disturbing is the company's commercial alliances with enemies of the United States, including projects in Iran, where they developed devices to track dissidents through their phones.

But that didn't stop Tony. If there was money to be made, he was right on it.

According to Bill Gertz of the *Washington Times*, former Secretary of Defense Donald Rumsfeld ordered American aircraft to join British warplanes in a "raid on an Iraqi air defense network that had been targeting US aircraft patrolling the skies over Iraq. Some fifty jets bombed an air defense control center for fiber optic cables that Huawei technicians had installed in violation of UN sanctions."[84] Huawei also assisted the Taliban by installing a phone system in Kabul, Afghanistan. These are the folks that Rodham was promoting. The United States doesn't want them here—and with good reason. They don't belong here. But Tony Rodham took money to be a front man in a company dedicated to helping them get the coveted visas.

Clinton family best friend and current governor of Virginia, Terry McAuliffe, brought Rodham in to a company he had set up. The fact that Rodham's sister was secretary of state was, of course, a big plus. The Huawei Company evidently thought so, because even as brother Tony was trying to get their executives into the country, the company was lobbying the White House and the State Department over a variety of issues. Guess that Rodham name might help? Did it help to have the name Rodham on an application to the government while his sister is secretary of state?

Rodham, of course, had no professional experience in this area and only a year before becoming CEO of the company was a deadbeat dad sued for over $100,000 in back child support. His entire adult life has been spent trying to make money off his family connections—from selling hazelnuts in the nation of Georgia to selling pardons in the White House. It's highly unlikely that Hillary had no idea what Tony was up to. Make that impossible that she didn't know. And he's still at it.

All in the Family: Tony and Roger Go to Haiti

Following the Haiti earthquake, Bill and Hillary Clinton became the most powerful people in Haiti. Through the State Department, the Bush–Clinton Haiti Fund, and the Clinton Foundation, they controlled the granting of all contracts for rebuilding Haiti.

Bill Clinton ran Haiti after he was appointed as the UN Special Envoy to Haiti. In addition, he and Jean-Max Bellerive, a former prime minister, headed the Interim Haiti Recovery Commission (IHRC) that had to give final approval to every reconstruction project. Cheryl Mills, Hillary Clinton's Chief of Staff and a longtime Clinton Foundation board member, was the State Department liaison to Haiti and was a member of the IHRC. So anyone who wanted to get anything done in Haiti had to get the OK from the IHRC . . . and, presumably HRC. Let's leave aside for the moment Bill's and Hillary's own greed and malfeasance, which could fill a book, seeing yet another opportunity for trading on their famous names, Tony Rodham and Roger Clinton prowled around for a new project. Not surprisingly, both of them found something in Haiti.

Tony's Mining Company Connection

Tony was given a seat on the board of a company that received the first permit to mine for gold in Haiti, again exploiting and making money, this time off Hillary and Bill's role as the savior of Haiti. How did Tony get the gold-mining gig? At a meeting of the Clinton Global Initiative, he met the chief executive of the Delaware-based VCS Mining Company. Guess the CEO was blown away by Tony's talents . . . or maybe he looked around and saw just how things worked. One thing is certain: Bill Clinton had to know about Tony's mining deal. When the details became public in 2013, the Haiti Senate passed a resolution calling for a moratorium on all activities connected to gold mining permits, citing the historic "pillaging" of Haiti's natural resources. The IHRC would know all about it—and so would HRC and WJC. They just chose, once again, to look the other way.

Tony's Land Grant in Haiti: A Gift of 10,000 Acres

According to the *New York Times,* Tony also tried to get approval from the Clinton Foundation Haiti Fund for a $22 million project to rebuild housing in Haiti from which he expected to make $1 million profit. Tony admitted that "a guy in Haiti" had "donated" 10,000 acres of land to him. So who was this very generous guy? And why would anyone give anything to Tony Rodham—except to try to influence the Clintons, who were running the show in Haiti. Tony testified under oath in a lawsuit filed by his former lawyer that he was in regular contact with Bill Clinton, nudging him to grant the $22 million from his Fund, and that he was assured that it would happen soon. In his testimony, Tony made it clear that the Clinton Foundation was the vehicle for his dealings. According to the *New York Times*, he said that it was the foundation that got him in touch with officials in Haiti. The Clinton Foundation denied knowing anything about it. Sure.

Roger's Haiti Consulting Deal

Meanwhile, Roger was able to pick up a $100,000 consulting gig with a group of builders who wanted to build houses in Haiti. His benefactor, businessman Wayne Coleman, told the *New York Times*, "I paid Roger $100,000 . . . Basically, he promised to get us a contract through the Clinton Foundation for a project over there. What he was really trying to do was sell the influence of his brother."[85] Neither Roger's nor Tony's Haiti schemes have worked out.

Roger's Foreign Cash

During the Clinton presidency, Bill Clinton's brother Roger collected $700,000 in cash, money orders, and American Express

Travelers Cheques issued in foreign countries. Roger told FBI agents that he "received money for President Clinton from foreign governments"[86] during Bill's presidency. Roger says that the first few times he came to Washington bearing cash, he gave it to his brother. But after that, he told the FBI that either Bill or his staff told him that the president could not accept money from foreign governments and that he should send the money back.

Now that's a good one, isn't it? What are the odds that Roger Clinton packed up wads of cash and sent it back to where it came from? And what about the first few times? What happened to that money? In 2002, the House Committee on Government Reform issued a scathing report on the Clinton presidential pardons with disturbing findings about Bill's brother. "Roger Clinton engaged in a systematic effort to trade on his brother's name"[87] during the Clinton administration, the report found. The section of the Committee report on Roger went well beyond just pardons and included a number of his other schemes to trade on his relationship to the president.

His combined take was $700,000—and that's just what he deposited in his bank account and could be traced. It seems likely that he pocketed or spent at least some additional cash. Roger insisted that his brother was aware of his activities and approved of them. Roger admitted to receiving $335,000 in cash and traveler's checks from foreign sources such as South Korea, Venezuela, and Taiwan that were deposited into his account during Bill's presidency, as well as an additional $150,000. Roger refused to tell the Committee why he had received the checks, but apparently told the FBI that a lot of it was for overseas "concerts" by his band. Let's get real. Roger wasn't exactly Mick Jagger and the Rolling Stones.

The committee noted that the fact that the traveler's checks were provided blank, "suggests that the funds were intentionally provided to Clinton in a manner calculated to conceal their origin."[88] All of the traveler's checks were purchased overseas and brought to the United States by Roger Clinton, who did not disclose them to Customs officials as required by federal law. The Committee also noted that it was likely that there were more traveler's checks and cash that were not deposited into his account.

The House Committee uncovered these checks totaling $335,000 in Roger Clinton's bank account:

Date Deposited	Type of Check	Origin	Purchaser Name	Amount
November 30, 1998	American Express	Unknown	Chen Jianxing	$1,000
November 30, 1998	American Express	Unknown	Chen Jianxing	$1,000
December 1, 1998	American Express	Taiwan	Huang Xian Wen	$15,000
December 8, 1998	American Express	Taiwan	Huang Xian Wen	$23,000
December 15, 1998	Citicorp	Taiwan	Unknown	$90,000
December 15, 1998	Unknown	Unknown	Unknown	$29,000
December 15, 1998	Visa-Sumitomo	Taiwan	Lin Mei Guang	$4,000
December 15, 1998	American Express	Taiwan	Huang Xian Wen	$2,000
July 12, 1999	American Express	Unknown	Unknown	$20,000
July 12, 1999	Citicorp	South Korea	Sook-Eun Jang	$5,000
November 30, 1999	Citicorp	Taiwan	Unknown	$3,000
November 30, 1999	Citicorp	Taiwan	Unknown	$10,000
November 30, 1999	Citicorp	Taiwan	Unknown	$5,000
November 30, 1999	Visa	Taiwan	Unknown	$1,000
November 30, 1999	Visa	Taiwan	Xu Jingsheng	$3,000
November 30, 1999	Citicorp	Venezuela	Pedro Jose Garboza Matos	$38,000

Date Deposited	Type of Check	Origin	Purchaser Name	Amount
November 30, 1999	Unknown	Unknown	Unknown	$40,000
February 22, 2000	American Express	Taiwan	Qu Guang Yin	$7,000
March 24, 2000	Citicorp	Venezuela	Pedro Jose Garboza Matos	$3,000
April 5, 2000	American Express	Taiwan	Mou Chuanxue	$4,000
April 17, 2000	American Express	Taiwan	Qu Guang Yin	$13,000
April 17, 2000	American Express	Unknown	Suk Eun Chang	$5,000
May 15, 2000	American Express	Unknown	Unknown	$5,000
July 13, 2000	Citicorp	South Korea	Seung-Chul Ham	$1,000
July 27, 2000	Citicorp	South Korea	Seung-Chul Ham	$2,000
July 31, 2000	Citicorp	South Korea	Seung-Chul Ham	$4,000
August 2, 2000	American Express	Unknown	Unknown	$1,000
August 11, 2000	American Express	Unknown	Unknown	$1,000
Total Payments Received				$335,000

In addition to the $335,000 listed above, Roger also deposited $85,000 in cash in his personal bank account between January and November 1998. In December 1999, he deposited a $70,000 traveler's check from "Suk Eun Chang" as well as a $10,000 traveler's check from the same source. Clinton refused to disclose the source of these funds, saying only that he got some of the money for performing in foreign countries with his band. The Committee was unable to find Suk Eun Chang to get any further information.

Hugh Rodham Lobbied for Pardon for Crack/Cocaine Dealer and Claims Hillary Supported Him

Hugh Rodham was paid $204,000 by the father of Carlos Vignali, a predatory crack/cocaine kingpin who was convicted of transporting and distributing massive kilos of addictive drugs in poor neighborhoods in Minnesota. Both the pardon attorney at the Justice Department and the US Attorney in Minnesota who had prosecuted the case adamantly opposed the pardon.

But Vignali's father was a local politician in Los Angeles who began calling in his chits. Soon Vignali supporters were attending meetings and talking to key White House Staff—all arranged by Rodham. One of them was Alejandro Mayorkas, then US Attorney in Los Angeles. He later helped Tony Rodham in his own influence-peddling business. Bill Clinton granted a commutation of Vignali's remaining sentence.

When the House Government Operations Committee investigated the pardons, they interviewed Hugh Rodham. In meeting after meeting, Rodham repeatedly cited his sister's support for his activities. According to the committee report, he told the White House staff that Hillary was aware of and very concerned about the pardon.

Rodham was also able to get another pardon. This one was for Glenn Braswell, a convicted fraudster who paid Rodham $230,000 and purportedly "loaned" him an additional $79,000 after his success in getting the pardon. Hugh also represented Gene and Nora Lum, who were convicted of money laundering and making illegal campaign contributions to Democratic Party campaigns. Hugh failed on that one.[89]

Tony Rodham Gets Pardon for Bank Fraudsters

Hillary's younger brother, Tony Rodham, got in on the gravy train. He was paid $244,758 for getting a pardon for Vann Jo and Edgar Gregory, carnival owners who had received suspended sentences for bank fraud. Tony also tried on several occasions to solicit money from the daughter of Fernando Fuentes-Coba, who had been convicted of violating the Cuban embargo. When she declined to pay the $50,000 fee he quoted, he then offered a discounted price of $30,000.[90]

Roger Clinton Was Paid $50,000 to Get Mob Pardon

Roger Clinton tried unsuccessfully for several pardons, although he and the Clintons initially denied that he had lobbied his brother. The FBI found that Roger had been paid $50,000 by members of the Gambino crime family to get a pardon for mob lieutenant Rosario Gambino. He was also paid $43,500 by Garland Lincecum, who was told that he could purchase a presidential pardon for $30,000. None of Roger's pardon requests were granted, but Roger himself was given a pardon by his brother.

Throughout the FBI interviews, Roger insisted that Bill Clinton was aware of his pardon activities and made tactical suggestions.

Bill and Hillary have had more than ample evidence of their siblings' shenanigans over the past two decades. And by opening doors, making introductions, granting pardons, and the like, the former first couple are enablers, not bystanders. Look for much more of the same in a Hillary Clinton White House. They're all poised to move into their old rooms.

CHAPTER 2

How to Beat Hillary

THE KEY TO DEFEATING Hillary is to run against her the way Bernie Sanders did. While he failed to win the nomination, Sanders defeated Hillary in state after state, scoring upsets where she least expected them. Bernie's appeal was so strong, and Hillary's so weak, that their battle came right down to the wire.

Sanders exposed all of Hillary's weaknesses.

· She has to win Independents in November, but she lost them overwhelmingly in the primaries.

· She needs to carry voters under 35 by top-heavy margins in the general election, but she lost them by 3:1 and 4:1 in the primaries.

· Hillary has to carry the blue states to win the election, but in the primaries she lost a slew of states, including Michigan and Wisconsin—that she must carry in November.

Hillary's margin over Bernie came largely from states she has no chance of winning in November. Hillary carried South Carolina, Georgia, Alabama, Mississippi, Louisiana, Texas, and more than a dozen other red states. But although they sided with Hillary in the primaries, she has not a prayer of carrying them in November.

In order to exploit that vulnerability and to benefit from the Democratic Party's divisions, Republicans must run against Hillary the way Bernie did. We cannot embrace his left-wing agenda of tax increases, gun control, environmental extremism, and socialism. But we can make the same critique of the special interests that dominate the Democratic Party that Sanders did.

We can hammer away at the need to regulate Wall Street and say bluntly that we will not rescue any bank that is thought to be too big to fail. And we can draw the correlation between massive illegal immigration and job loss, unemployment, wage stagnation, and income inequality that animated and invigorated the Sanders campaign.

Hillary: Teflon No More

Hillary and Bill have successfully dodged scandals ever since they entered public life, not because they were innocent, but because a variety of circumstances made it impossible to prove beyond a reasonable doubt that they were guilty. Scandal follows them everywhere. They're still standing, but that doesn't mean they are unscathed. During Bill Clinton's presidency, Hillary had two narrow escapes from federal indictment, and Bill lost his law license and was fined close to a million dollars after a federal judge found him in civil contempt of court for lying in the Paula Jones deposition.

At this writing, the FBI is still investigating Hillary's handling of classified documents at the State Department and has apparently expanded that investigation to determine whether the overlapping activities of the Clinton Foundation, Bill Clinton's paid speaking clients, and State Department actions violated corruption laws. The outcome of these serious, serious inquiries could derail Hillary's candidacy.

But what if this political Houdini escapes being held responsible for her crimes once again? What is the lasting impact of the scandals that have engulfed her?

The constant attacks on the integrity of the Clintons, especially Hillary, have left a deep legacy of distrust and dislike by American voters. A Quinnipiac poll in the summer of 2015 found that 61% of the respondents felt that Hillary was not "honest and trustworthy," while only 34% felt these adjectives fit her.[1] Hillary's favorability ratings have suffered and her vote share in a prospective general election seems to have fallen as a result. But she is not in jail or on her way. So will these attacks matter? Damn right they will. Each hit has taken a chink out of her armor and made her more vulnerable and less believable.

A candidate is like a gladiator with only one weapon in her arsenal: her own voice. If she is disbelieved on a fundamental level, she loses the ability to speak and ever be credited with telling the truth. A candidate who cannot be believed is one who cannot campaign effectively, who cannot give a speech with any credibility, who cannot take a position on an issue and be taken at her word. That's Hillary—stripped of maneuverability, unable to cope with changing events and situations. Naked in the face of attacks, she becomes a ship without a navigational system. Still afloat, but dead in the water.

But strategically, in order to defeat Hillary, we must go beyond her scandals and her character flaws. We have to come to grips with how Obama has changed America. He has not only transformed our economy and health care, but he has kept his most basic promise: to fundamentally change America. Just as he has changed our country, so we must change the way we plan to beat Hillary.

A self-defeating cycle has gripped the GOP. Many Republicans try to win elections by moving to the center, mimicking what Clinton did in 1996. They tone down their opposition to gun control, moderate their views on abortion, grudgingly accept same-sex marriage, go along with the bulk of the Democratic spending programs, and promise to "fix" but not to "repeal" Obamacare. But the more Republicans move to the center, becoming the "pale pastel" shades Reagan condemned instead of the "bold colors" he proclaimed, the more the base stays home.[2] They see no reason to elect go-along, get-along Republicans who will submit to the dictates of the liberal media and sell out their ideals once they take office. The base comes to see the candidates as the "Tweedledum" and "Tweedledee" of Alice in Wonderland, different only in their party labels. Hence the complaint one hears all over: "I have nobody to vote for!"

The Key to Victory: Get Out Our Base Voters

In 2008, Obama won by turning *his* voters on and, in the process, turning them out. But in 2012 he won by turning *our* voters off and keeping them at home. In 2008, his program of "hope and change" resonated with a broad spectrum of Americans. He got people of both races to come out to vote enthusiastically for his view of the political promised land. He got nine million new voters to the polls in 2008. (In 2004, 122 million Americans voted. In 2008, 131 million did, inspired by Barack Obama).

But as president, Obama turned out to be an old-fashioned African American liberal, backing more handouts, food stamps, welfare, and benefits of every description while raising taxes on everybody (not just the rich) and cutting defense to the danger point. He passed a modified version of socialized medicine and jammed through measures that doubled the national debt. His program appalled the moderates in the center, but his handouts bought him greater support from the "takers," people who depended on the labor and taxes of others to make ends meet. Even as his policies expanded his base, they angered what had been the middle, driving them into the arms of the GOP, allowing the Republicans to win first the House and then the Senate. By the time he ran for reelection in 2012, it was not enough just to get his people out to vote. He needed to turn his base on—and the Republican supporters off! He had to combine a big turnout from his voters with a low turnout of everyone else.

He kept his voters turning out by increasing handouts and goodies to bring the dependent population to the polls. And while he did that, he ran negative ads savaging Romney in order to turn off Romney's potential supporters and keep them home on Election Day. He bought the Left and so depressed the Middle and the Right that they wallowed in cynicism and didn't even vote.

In the election of 2012, voter turnout dropped after years of increasing. Only 129 million voted, two million fewer than in 2008, even though the US population had risen by 10 million in the interim. In 2008, 62.3% of eligible citizens voted, but in 2012, only 57.5% showed up. Ten million would-be voters stayed home. While Obama brought in millions of new black and Latino voters in 2008, the real swing in 2012 was that the white vote stayed home.

Why Didn't Whites Vote in 2012?

Between 2004 and 2012, white voter turnout dropped by 10 million and black and Hispanic turnout rose by four million. In fact, in 2012, blacks voted at a higher percentage of those eligible than whites did. Republicans carried the whites who did vote by 61 to 39, but 10 million stayed home and didn't show up at the polls. It wasn't that whites lost population; there were 10 million more white Americans in 2012 than in 2004. They just did not vote.

To understand the decrease in white turnout, we have to go back to the year 2000 when a tied election showed everybody the value of each single vote. Add to that the sense of urgency engendered by the 9/11 attacks and the result was a dramatic 10-million-vote surge in white turnout in just the four years between 2000 and 2004. Voters had something to believe in: George W. Bush's courageous stand against international terror. But then disillusionment and disenchantment set in. The Iraq War ground on with mounting body counts. The crash of 2008 wiped out more than a decade's economic gains. And under Obama, things just kept getting worse. Rather than galvanize these absent voters into turning out, the depressing conditions left them feeling apathetic and passive. Hopeless. So they stayed home on Election Day. And most of the absentee voters were whites who would have voted for Romney. To win in 2016, we have got to get those voters back.

VOTER TURNOUT BY ETHNIC GROUP, 2004–2012

	WHITE (%)	BLACK (%)	HISPANIC (%)
2000	61.8	56.8	43.3
2004	67.2	60.0	44.2
2008	66.1	64.7	47.6
2012	64.1	66.2	47.3

Note, in this table, how white turnout surged in 2004 from 61.8% in 2000 to 67.2% in 2004. That reelected Bush. Then it dropped from 67.2% in 2004 to only 64.1% in 2012. That reelected Obama. Meanwhile, look at how black turnout soared from 56.8% in 2000 to 66.2% in 2012. Hispanic turnout rose as well, though by not as much, from 43.3% to 47.3%.[3]

How to Get the Disappearing White Vote to Show Up

To win, the Republican Party needs to appeal to all segments of the electorate, and the process has to start with an answer to the question, How do we get white turnout back up? The election of 2012 proved that these disenchanted voters won't show up to vote *against* something. To get them to come to the polls, they have to have something to vote *for*. The stay-at-home voters disliked Obama—his job approval was at record lows. But Obama had a secret weapon: Mitt Romney.

Obama drove a fissure into the white vote separating those who had graduated from college and had adequate income from those who did not. These downscale white voters wouldn't swallow Mitt Romney, even if the alternative was reelecting Obama by staying home and not voting. They understood that the American branch office of the global economy couldn't care less about them and left them behind at every turn. These voters got it that Romney was no businessman; he was a speculator. He was the poster boy for the fabulous incomes of the richest 1%, while those whose votes they sought were just treading water, stagnating in income and wealth. But now we have a secret weapon of our own: Donald Trump.

Trump's campaign has energized the very voters we need to bring out in order to win. With Trump stimulating turnout, the Republican primaries generated vastly more voters than they did just four years ago. The Republican race drew 33 million voters, almost twice the 19 million who voted in 2012. Where did these extra 14 million come from? Likely many were from the ranks of those who stayed home in the general election of 2012.

It is Donald Trump who brought them out in the primaries, and it will be the Donald who brings them out in the general election. Indeed, exit polls by CBS suggest that half of the Republicans voting in the Michigan primary, which was typical of the other primaries, were first-time GOP primary voters.[4] Trump's voters, in particular, were precisely the ones who sat out the 2012 election and led to Obama's victory: white voters who had not been to college. As they pump gas and look forlornly at the closed factory where they once had good jobs at good pay, their resentments fester. And when they see the Wall Street kids making money hand over fist, their anger explodes.

It is at that point that their resentments and opinions merge with the Bernie Sanders voters who decry that 95% of the income gains of the past eight years have gone to the top 1% of the population. These leftists once sought to "occupy Wall Street" and used their votes to give Hillary the scare of her life as they propelled Bernie to the verge of the Democratic nomination. Ultimately, the Left and the Right fuse in their outrage at income inequality. And they have a good case.

The fact is that the downscale, non-college-educated white voter is the one who has been left behind by the global economy. It's hard to believe, but white high school graduates with no college education get a median weekly paycheck of only $700! How can you support a family on that?

If they have completed a two-year associate degree or have some college, their weekly income goes up by all of $91 to the princely sum of $791. It isn't until they get a four-year college degree that whites make any kind of decent money—$1,132 per week, or $59,000 a year Blacks and Hispanics do even worse. A four-year college degree still leaves blacks $12,000 below white income levels and Hispanics $10,000 behind.

MEDIAN WEEKLY INCOME[5]

	WHITE	BLACK	HISPANIC
HIGH SCHOOL GRADUATE	$696	$579	$595
SOME COLLEGE EDUCATION	$791	$637	$689
FOUR-YEAR DEGREE	$1,132	$895	$937

With their incomes depressed, their factories closed, and opportunities seeming to vanish, non-college-educated whites are truly the jump ball in our politics.

At the start of the modern era, these non-college-educated voters were attracted to the Democratic Party as FDR pushed his New Deal, urging workers to join labor unions and reinforcing their determination to oppose the "economic royalists" who Roosevelt condemned during his 1936 reelection campaign. FDR had governed in close coordination with the capitalist class in his first term. But as he ran for his second term, he pivoted sharply to the left and attacked those whom he had supported in the past. Democrats picked up the FDR theme. They pounded into the heads of blue-collar whites that they needed to vote Democrat to protect their families, jobs, and paychecks.

As a result of the FDR/Truman/Johnson rhetoric, blue-collar whites came to believe that they needed to vote Democrat to protect their economic interests against rapacious and greedy employers. Class warfare became the Democratic Party's motif. Decades later, Richard Nixon, and later Ronald Reagan, turned everything on its head and stole the blue-collar white vote from the Democratic Party, luring millions of them to the GOP. Nixon used social populism while Reagan used taxes to this end.

Nixon played off student antiwar demonstrations to craft the "silent majority" who, he said, shared traditional American values. Condemning hippies and yippies and flag burners, he rallied blue-collar whites to the Republican Party. Archie Bunker, the blue-collar hero of the hit TV show *All in the Family*, became emblematic of the backlash against the radical students.

Social populism had an ugly side too as Nixon rallied Southern whites against court-ordered integration. As racial animosities and intrusive court decisions found their way north, white resentment followed it. First, Alabama Governor George Wallace, an avowed racist, and then Nixon, whose act was cleaner, tapped into the backlash and piled up white blue-collar voters.

But the conversion of these former Democrats to the Republican Party really only reached its zenith under Reagan who rallied them against high taxes that sapped the paychecks of the working class whites. While Reagan attacked the welfare state, his appeal was more economic than racial, and on this surer footing, he triggered the desertion of an entire class of voters from the Democratic Party of their fathers. They came to be known as "Reagan Democrats," a kind of political boat people who drifted to various parties and candidates in search of a political home.

Then Obama made the brilliant move of reshaping antitax rhetoric to aim at holding down taxes, but only on the middle class and the poor—those making under $250,000 a year. Obama's line in the economic sand exploited the wedge between the rich and the not-rich as he focused resentment over taxes on the rich "not paying their fair share." In stoking this resentment, he turned the antitax rhetoric of the Republicans on its head. When the GOP lined up against all hikes in taxes, he was able to accuse them of protecting the rich at the expense of the middle class. The antitax impulse that lay at the core of the program that had attracted the Reagan Democrats to the GOP in the first place now worked against the Republican Party as it manifested itself in anger against tax loopholes that let the rich escape heavy taxation.

Even though the top 1% paid 47% of all federal income taxes,[6] Obama could point out that they earned about 20% of all income.[7] (Estimates of their income vary, ranging from 17% to 25%, and are quite volatile from year to year.) As the income disparity between the top and the rest of America widened, so did the resentment of the blue-collar voters. By 2008, the gap between the rich and the poor had become not only noticeable but unavoidable. And Obama drove a truck through it—all the way to the White House.

It was Obama's genius to use FDR's class-based rhetoric to undermine Reagan's antitax pitch and to distract voters from Nixon's social and racial arguments. When Obama ran in 2008, he often spoke of the Warren Buffet rule, quoting the billionaire investor as saying, "No household making more than $1 million each year should pay a smaller share of their income in taxes than a middle-class family pays."[8] Poverty became Obama's friend. The more the middle class stagnated and slipped back, the more they came to resent the rich and lined up behind Obama. And income inequality got worse and worse.

- Under Bill Clinton, 45% of all gains in personal income went to the top 1% of the country.[9]

- Under George W. Bush, 65% of the gain in income went to the top 1%.[10]

- And according to Emmanuel Saez, a top liberal economist from Berkley, under Barack Obama, 91% of the increase in earnings went to the top 1%.[11]

So the national ups and downs of the economy, to say nothing of the stock market, are but a distant echo to the 71% of American whites who have no four-year college degree.[12] When the Dow rose, it created a prosperity they could see all around them but could not share. The resulting envy metastasized into a class consciousness that dominated their voting habits.

They simply could not feel empathy coming from a Mitt Romney, a super wealthy example of the process of wealth creation that left them out. There could be no better symbol of their exclusion than this wealthy son of a tycoon who spent his life amassing a vast fortune. Even worse, they saw Romney as typical of the ruthless deal maker who encourages mergers, acquisitions, and outsourcing to save money by laying people off in the millions. The fact that Republicans didn't see how Romney would be anathema to the swing voters they needed attests to their nearsightedness. But even as we began to realize Romney's vulnerability, he hurtled toward the nomination, using his vast wealth and his even more wealthy connections to pay for negative ads that eviscerated his opponents one after the other. Michele Bachmann, Rick Perry, Herman Cain, and Newt Gingrich all fell under his sword, leaving us with no choice but Romney.

But Romney was a disaster. He alienated the very voters we needed to attract to the polls. When Obama attacked Romney for his work at Bain Capital, the Republican, inexplicably, failed to answer the charges and let them sit out there, undermining his support and convincing his white blue-collar would-be supporters to stay home. Obama exploited the boiling resentment of white blue-collar voters who worked hard at one or two or three jobs each but still couldn't get ahead while they watched the Wall Street rich pile up treasure.

In 2008, Obama had run for office on a positive theme of hope, change, and inclusion. But in 2012, he got reelected on a campaign of vicious class hatred, stoking the fault lines that divide us, capitalizing on the very income inequality that his policies and those of his Federal Reserve Board had created.

To defeat Hillary, we must bring back the white blue collar vote. In Donald Trump, we have the perfect candidate to do so. He articulates their resentment in a way no other modern political figure has been able to do. He speaks right to them. He uses the issues of terrorism, Obamacare, trade and immigration to rally their support.

We need to get the blue collar white vote back by throwing the right jab, hitting Hillary over these Republican issues.

CHAPTER 3

Use the Right Jab to Bring Out Our Base

A S WE DID IN 2004, we can hit Hillary and the left over their failure to rein in terrorism and to fight it with passion and vigor. With President Obama seemingly asleep at the switch and his former secretary of state impotent as well, our way forward is clear.

What is the key issue of 2016? . . .

The Key Issue? It's Terrorism, Stupid

The ISIS attacks of 2015 and 2016 have set the stage for a massive Republican victory. Terrorism clearly, and cruelly, transcends all the careful class, race, and gender divisions into which Obama has carved America. When an ISIS bomb goes off in a shopping mall, the shrapnel hits all in its path. An ISIS terrorist with a suicide vest or an assault rifle or a handgun will not play favorites in choosing his victims.

After the 9/11 attacks, we all looked up into the sky to see if any airplanes were overhead ready to crash into nearby buildings. But in the aftermath of the random terror of the ISIS attacks, we need to look all around us—360 degrees. As we go shopping, walk up to an airline counter, step on a subway, see a movie, cheer at a sports event, or even just stay at home, we could become victims. It is not just a few of us in the nation's largest buildings or cities who are at risk.

This pervasive feeling of danger—that's why it is called "terrorism"—has created a sense of unease in all of us. It may matter to Obama if his voters are black or Latino or young or single women or gay. But it matters not at all to ISIS. Keeping America safe will inevitably be the single biggest issue of the 2016 election. It is an issue that will just not go away. Even as economic concerns such as wage stagnation climb to the top of the national charts, they get knocked down into second place when every few weeks or months a new outrageous attack rears up and dominates the national news cycle.

Paris . . . San Bernardino . . . Brussels. Each attack provides a graphic demonstration of the abject failure of President Barack Obama and Secretary of State Hillary Clinton to keep us safe. Every time a bomb goes off, it brings us all back to the essential point: our country is in a war and Obama and Hillary are losing it.

As Obama ran for president in 2008, he was bedeviled by tapes of his pastor, Rev. Jeremiah Wright, ranting and raving about how evil America was. Commenting on the 9/11 attacks, Wright said that we had brought them on ourselves by our lawless international conduct. He famously said, "The chickens have come home to roost."[1] Now they have truly come home as Obama's and Hillary's weakness, appeasement, and failure to protect our country is resulting in massive new terrorism unseen since the 9/11 attacks.

When Obama took office as president and Hillary Clinton became his secretary of state, Iraq was quiescent after the successful surge in US forces. ISIS did not exist. There had been relatively few terror attacks in the United States, and those that had occurred were dwarfed by the hundreds that were thwarted. The shoe bomber's footwear failed to explode. The taxi bomb in Times Square was discovered and defused before it could detonate. The underwear bomber failed to bring down the airplane on which he was a passenger as his fellow travelers disarmed him. But now the world is a very different place.

Paris's heart has been ripped open by a series of ever-more-deadly terror attacks. Dozens were killed in Brussels, many within sight of the headquarters of the European Union. Shooting rampages by Muslim jihadists have become a weekly occurrence in the United States. ISIS controls territory equal in size to the state of New Jersey. But Obama continues to put everything else first—ahead of protecting us from terrorism.

- He won't use our technology to pick up conversations involving terrorists. That violates their civil liberties.

- He won't keep refugees out of the country, despite the likelihood that their ranks are salted with terrorists. That would violate our principle of diversity and it's not "who we are."

- He won't stand up and condemn radical Islam. In fact, he won't even say the words. That would violate pluralism and imply intolerance.

- He won't even go after the most likely terrorists. That would be profiling.

- Instead, he wants to disarm honest, innocent Americans who are trying to protect themselves by purchasing guns.

Everything comes before fighting terror with Obama.

And with no condemnation from Hillary or Obama, New York City's Mayor Bill de Blasio disbanded the municipal agency within the Police Department tasked with keeping tabs on the locations (including mosques) where Muslim extremists congregate. And so, just as 9/11 dominated the presidential elections of 2004, so ISIS's attacks will loom large in the 2016 contest.

Back in 2004, voters told pollsters that they tended to prefer Democrat John Kerry's ideas on education, Social Security, the environment, and poverty. But they voted for Bush because of one issue: His fight against terror. So it will be in 2016. In a RasmussenReports.com survey in December 2015, general election voters reported that they trusted Republicans more than Democrats when it came to national security and the war on terror by a margin of 46% to 35%.

This finding by Rasmussen is no surprise, nor is it likely to change. Ever since the days of Richard Nixon and Ronald Reagan, Republicans have had the edge on national security as an issue. And when President George W. Bush proved so aggressive and effective in pursuing the terrorists and President Obama so inept, the Republican lead on the issue widened.

So now only the core Democratic base of about one-third of the electorate gives their party the edge on the terrorism issue. Not only Republicans, but also the majority of Independents, say that they trust the GOP more on the issue. As the 2016 campaign unfolds, Democrats all face a key dilemma: the more they discuss and debate terrorism, the more the issue will come to dominate the campaign, inuring to the Republican advantage. But if they don't spend a lot of time talking about terrorism, the perception of their weakness on the issue will only grow sharper.

Of course, they may not have any choice. ISIS will do what it can to keep terrorism at the top of the national agenda by attacking Americans wherever they can. Their hideous videos of beheadings and the images of their terror attacks on our televisions will serve to keep the focus of national attention on the issue. But since the Democrats are running a former secretary of state who did little to stem—and much to inadvertently encourage—terrorism, the issue will cut even more strongly for the Republican candidate in the election.

And Donald Trump is just the right person to hammer away at the issue. By blaming political correctness for the Administration's failure to protect us, he has hit the issue head on. Trump's proposal to end all Muslim immigration while the current tide of terrorist infiltration is high, will work well to bring back our base voters.

Hillary Let Terrorism Grow on Her Watch

Nothing could more squarely link Hillary Clinton to the dismal record of Obama in fighting terrorism than her inept record at the State Department. As former secretary of state, she bears more responsibility than anyone else in the administration except for the president for the spread of ISIS and the growing number of terrorists salivating for a chance to attack us. New York City's former mayor Rudy Giuliani even went so far as to say that Hillary created such an encouraging environment for ISIS to sprout that he said Hillary "helped create ISIS." He argued that she "could be considered a founding member of ISIS."[2] The former mayor, who won national recognition for his leadership of New York after the 9/11 attacks, said that she helped ISIS to grow "by being part of an administration [that] withdrew from Iraq. By being part of an administration that let (Iraqi prime minister Nouri al-Maliki) run Iraq into the ground, so you forced the Shiites to make a choice. By not intervening in Syria at the proper time. By being part of an administration that drew twelve lines in the sand and made a joke out of it."[3]

Indeed, terrorism has grown like a weed in the gardens Hillary was supposed to tend as secretary of state. While she gallivanted around the world, racking up frequent flyer mileage, the terrorists were gaining ground.

Foreign policy is the area of American politics in which the executive branch can make no excuses. Because of the president's and the secretary of state's exclusive control over policy and its execution, success works to their benefit while failures are also charged to their account. (Look at how much mileage Obama got in the 2012 election from killing bin Laden). Now the battle against terror has turned sour and the blame lies clearly with Barack Obama and Hillary Clinton. Every aspect of the Obama/Hillary foreign policy has encouraged the rise of terrorism.

For example, had America kept ground troops in Iraq after our 2011 pullout, there would have been no space for ISIS to develop. A small garrison of 10,000 or so would have been sufficient to keep things under control. But we repeated in Iraq the mistake we made 20 years earlier in Afghanistan by pulling out and letting the forces of chaos reign. Obama, who originally surfaced in our politics as an early opponent of the war in Iraq was determined to honor his commitment to pull all of our troops out before the 2012 elections. During the 2008 elections, he and Hillary (his primary opponent) excoriated Senator John McCain, the Republican candidate, when he proposed a continuing presence in Iraq to prevent the rise of groups like ISIS. McCain said "It's not a matter of how long we're in Iraq, it's if we succeed or not." Asked by a heckler at a campaign rally about whether we should keep troops in Iraq for 50 years, "Maybe 100," was McCain's reply. "As long as Americans are not being injured or harmed or wounded or killed, it's fine with me and I hope it would be fine with you if we maintain a presence in a very volatile part of the world where al Qaeda is training, recruiting, equipping and motivating people every single day."[4]

Hillary pounced, saying, "He [McCain] said recently he could see having troops in Iraq for 100 years. Well, I want them home within 60 days of my becoming president of the United States."[5] Obama echoed her criticism, saying, "Senator McCain said the other day that we might be mired for 100 years in Iraq—which is reason enough not to give him four years in the White House."[6]

Hillary had always played politics on Iraq and on the War on Terror. When New York was attacked on 9/11, Hillary had just taken office as its US senator, despite never having lived in the state. She felt she needed to show toughness on terror and voted for the Patriot Act and the war in Iraq in 2003. But by 2008, the war was unpopular, so she opposed additional troops, dubbed "the surge."

Having both vowed during the election to remove all our troops from Iraq, neither Obama nor Hillary was willing to back a continuing presence there, however much sense it might make. Both agreed that our ongoing troop commitment in Korea and Germany had played a large role in deterring aggression, but neither one would apply that logic to Iraq.

ISIS grew out of Obama's and Hillary's obstinate refusal to listen to the advice of people like McCain. Determined to produce a full pullout in time for the 2012 elections, Obama left in our wake a sectarian war between Sunni and Shia Muslims that metastasized into the formation of ISIS, the most deadly terror gang yet.

As we left Iraq, we lost our leverage to force the Shia governments of Nouri al-Maliki and then Haider al-Abadi to moderate their course as they appointed anti-Sunni men to their new governments, alienating the 20% of Iraq's population that is Sunni. Hillary and Obama vainly warned the Iraqi leaders to include Sunnis in their government, but lacking a troop presence there, they could do nothing to make their concerns stick.

Instead, the Sunnis—who dominated the former government of Saddam Hussein—found themselves cut out. Their solution was to wage continued war against the government just as they had during the years when the United States had troops on the ground. Now reorganized and energized by the increasing anti-Sunni bias of the Baghdad government, they set up a new organization to fight for them: ISIS. Sunni-ism on steroids: ISIS.

Obama's CIA director John Brennan summarizes what happened. The Islamic State, he said, was virtually destroyed under President George W. Bush after his surge in US troop levels. Brennan said that ISIS was "pretty much decimated when US forces were there in Iraq. It had maybe 700-or-so adherents left. And then it grew quite a bit in the last several years, when it split then from al-Qaida [*sic*] in Syria, and set up its own organization." But, Brennan notes, "[ISIS] can [now] muster between 20,000 and 31,500 fighters across Iraq and Syria . . . This new total reflects an increase in members because of stronger recruitment since June [2015] following battlefield successes and the declaration of a caliphate, greater battlefield activity, and additional intelligence."[7]

As ISIS (called ISIL by Obama) was growing and recruiting, Deputy National Security Adviser Ben Rhodes was minimizing the threat it posed to the United States. He said the major danger was al-Qaeda, not ISIS: "While both are terrorist forces, they have different ambitions. Al-Qaida's principal ambition is to launch attacks against the west and US homeland. . . . Right now, ISIL's primary focus is consolidating territory in the Middle East region to establish their own Islamic State. So they're different organizations with different objectives."[8]

The Obama administration has consistently underestimated the goals of ISIS. In an August 8, 2015, interview with CNN, Deputy National Security Adviser Tony Blinken echoed Rhodes's dismissal of the danger ISIS posed. He declared that "unlike core al Qaeda, right now, their focus is not on attacking the US homeland or attacking our interests here in the United States or abroad. It's focused intently on trying to create a caliphate now in Iraq."[9]

President Obama famously weighed in, showing how lightly he took the rising power of ISIS. In an interview with *New Yorker Magazine* editor David Remnick on January 7, 2014, Obama said, "The analogy we use around here sometimes, and I think is accurate, is if a jayvee team puts on Lakers uniforms that doesn't make them Kobe Bryant."[10] After the ISIS attacks in Paris and San Bernardino, it is clear how stupidly, grievously, and tragically wrong the administration's assessment was. It now is becoming clear that ISIS exists to attack the West. But still Obama—with Hillary following after him—fails to grasp the true nature of the threat ISIS poses.

After all, Hillary has stood solidly behind Obama's inept treatment of ISIS. In the third Democratic presidential debate, Hillary incredibly said, "We finally have ISIS exactly where we want them."[11] And Obama insisted during a visit to Turkey in November 2015 that "the strategy that we are pursuing is the right one."[12] As the ISIS threat became clearer, Obama stuck with his refusal to make the kind of troop commitment that would hobble these terrorists. Committed to a strategy of air strikes and no ground troops, Obama has imposed such restrictions on our air campaign that pilots report coming back from sorties with only a quarter of their bombs dropped. Where Republicans vow to do what it takes to beat ISIS, Obama keeps our efforts to a minimum.

Nor have Obama or Hillary has gotten the message that toppling secular dictatorships in the Middle East opens the door to ISIS-like groups taking over, just as they did in Iraq. Throughout the Middle East, they are not content to leave well enough alone, and insist on ousting dictators wherever they find them, regardless of the risk that somebody worse will succeed them.

Donald Trump puts the American policy options in a broader perspective. "The United States owes $19 trillion," he said. "We have to straighten out our own house. We cannot go around to every country that we're not exactly happy with and say we're going to recreate [them]. It hasn't worked," Trump added. "Iraq was going to be a democracy. It's not gonna work, OK? It's not gonna work and none of these things will work." Referring to Iraq, he said, "We're nation-building. We can't do it. We have to build our own nation. We're nation-building, trying to tell people who have [had] dictators or worse for centuries how to run their own countries. . . . Look what's happened in Iraq. We got rid of Saddam Hussein. I don't think that was a helpful thing. Iraq is a disaster right now and it's going to be taken over by Iran and ISIS, so I think we have to focus on ourselves."[13]

But Obama and Hillary have not gotten the message. They backed the overthrow of Egyptian dictator Hosni Mubarak and almost opened the door to domination of that strategic country by the likes of the Muslim Brotherhood. Only the determined efforts of the Egyptian Army were able to depose the extremist government that had taken over in Cairo.

Hillary's complicity in allowing a Muslim Brotherhood–dominated regime under Mohamed Morsi may have been influenced by her close connection to the Brotherhood's leader. Morsi's wife Nagla Mahmoud spoke of the "special relationship" between her husband and Hillary. Indeed, when Clinton criticized Morsi in public—likely in an effort to appease his successor Abdel Fattah el-Sisi, a former Field Marshall in the Egyptian Army—Mrs. Morsi threatened to "publish letters exchanged between her husband and Hillary."[14] Indeed, Hillary's Clinton Foundation and the Muslim Brotherhood shared a high-ranking employee, Gehad el-Haddad, who worked for the foundation right before going to Egypt and serving as Morsi's top communication official.

Next door to Egypt, in Libya, Hillary again worked to oust a dictator, opening the door to massive terrorist and Islamist infiltration of the government. Muammar Gaddafi was no angel. He was a vicious dictator who was behind the Lockerbie jetliner attack that killed 270 people. The Libyan tyrant was defanged when President Reagan ordered an aerial attack on his home, killing his son in retaliation for Lockerbie.

After that raid, Gaddafi stopped his attacks on the West. Then, when President George W. Bush toppled Saddam Hussein from power, Gaddafi saw the handwriting on the wall and voluntarily gave up his arsenal of biological and chemical weapons and ended his efforts to develop or acquire nuclear weapons. He was still a miserable excuse for a human being, but he was minding his own business. Then Hillary decided he was committing human rights abuses. Eager to please Obama's key aide, Samantha Powers, who made her name speaking out against genocide in Rwanda, she set her sights on ousting Gaddafi.

Egged on by Hillary, Obama joined NATO in mounting air attacks that supported rebel ground troops. When they succeeded in toppling Gaddafi, the world saw that there was no genocide taking place, a situation reminiscent of George W. Bush's surprise at not finding weapons of mass destruction (WMDs) in Iraq. But at least Bush followed the intelligence of his government in assuming that Iraqi dictator Saddam Hussein had WMDs. Hillary, by contrast, deliberately overrode the findings of the US intelligence agencies and decided that genocide was, indeed, taking place.

After Gaddafi fell, all hell broke loose. Naively, Hillary hoped that "good" rebels who advocated a democratic, sectarian government for Libya would take over. But as many experts had warned, they were thrown into retreat by Islamic fundamentalists allied with ISIS and al-Qaeda. Our consulate in Benghazi was attacked and our ambassador Chris Stevens was killed along with three brave American guards. But Hillary still didn't learn the lesson.

Hillary then clamored for Obama to intervene in Syria to depose yet another dictator, Bashar al-Assad. At first, after al-Assad took over from his father who had ruled Syria with an iron hand for decades, he promised reform. Hillary, deceived as usual, promoted him as a "possible reformer" in March 2011. But when al-Assad Jr. used poison gas against his own people as his nation erupted into civil war, Hillary swung over to the other side, calling for bold American action to depose him. Led by around by the nose by his secretary of state, Obama worked to arm the prodemocracy rebels in Syria.

Idiotically, Obama and Hillary said that the weapons were only for pro-Western Syrian rebels who rejected both al-Assad's horrific dictatorship and ISIS's terrorism. But the fact is that they had no idea who was really getting the weapons. And sure enough, they next surfaced in the hands of the ISIS forces, giving the organization the arms it needed to conquer large swaths of Iraq and Syria. The idea of prodemocracy rebels in Syria proved as illusory as it had in Iraq, Libya, and Egypt. ISIS took over, merging with affiliates in Iraq to present an unprecedented crisis to the West.

So here's Hillary's record:

- She did nothing to stop President Obama from pulling our troops out of Iraq, opening the door to the growth of ISIS.

- She assisted in the overthrow of Mubarak in Egypt and acquiesced in his replacement by Morsi, a Muslim Brotherhood leader.

- She led efforts to topple Gaddafi in Libya, setting up an opportunity for Islamist terrorists to infiltrate and fight for control of that government.

- She pushed for arms shipments to the "prodemocracy" rebels in Syria who proved too weak to keep control of the armaments and they now arm ISIS in its battle against us.

Quite a record!

Even as ISIS and its allies took hold in Iraq and Syria, Obama—with Hillary's backing—refused to take bold action against it, eventually settling for limited, pinpoint air strikes that do little to crimp the terror organization's growth.

With Hillary's support, Obama even refused to attack the oil fields that provided ISIS with half of its revenues. These oil wells, formerly controlled by the Baghdad government, pumped an estimated 120,000 barrels a day, bringing in at least $2 million each day to fund the army of mercenaries who fought at ISIS's behest. Why not attack? Because, according to Obama's former CIA director Mike Morrell, the president feared doing so would inflict "environmental damage."[15]

Donald Trump will not abide such nonsense. He said he'd "bomb the hell" out of oil sites that are controlled by ISIS. He said "the situation with [ISIS] has to be dealt with firmly and strongly when you have people being beheaded. I would do things that would be so tough that I don't even now if they'd be around to come to the table." He continued, "I would take away their wealth. I would take away the oil. What you should be doing now is taking away the oil."

In explaining what would happen after he "bombed the hell out of the oil fields," Trump said "I'd then get Exxon, I'd then get these great oil companies to go in—they would rebuild them so fast your head will spin . . ."[16]

Hillary is all for intervening when the adversary is some geriatric dictator whose worst days are behind him but with a fledgling, vigorous, and robust terror threat in ISIS, Hillary is backing away from the conflict. During the Democratic primaries, she said, "In terms of thousands of combat troops, like some on the Republican side are recommending, I think that should be a non-starter." Hillary warned, "I don't think it's the smartest way to go after ISIS. I think it gives ISIS a new recruitment tool."[17]

She says that sending ground troops to battle them is "exactly what ISIS wants. They've advertised that. They want American troops back in the Middle East. They want American soldiers on the ground fighting them."[18] Once again, Hillary is showing her gullibility. While ISIS may brag, boast, and say, in effect, "bring it on," they will actually welcome US troops about as much as a boxer would welcome Mohammed Ali climbing into the ring to fight him.

The contrast between George W. Bush's obsessive focus on fighting terrorism and Obama's dismissal of ISIS as "the junior varsity" could not be more obvious. And disparate results flow from that contrast. During the Bush administration, after 9/11 only three Americans were killed within our borders by terrorists. Under Obama and Hillary, 42 Americans have been killed on our soil (through December 10, 2015).

Terrorism is the legacy of the Obama/Hillary foreign policy. The entire election will be a referendum on their policy and its obvious failure. Nor will the terror issue fade. Unfortunately, it will remain front and center. ISIS will keep it there. Hillary's candidacy is, literally, hostage to each demented terrorist who kills innocents in hope of a reward in heaven. Each attack diminishes her credibility and makes terrorism, her weakest suit, the central issue. Why will Hillary lose? Terrorism, stupid.

Hillary's Anti-Israel Policy

The breeding ground for anti-Western sentiment in the Arab world is the West Bank and the Gaza Strip where millions of Palestinians live in self-imposed exile in refugee camps, thinking of little but eventually returning to Israel and taking back the land they abandoned 70 years ago.

Because the United States and Europe have largely sided with Israel, the Arab street has been violently anti-American and creates thousands of would-be terrorists every year. Their animosity toward the United States and Europe is odd given the massive amount of aid the West gives the Palestinian Authority each year.

INTERNATIONAL AID TO PALESTINIAN AUTHORITY, 2013[19]

UNITED STATES	$294 MILLION
EUROPEAN UNION	$216 MILLION
SAUDI ARABIA	$151 MILLION
SWEDEN	$94 MILLION
GERMANY	$55 MILLION
NORWAY	$53 MILLION
JAPAN	$34 MILLION
SWITZERLAND	$28 MILLION
AUSTRALIA	$23 MILLION
NETHERLANDS	$20 MILLION
DENMARK	$19 MILLION
KUWAIT	$17 MILLION
FRANCE	$13 MILLION
ITALY	$11 MILLION
BELGIUM	$10 MILLION

In all, the world gave the Palestinian Authority $1.1 billion in 2013. With a population of 4.7 million, the aid comes to $234 per person, per year. For a family of four or five or six, this amounts to a princely subsidy, if ever the people could see the money before the Palestinian Authority steals it.

Obama and Hillary have sought to appease Arab anger over the West Bank by justifying their complaints and drawing a parallel between Palestinian terrorism, which murders innocents, and Israel's construction of homes for Jews in the region. Every time a terror attack kills Israelis—and often Americans too—Obama and Hillary say that Israel shared part of the blame because it enraged the Arabs by helping Jewish settlers build homes on the West Bank. This rationale ignores completely the fact that the real epicenter of Palestinian terror is Gaza, where, in 2005, Israel pursued the very policy Obama and Hillary want them to adopt on the West Bank. Back then, Israel forced the Jewish settlements to close down and pulled out all of its troops. But the withdrawal didn't stop the terror attacks on Israel. It just gave the terrorists a new base from which to operate.

Obama and Hillary have given the Arab terrorists what they lack and so desperately seek: legitimacy for their hateful anti-Semitic point of view. At the State Department, Hillary urged a so-called two-state solution (Israeli and Palestinian) based on the pre-1967 war borders of Israel. Those borders left Israel with a waist of only nine miles, a border Israeli prime minister Benjamin Netanyahu called "indefensible," noting that it left Israel with a width that was only "half the width of the Washington Beltway." He added, "These were not the boundaries of peace; they were the boundaries of repeated wars, because the attack on Israel was so attractive."[20]

Hillary and Obama began the new administration by demanding that Israel stop all construction on West Bank settlements, where over half a million Jews now live. Their idea was that the building was a de facto effort by Israel to annex the West Bank permanently by creating a Jewish majority.

Even Hillary admitted what a mistake her anti-Israel policy was. In her memoir of her State Department years, *Hard Choices,* she writes, "For the Israelis, we requested that they freeze all settlement construction in the Palestinian territories without exception. In retrospect, our early hard line on settlements didn't work. Israel initially refused our request, and our disagreement played out in public, becoming a highly personal standoff between President Obama and Netanyahu, with the credibility of both leaders on the line."[21] She added, "This demand hardened [Mahmoud] Abbas's position at the negotiating table, as the Palestinian leader could now credibly argue that halting settlements was not simply a Palestinian demand but a precondition laid down by the United States and the White House's official position. This move by the U.S. snatched a major bargaining chip out of the hands of Israeli negotiators."[22]

Obama's and Hillary's efforts to bully Israel into abandoning the West Bank became an obsession with them both. *Breitbart News* reported that, in March 2010, Obama followed up "on his threatening language about settlements by deploying Vice President Joe Biden to Israel, where Biden [ripped] into the Israelis for building bathrooms in Jerusalem, the eternal Jewish capital. Hillary Clinton then [yelled] at Netanyahu for nearly an hour on the phone, telling him he had 'harmed the bilateral relationship.' David Axelrod [called] the building plans an 'insult' to the United States. When Netanyahu [visited] the White House a week and a half later, Obama [made] him leave via a side door."[23]

Meanwhile, Israel faces a growing international movement to treat it with the same harsh measures as were meted out to South Africa in the '80s for its policy of apartheid. Arab apologists have long condemned Zionism as racist, and that rhetoric has blossomed into the BDS movement that seeks to "boycott, divest, and sanction" the only democracy in the Middle East. The BDS movement tries to persuade corporations, colleges, and pension funds to divest themselves of investments that benefit Israel while boycotting Israeli products and services, particularly those from the West Bank.

Such heated rhetoric and outrageous proposals seem to come with the territory in the Middle East, but Hillary's successor, John Kerry, has increasingly enlisted in the effort to isolate Israel. In July 2015, he warned Israel that its opposition to the Iran nuclear deal and its settlement construction policies would only stoke efforts to increase its global isolation. "I fear that what could happen is if Congress were to overturn it, our friends in Israel could actually wind up being more isolated and more blamed," Mr. Kerry said in an appearance at the Council on Foreign Relations.[24]

Kerry further implied that he, as secretary of state, would do nothing to stop the BDS movement from gaining steam. He even implied that he might endorse United Nations' recognition of the Palestinian Authority as the legitimate government of the West Bank. With such provocative words coming from the Foggy Bottom headquarters of the State Department, Hillary's silence—despite her avowed support for Israel—speaks volumes. Obama's, Kerry's, and Hillary's efforts to appease the Arabs have led to nothing good. Far from softening Arab resolve to destroy Israel—and its chief ally, the United States—the policy has led where appeasement always leads: to empowering the bad guys.

In fact, ISIS is making huge gains in its effort to bring its brand of barbaric terrorism to America's shores. Both Obama and Hillary are terrified of the left wing of the Democratic Party—Hillary all the more so as the Bernie Sanders campaign gained momentum. Determined to appease their own party's left as surely as they appease America's Arab enemies, Obama and Hillary are throwing open the doors of America to a refugee population from Syria that inevitably will include ISIS terrorists salted among their number.

Now, with Obama's help and Hillary's approval, ISIS operatives are breeching our borders with impunity, bringing terror to far flung corners of our nation.

Obama and Hillary Are Letting Terrorists into America

Even as President Obama refuses to identify those who wear suicide vests filled with bombs and detonate them in our malls and streets as "Islamic extremists" or "Islamic terrorists," he works overtime to appease the Islamic community. We are seeing the results of his weakness.

The contrast between the assiduous efforts of President George W. Bush and Obama's lackadaisical approach to the issue shows up in the grisly results. After 9/11, only three Americans were killed by Islamic terrorists on US soil during the Bush administration. Under Obama, the total has swelled to 42 (as of December 10, 2015). This explosion of terrorism will dominate the 2016 election. It has edged out everything else as the key issue in the coming election.

The ISIS brand of terrorism is more threatening than even the al-Qaeda model that destroyed the World Trade Center. Even as we learned to contain and frustrate large terror plots like 9/11, ISIS has pioneered the "lone-wolf" attack using simple armaments and small groups of suicide attackers who enter crowded auditoriums, gyms, or classrooms and annihilate dozens of innocent people who happened to be in the wrong place at the wrong time.

The vast intelligence apparatus the United States and its European allies has developed is finding it hard to spot such lone-wolf attacks and harder still to disrupt them and arrest the terrorists before they carry out their deadly missions. The al-Qaeda model of terrorism required vast organization, intricate planning, and lots of equipment, all making the plotters vulnerable to detection. But the lone wolf needs nothing more than a gun, so he can be impossible to spot before he strikes.

A multitude of lone-wolf attacks can paralyze America, just as the DC area was frozen in fear in 2002 as snipers John Allen Muhammad and Lee Boyd Malvo proceeded to pick off 13 people, one by one, as they pumped gas or mowed their lawns. Ultimately, lone-wolf attacks could induce us all to be looking over our shoulders—more menacing than having to look skyward after 9/11.

Once the gunfire died down in Paris in November 2015 and in Brussels in March of this year, we all realized that the terror threat was back, as bad as ever. But as we face this threat, we know that, while Muslims are only nine-tenths of 1% of our population, they constitute the vast majority of these terrorists. Their mission is, simply put, to kill the infidel in order to establish a global Islamic caliphate. While the vast majority of Muslims are peace loving, we cannot forget what Warren Delano, FDR's grandfather, said: "While not all Democrats are horse thieves, in my experience, all horse thieves are Democrats."[25]

Are American Muslims peaceful? Overwhelmingly, yes. But it only takes a handful to mount a terrorist attack. The Pew Research Foundation asked American Muslims the following:[26] "Some people think that suicide bombing and other forms of violence against civilian targets are justified in order to defend Islam from its enemies. Other people believe that, no matter what the reason, this kind of violence is never justified. Do you personally feel that this kind of violence is often justified to defend Islam, sometimes justified, rarely justified, or never justified?"

Here's how US Muslims answered:

OFTEN JUSTIFIED	1%
SOMETIMES JUSTIFIED	7%
RARELY JUSTIFIED	5%
NEVER JUSTIFIED	81%

While it is comforting—and we must bear in mind—that four of five say violence is "never justified," another 13% could approve of it in certain circumstances, and 8% say it is either "often" or "sometimes" justified.

With almost three million Muslims in the United States, that's a lot of potential terrorists.

(And consider the inherent bias in the survey. Who is going to admit, in effect, to supporting a crime in an interview with a stranger who could work for the FBI?)

The Middle East has become a cauldron of terror, an incubator for mass murderers who are indoctrinated to sacrifice their lives for the Jihadist cause. Trained as terrorists, they are skilled at the art of random destruction.

Our problem is how to stop this flow of death into our country. One approach, of course, would be to destroy ISIS in its lair in Syria and Iraq. But President Obama, elected on a peace platform, is so eager to preserve his legacy as having ended the Iraq War that he is loath to start another one. Relying on very limited air strikes and resolutely refusing to commit significant numbers of ground troops, he is unlikely, unqualified, and unable to bring the kind of determination we need to stop ISIS before it kills again. So we are left, by the president's refusal to act, with no option but to try to stop potential terrorists from coming into our nation.

Would Hillary be any better? Not very likely. Her opposition to ground troops in the Middle East is already noted and her cooperation in Obama's policy of appeasing terrorists is well documented. With ISIS working to infiltrate its highly trained, motivated, and demented terrorists into our country, immigration is the new national security issue of our time.

Donald Trump has ignited enthusiasm in tens of millions of Americans with his proposal that we ban all Muslims from entering the United States, at least for now. Nationally, the latest U-Gov/ *Huffington Post* poll revealed that, by 51–45, Americans support "a total and complete shutdown of Muslims entering the United States until our country's representatives can figure out what is going on."[27]

Currently, the State Department designates Iran, Syria, and Sudan as nations that have "provided support for international terrorism."[28] Cuba, Yemen, Iraq, North Korea, and Libya had been on the list but were removed by Obama, taking, on faith, the promises of their despotic leaders to behave themselves. All these nations should also be subject to an immigration ban. We should ban all immigration from people of any religion from nations in which terrorists operate, whether with or without government sanction. We should keep all immigrants, students, workers, and tourists from Saudi Arabia, Qatar, the United Arab Emirates, Kuwait, Nigeria, and other such countries out of the United States. We must not be deluded by protests from these nation's governments that they too oppose terrorism. Where terrorists have a significant presence, we cannot vet who is coming into our country and we must keep people from such nations out of America.

We are under no obligation to admit anyone to the United States. We can exclude whomever we want. And we should. Hillary will ask, "Where will the Syrian and other refugees go?" To the Muslim world! Let Saudi Arabia, Egypt, Pakistan, Bangladesh, Indonesia, the Philippines, Algeria, Jordan, Tunisia, Morocco, Libya, Turkey, and even Russia take them. What if they refuse? Exactly how is that *our* problem? *Our* problem is with those who came here and perpetrated acts of horror and terror. Read the list of immigrant/terrorists compiled by Leo Hohmann for WND.com.[29]

- Twenty-four-year-old Muhammad Abdulazeez killed five US servicemen in Chattanooga in 2015. He came from Kuwait.

- An immigrant from Bangladesh tried to incite people to travel to Somalia and conduct violent jihad against the United States. He was arrested in Texas in 2014.

- In July 2015, a Cuban immigrant inspired by Islamic extremists plotted to explode a backpack bomb filled with nails on a beach in Key West.

- An immigrant from Ghana plotted a terrorist attack on US soil. He attacked an FBI agent during a search incidental to the arrest of his fellow terrorist, Munther Omar Saleh, who was charged with conspiring to provide material support to ISIS.

- A Sudanese immigrant pleaded guilty in June 2015 to providing material support to ISIS.

- A Muslim refugee couple from Bosnia, along with five of their relatives living in Missouri, Illinois, and New York, were charged in February 2015 with sending money, supplies, and smuggled arms to ISIS.

- A Muslim immigrant from Yemen, along with six other refugees living in Minnesota, was charged in April 2015 with conspiracy to travel to Syria and to provide material support to ISIS.

- A Somali refugee was charged on July 23, 2014, with leading an al-Shabaab terrorist fundraising conspiracy in the United States, with monthly payments directed to the Somali terrorist organization.

- A Kazakhstani immigrant conspired to purchase a machine gun to shoot FBI and other law enforcement agents.

- Two female immigrants, one from Saudi Arabia and one from Yemen, pledged to explode a propane tank bomb on US soil. They were arrested in April 2015.

- An Uzbek man in Brooklyn raised funds for terror organizations.

- The Boston Bombers were invited in as asylum seekers. The younger brother applied for citizenship and was naturalized on September 11, 2012. The older brother had a pending application for citizenship when he struck.

- A Moroccan Muslim who came to the United States on a student visa was arrested and charged in April 2014 with plotting to blow up a university and a federal courthouse.

- Six members of Minnesota's Somali American refugee community have recently been charged with trying to join ISIS.

- An Uzbek refugee living in Boise, Idaho was arrested in 2013 and charged with providing support to a terrorist organization in the form of teaching terror recruits how to build bombs to blow up US military installations.

- A teenage American citizen living in York, South Carolina, whose family emigrated from Syria, was sentenced in April 2015 for plotting to support ISIS and rob a gun store to kill members of the American military.

- A Muslim immigrant from Syria living in Ohio, who later applied for and received US citizenship, was accused by federal prosecutors of planning to "go to a military base in Texas and kill three or four American soldiers execution style."

- A college student who came to America as a refugee from Somalia attempted to blow up a Christmas tree lighting ceremony in Oregon.

- Immigrants from Afghanistan and the Philippines were convicted on September 25, 2014, for trying to "join Al Qaeda and the Taliban in order to kill Americans."

- An Iraqi immigrant was arrested in May 2015 for lying to federal agents about pledging allegiance to ISIS and his travels to Syria.

- Two Pakistani American brothers living in New York were sentenced in June 2015 for plotting to detonate a bomb in New York City.

- A Yemeni immigrant was arrested in September 2014 in Rochester, New York for attempting to illegally buy firearms to try to shoot American military personnel.

How many more of these examples do we need until we all see the need to restrict immigration from terror-harboring countries? Notice how geographically spread out these threats are—no longer concentrated in New York City, but spread to all parts of our nation. How did that happen? How did we export terrorists to formerly calm and loyal parts of America? Our own government did. In the refugee resettlement program, the federal government decides who to send where and makes an effort to spread the refugees out across the nation to hasten their integration into our population. Instead, we have enabled their infiltration!

Democrats, including Hillary Clinton, have lined up to oppose restrictions on immigrants and in favor of opening our arms to refugees even if there is a risk that they are terrorists in disguise. But Muslim immigrants keep pouring into the United States. *Breitbart.com* reported that, according to the Department of Homeland Security, the United States has issued green cards (i.e., permanent resettlement documents) to "more than 1.5 million [migrants] from majority Muslim nations" since 9/11.[30]

The United States has awarded 11,000 green cards to immigrants from Afghanistan (mostly Muslim) from 2009 to 2013. We have also given green cards to 83,000 Iraqis and the same number of Pakistanis in the same time period. Turks got 22,000 green cards and Kazaks got 7,000.[31]

Hillary conditions her support for ongoing Muslim immigration by saying that we can vet those who want to come here. Vet? What nonsense! How on Earth can we vet people coming in from Syria? We can't just call up their high school guidance counselor or pull up their Social Security employment history. We have no way of separating real refugees from terrorists posing as refugees.

Former Homeland Security Administrator Tom Ridge made clear in a radio interview last December just how absurd Hillary's claim that we will vet Syrian refugees really is. He said, "I'm just not sure that we've got the background information. . . . They talk about screening. They talk about being able to review everybody in a timely way. I'm just not confident they have sufficient information for law enforcement, the intelligence community, to do effective screening. . . . A pause for refugees from that part of the world is very appropriate at this time."[32] And the FBI warned Congress on October 21, 2015, that "admitting people displaced by the Syrian civil war into the U.S. is a highly dubious venture, fraught with risks that terrorist fighters could slip in posing as 'refugees.'"[33]

There is a vast difference between immigrants and refugees. Immigrants are admitted to the United States legally, pursuant to legislation adopted by Congress and administered by Immigration and Customs Enforcement (ICE). Many evade ICE and enter illegally, but they are still immigrants, subject to deportation if they are apprehended. Refugees come here as a result, not of congressional legislation, but under agreements between the administration and the United Nations, not subject to congressional approval. And refugees are eligible to become citizens while illegal immigrants are, of course, not. Obama and Hillary are using refugees to circumvent congressional restrictions on immigration to get more Muslims into America.

Why would they want to do that? Pew Research has found the answer: 70% of Muslims, in their survey, said they mainly vote Democrat while only 11% sided with the Republicans.[34]

Of course, Hillary cannot change her record. But she can try to change her positions. During the primaries, Hillary was obliged to toe the Obama line on terror and immigration. With Bernie Sanders crawling up her left flank, she could not move to the center. But what about the general election? Will she change her support for immigration or her refusal to send ground troops to fight ISIS?

She'll want to. But it will be tough. Will Hillary seek to maximize the enthusiasm and turnout of her liberal base, as Obama did, or pivot to the center as her husband did in 1996?

If she hopes to move to the center on issues like ISIS, terror, and immigration, she will pay the price in liberal voter turnout. Many on the Left—a notoriously picky bunch—will feel that they have nobody to vote for and stay home. She can't mount an Obama-like crusade by standing in the middle. Even if she chooses to modify her position, her past record of repeated flip-flops undermines her credibility. Those who had agreed with her before she changed are likely to be disenchanted as she moves to the center. And those who used to disagree with her will find themselves very skeptical of her newfound centrism.

Now that terrorism has resurfaced with a close nexus to the immigration issue, the combination of the two will work even more strongly on behalf of the Republicans in 2016. The Democratic Party and Hillary have gone over a cliff and are articulating ideas and policies so totally out of sync with the average American that it is hard to conceive of their winning an election on that platform. Americans do not feel a duty to open their borders to possible terrorists and will not vote for anyone who does.

No issue cuts across all racial, class, gender, income, and ethnic lines more than terrorism. Obama's inept response to terrorism and his Secretary of State Hillary Clinton's failures make the Democrats extremely vulnerable on the issue. Obama's strategy of dividing the electorate along race, gender, age, and ethnicity falls in the face of the terrorism issue. As random as the terror attacks have become, they reach everyone equally. People of all races, ages, and both genders are vulnerable. It is the transcendent issue of our times. We are in danger not because we are white or black, Anglo or Latino, men or women, gay or straight, young or old, but because we are Americans. But the terror threat is growing on both the macro and micro level. Even as ISIS shows the potential for awful destruction from lone wolves or small groups with rudimentary weapons, Iran speeds toward the development of nuclear weapons, impelled by both Obama's and Hillary's policies of appeasement.

Hillary Enables Iran

The horrible giveaway Obama negotiated with Iran will be one of the Republican Party's best issues in 2016. Voters don't trust Iran. They see Iran as still intent on backing and funding terrorism and focused on developing a nuclear weapon. They feel Obama's deal is predicated on a level of trust in Iran's government that they do not share and feel the procedures to verify it and detect cheating are inadequate. Few issues unite Americans more than their skepticism of Iran.

Rasmussen reported that, by a margin of 62 to 35, American voters do not think it is likely that Iran will "uphold its end of the deal that ends some economic sanctions on that country in exchange for cutbacks in the Iranian nuclear weapons program." Indeed, 39% say it's "not at all likely" that Iran will abide by its word.[35]

So in the Rasmussen poll, taken in December 2015, only the die-hard Democratic Party base believes Iran will keep its word. A strong majority of Independents and almost all Republicans think Iran will cheat.

Hillary has tied herself to the Iran deal, giving it what the *New York Times* called her "strong endorsement." As usual, she hedged, saying that it could only work as part of "a larger strategy toward Iran" that contained Tehran's power in the region as sanctions are lifted.[36]

Since Iran has no intention of abiding by the deal, Hillary will need all the wiggle room she can get on the issue. But Trump can cut her off and pin her down by listing all the ways in which Iran has already violated the deal even before the ink was dry.

In the nine months after the deal was signed, Iran has conducted a series of ballistic missile tests that could be used to perfect nuclear weapons technology. Iran was barred from any ballistic missile development by UN resolution 1929, which read, "Iran **shall not** undertake any activity related to ballistic missiles capable of delivering nuclear weapons."[37] But the final deal with Iran on nuclear weapons watered down the prohibition into a mere request. The new UN resolution 2231, adopted July 20, 2015, superseded the old resolution 1929 and says, "Iran *is called upon not* to undertake any activity related to ballistic missiles designed to be capable of delivering nuclear weapons."[38] And even this resolution is slated to expire in eight years, leaving Iran free to do whatever it wants.

To celebrate its liberation from UN controls, in March 2016 Iran launched multiple 800 km and 2,000 km missiles from silos across the country. What did the United States do? Nothing. If the UN does anything, it will likely pass a toothless Security Council resolution critical of Iran. Meanwhile, the torrent of money released to Iran by the US government continues to flow unabated.

As Donald Trump said "we give them $150 billion. We get nothing."[39]

Senators Mark Kirk (R-IL) and Kelly Ayotte (R-NH) demanded that the administration take concrete action to address Iran's violations of the agreement. They said that the administration is "inviting" Iran to continue breaking international agreements. Obama claims that the issue of ballistic missiles is separate from the deal on nuclear weapons. He says one has nothing to do with the other. He implies that Iran can develop all the missiles it wants as long as it doesn't build a bomb. But Director of National Intelligence James Clapper told Congress that "Iran is developing [intercontinental ballistic missile] capabilities and the sole purpose of an Iranian ICBM is to enable delivery of a nuclear weapon to the United States."[40]

Sen. Bob Corker (R-TN), chair of the Senate Foreign Relations Committee, also cited Iran's violations. "Iran violates U.N. Security Council resolutions because it knows neither this administration nor the U.N. Security Council is likely to take any action," Corker said in a statement. "Instead," he added, "the administration remains paralyzed and responds to Iran's violations with empty words of condemnation and concern."[41] "If we cannot respond to a clear violation of a U.N. Security Council resolution, I have no faith that the U.N.

and the Obama administration will implement any form of snap-back in response to Iranian violations of the nuclear agreement," Corker said. The Obama administration, he added, "has the authority to penalize" Iran and its allies, but is refusing to exercise it.[42]

During the winter and spring of 2015–2016, in the run up to the elections, the Iranian violations received scant notice in American media. But during the fall campaign, Trump must hammer away at the violations, let Hillary have it, and demand action from Obama. Hillary, who endorsed the Iran deal after it was signed and urged Senate approval, must be held to account both for the flaws in the deal and for Iran's violations of it.

And the money keeps on flowing to Iran. The Ayatollah has gotten $11.9 billion from the United States since the nuclear talks began. How much does that mean to Iran? Life and death.

Before the sanctions relief, Iran's inflation rate was north of 30%, the government had to curtail subsidies for food and fuel, and political instability threatened. Now all is calm and all is good.

Iran's GDP is $416 billion. Proportionately, getting $12 billion in cash is like America getting a grant of over $500 billion—enough to pay for all defense spending for a year or enough to pay for Social Security and Medicare. And the funds we are sending them are not mainly going to their domestic economy and certainly not to their impoverished people, but to Iranian terrorists bent on destroying us.

But the Iranians claim it is their money that the United States is giving back to them. Yes, it is Iranian money, but it was amassed by the Shah in the days before the Ayatollah took over. For the current regime, in power since 1978, it is an undeserved and unearned windfall.

Hillary the Hypocrite claims credit for the tough sanctions on Iran that forced it to the bargaining table. But the truth is the exact opposite. She, in fact, moved heaven and earth to block the sanctions from passing Congress. Hillary pretends that she and Congress worked hand-in-glove to get sanctions passed. "With the help of Congress," she said, "the Obama administration imposed some of the most stringent crippling sanctions on top of the international ones . . . our goal was to put so much financial pressure on Iran's leaders that they would have no choice but to come back to the negotiating table with a serious offer."

She continued, "We went after Iran's oil industry, banks, and weapons programs, enlisted insurance firms, shipping lines, energy companies, financial institutions and others to cut Iran off from global commerce."[43]

All true. But she omits one part of the story: That she was against the sanctions and did her best to defeat them. Yet, as Ronald Reagan (and President John Adams) said, "Facts are stubborn things."[44]

Republican Senator Mark Kirk (R-IL), who worked closely with former chairman of the Senate Foreign Affairs Committee Bob Menendez (D-NJ), says that Hillary's claim to have supported the Iran sanctions are "a blatant revision of history." The senator added, "The fact is, the Obama administration has opposed [the effort to impose] sanctions against Iran led by Senator Menendez and me every step of the way, as was thoroughly documented at the time."[45]

In late 2011, for example, Hillary sent a key aide, Undersecretary of State Wendy Sherman, to Capitol Hill to express the administration's "strong opposition" to the amendment sponsored by Kirk and Menendez to sanction the Central Bank of Iran, one of the key measures that Congress imposed. Sherman argued that the action would "anger [our] allies by opening them up for punishment if they did not significantly reduce their imports of Iranian oil."[46]

When the senators refused to back off their amendment, Hillary upped the ante by sending her number two at the State Department, Bill Burns, to an "emergency" meeting with top senators to try to kill the amendment. He and Hillary failed and the Senate passed the bill 100–0. Commenting on the battle over the amendment, Menendez told Hillary and Obama, "At your request we engaged in an effort to come to a bipartisan agreement that I believe is fair and balanced. And now you come here and vitiate that agreement. . . . You should have said [that you] want no amendment."[47]

Menendez's successor as Foreign Relations chairman, Senator Bob Croker (R-TN), saw Hillary's and Obama's attempts to take credit for the sanctions as a kind of backhanded compliment. "I take comments from administration officials saying they were so involved in this as a compliment. It was Congress who pushed this on a bipartisan basis," said Corker. "Let's face it. You saw the public pushback from the administration. People can say what they wish, but there's no way we would be where we are today without Congress's actions."[48]

Hillary's opposition to Iran sanctions goes back to 2009 when she and Obama worked to kill an amendment by Kirk and Democrat Evan Bayh (D-IN) to impose sanctions on Iranian exports of refined petroleum. Rolled into a subsequent omnibus sanctions bill, it passed—over Hillary's objections—by 99–0 in the Senate and 408–8 in the House.

The most effective of the various sanctions imposed on Iran was the bill to bar Iranian financial institutions, including its Central Bank, from doing business with the Society for Worldwide Interbank Financial Telecommunication (SWIFT), the Brussels-based global financial clearinghouse. This sanction made it virtually impossible for Iran to do any kind of business internationally.

The *Wall Street Journal* reported that "the administration was afraid that the SWIFT-related sanctions would cause too much disruption to the system and unnerve allies. Lawmakers said the sanctions were needed to close a huge loophole through which Iran was laundering money."[49]

Mark Dubowitz, the executive director of the Foundation for Defense of Democracies, put it best: "The overwhelming success of Iran sanctions is certainly motivating many folks to claim credit. The reality is that there is no doubt that the toughest sanctions were imposed by Congress over the objections of the administration."[50]

After these sanctions forced Iran—on its knees—to enter negotiations, the administration agreed (and Hillary supported) a deal
that gave Iran everything it ever wanted. And on top of the giveaway
deal, the administration has since showered Iran with other conces-
sions that even go beyond the scope of those it won in the negotiations. All Iran has to do is whisper that it is somewhat unhappy with
something and Obama is right there offering more goodies. Almost
any scrutiny of its terms, whether superficial or detailed, reveals its
glaring defects. It is hard to conceive of a worse deal for the United
States, Israel, or the fate of the world.

Defects of the Deal

Israeli prime minister Benjamin Netanyahu called the Iran deal
"a historic mistake" and said that it "reduces the pressure on Iran
without receiving anything tangible in return, and the Iranians who
laughed all the way to the bank are themselves saying that this deal
has saved them."[51]

We need to use the Iran deal as a key campaign issue. To do so, we
have all got to understand why the deal is terrible. We have to be able
to argue it out with our undecided friends, point by point. The key
things to stress are discussed below.

Iran was wilting under the impact of American and international
sanctions. Originally, these sanctions targeted the nuclear program,
but over the years had expanded to hit every aspect of Iran's economy starting with its banking system. Eighty percent of Iran's government revenue comes from its sale of oil and gas to the rest of the
world. The United States has long boycotted Iranian oil, but under
the most recent round of sanctions—the ones that brought Iran to
its knees—the European Union joined the boycott. At the peak of
the sanctions, nobody in the United States or the European Union
could either buy Iranian oil or insure their tankers. At the same
time, the United States enacted legislation to punish countries that
continued to do business with Iran, sharply limiting their ability to
operate in the United States.

Driven by sanctions, inflation officially reached 22%, but most believe it had soared even higher. The International Affairs Review of the Elliott School at George Washington University wrote that "in one week alone, the price of chicken rose 30 percent and the price of vegetables almost 100 percent." It noted that prices became "unstable" and that household budgets were "being stretched thinner and thinner, and people [saw] the value of their savings quickly disappear."[52]

The government was forced to end its subsidy of food staples, electricity, water, and gas. Unemployment reached 35%. Factories and businesses laid off workers because they couldn't get raw materials. The Iranian rial lost half its value and Iranians were increasingly demanding US dollars in their commercial transactions. The black market thrived.

Then the United States and the European Union took its foot off the throat of Iran and agreed to lift the sanctions under the deal. National Public Radio reported as follows: "$100 billion: That's roughly how much the US Treasury Department says Iran stands to recover once sanctions are lifted under the new nuclear deal. The money comes from Iranian oil sales and has been piling up in some international banks over the past few years."[53]

The money was accumulating because the Iranians were able to skirt the sanctions and sell at least some of their oil on the global markets. But they couldn't get their hands on the cash the oil brought in. It was frozen in overseas banks.

Mark Dubowitz explained, "Those [mostly Asian] countries were buyers of Iranian oil. But they agreed to hold the funds in escrow until the sanctions are lifted. In other words, Iran sold them the oil but couldn't move the cash back home."[54] Dubowitz warns that all of the $100 billion could end up funding Hezbollah or other terrorist organizations.

Now the pressure on Iran is off. Subsidies can again flow. Inflation will now be tamed. All momentum for regime change is dissipated. And the cash bonanza could be higher. The *Foreign Policy*

Review estimates that the number is "north of $120 billion with an additional $20 billion per year in oil revenues, making the deal worth $420 billion over 15 years."[55] Not only is this torrent of cash being used to fund terrorism from Yemen to Lebanon to the West Bank to Iraq to Libya to Afghanistan to Pakistan, but it also keeps the Iranian regime afloat and in power.

By contrast, the United States has given Israel $148 billion in total military and economic aid in the 68 years since 1948, a sum dwarfed by the cash payout our worst global enemy has just received at the hands of President Obama.

Did Obama get the best deal he could? Donald Trump, for one, says absolutely not. He proclaimed that he would have doubled or tripled the sanctions when Iran proved obstinate at the bargaining table.

Now Obama—without a peep of protest from Hillary—is going even further in rewarding Iran with financial goodies beyond the scope of what was promised in the deal. The administration is telling foreign governments and banks that they can "start using the dollar in some instances to facilitate business with Iran."[56]

The AP was told the new rules "would permit offshore financial institutions to access dollars for foreign currency trades in support of legitimate business with Iran, a practice that is currently illegal. Several restrictions would apply, but such a license would reverse a ban that has been in place for several years and one the administration had vowed to maintain while defending last year's nuclear deal to skeptical U.S. lawmakers and the public."[57]

The more voters understand what a sweet deal Obama has given the Iranians, the angrier they will get. Hillary cannot avoid being caught in the crossfire. Her endorsement of the deal is clear and unequivocal. She will try to cloak her backing for its terms in anti-Iranian rhetoric. She has even vowed to go to war with Iran if they violate the deal. But Iran does not have to violate anything. Keeping to the terms of the deal will allow Iran to get the money to do anything it wants.

Nor does the treaty require that Iran give up its goal of developing nuclear weapons. The deal is only for 15 years. By 2030, all bets are off and Iran can go nuclear without fear of consequence. As Blaise Misztal, head of the national security program at the Bipartisan Policy Center, put it, "This isn't a deal that prevents a nuclear Iran. It's a deal that prevents a nuclear Iran for 15 years."[58]

"All Iran has to do is take the patience pathway to a nuclear weapon," said Mark Dubowitz, executive director of the Foundation for Defense of Democracies.[59] Even within the 15-year window while the deal is in effect, there is little in it to constrain Iranian nuclear ambitions. As Iran's atomic-energy chief, Ali Akbar Salehi, said, "The only thing that Iran gave Obama was a promise not to do things we were not doing anyway, or did not wish to do or could not even do at present."[60]

The deal permits Iran to continue enriching uranium and producing plutonium, although at lower grades. Iran would keep about one-third of its 19,000 centrifuges capable of separating explosive U-235 from uranium ore. For 15 years, Iran promises to refine uranium to no more than 5% enrichment—the level needed for nuclear power plants—and agrees to limit its enriched-uranium stockpile to 300 kilograms—3% of its stores before the deal. But will Iran keep the deal?

Originally, Hillary and Obama promised that any deal with Iran would provide for inspections "anywhere, anytime." But the deal has fallen far, far short of this pledge. To begin with, Iran may have nuclear enrichment facilities we don't know about. Iran only acknowledged its two main enrichment plants after they were exposed by foreign sources.

Inspections of its admitted enrichment facilities will be handled by the International Atomic Energy Agency (IAEA). The United States can only pressure the IAEA should we find that the inspections are inadequate. IAEA is an independent agency. Far from the "anywhere, anytime" standard for inspections that Obama, Hillary, and John Kerry promised before the deal was struck, it provides for, in effect, a 24-day notice period before an inspection could take place.

The IAEA would begin the inspection process, under the deal, by making a request for access to a nuclear site. Iran would have 14 days to grant access to inspectors. If it refused, an international panel of the United States, Britain, France, Germany, Russia, China, the European Union, and Iran would have another week to decide if access should be granted (a five-vote majority would be needed—presumably a coalition of the Western allies would suffice). If Iran agreed to let the inspections happen, they could still delay for three more days before providing access. A total delay of 24 days! More than enough time to hide what they are doing. And if they refused access, all we could do is refer the matter to the UN Security Council.

Good grief. Obama and Hillary claim that if Iran balked, economic sanctions would "snap back"[61] into place. But the idea that sanctions, once lifted, could "snap back" is delusional. After sanctions are lifted, countries and companies will resume their commercial relations with Iran—and many have started to do so. Reimposing sanctions would be a herculean task and, now that Iran has had a cash infusion and time to recover from the original sanctions, would take years to be effective.

By contrast, experts all agree that if Iran wanted to do so, it could probably have a bomb within a year, even if it had first dismantled its facilities as required by the deal. In other words, it could get the bomb before the sanctions were reimposed or became really effective. And once Iran gets the bomb, nobody will be able to control it.

Unbelievably, one of Iran's nuclear facilities—the Parchin military base, about 12 miles from Teheran—won't even be inspected by the IAEA, but will be "self-inspected" by Iran. According to leaked information, the still-secret deal between the IAEA and Iran would allow Iranian officials to take their own environmental samples at Parchin and turn them over to inspectors, in effect, allowing Iran to self-inspect the site. And even at the sites where the IAEA can inspect, could Iran cover up any violations of the agreement within the 24-day window the deal provides?

Olli Heinonen, a former director of the IAEA, said that Iran couldn't clean up its act in 24 days. But, he said, "the more likely risk is that the Iranians would pursue smaller-scale but still important nuclear work, such as manufacturing uranium components for a nuclear weapon. A 24-day adjudicated timeline reduces detection probabilities exactly where the system is weakest: detecting undeclared facilities and materials."[62]

David Albright, the president of the Institute for Science and International Security and a former weapons inspector in Iraq warns, however, that three weeks might be ample time for the Iranians to dispose of any evidence of prohibited nuclear work. Among the possibilities, he said, were experiments with high explosives that could be used to trigger a nuclear weapon, or the construction of a small plant to make centrifuges. "If it is on a small scale, they may be able to clear it out in 24 days," Mr. Albright said. "They are practiced at cheating. You can't count on them to make a mistake."[63]

In the campaign, we must make Hillary defend this absurd deal, forcing her on the defensive. By making her defend Iran or express any degree of confidence in Teheran, we can show how badly she has been conned by the Ayatollah. Bear in mind that the Iranian deal will have been in force for a year by the time the election is held. Evidence of Iranian cheating and of the IAEA's and the administration's inability to hold them to their word is already becoming obvious to all and by Election Day it will be even more obvious. . . . to all but Hillary and Obama.

Not only will there be abundant evidence of the deal's flaws, but there will likely be even more Iranian activity in promoting terrorism around the globe. The hundreds of billions of dollars that the deal has released to Iran will fund terror attacks in half a dozen countries. Its shortcomings will be on display for all to see.

Can't Hillary just attack the deal and disavow it? No way. This agreement is the most important foreign policy "achievement" of the Obama administration. Virtually all the Democratic senators and congressmen backed it. For the nominee of the party to abandon it or attack it would produce a giant schism in Hillary's ranks.

She is stuck with this horrible deal and it will help to drag her down to defeat.

Already Trump is all over the issue. Trump even wondered if there was some ulterior motive for Obama to OK the deal. "It's almost like there has to be something else going on," he said. "I don't think there is, I just don't think they're competent."

"Who would make that deal?" Trump asked, suggesting Tehran was celebrating as the agreement was being negotiated. And of Secretary of State John Kerry, he added, "I can't believe they didn't walk from that negotiation."[64]

Even during the treaty negotiations, Iran's leaders were avowing and reaffirming their intention to obliterate Israel. Iranian commander Mohammad Reza Naqdi, the head of the Basij paramilitary forces, came out and stated: "The destruction of Israel is non-negotiable." Even as Congress was voting on the deal, Supreme Leader Ayatollah Khamenei tweeted that "God willing" there would be no Israel in 25 years.[65]

Whether the issue is the proliferation of ISIS, the erosion of Israeli security, the increased terror threat to Americans in their daily lives, the admission of Syrian refugees (which could let terrorists into the United States), or containing Iran's nuclear ambitions, Hillary is vulnerable. Her tenure as secretary of state, rather than reinforcing her ability to govern, kindles serious doubts about her capacity for making sound policy choices.

Iran, Terrorism, and Obamacare are the three most potent issues we can use to win in 2016. Hillary is, of course, intimately tied to all three. She cannot escape blame for the first two since they metastasized on her watch as secretary of state. And she is the true mother of Obamacare, having spent all of 1993 and 1994 pushing its antecedent and close relative, Hillarycare.

Obamacare: The Bills Are Due
Obamacare has gone from being the poster child for the Obama administration, its chief legacy, to standing as a prime example of

what is wrong with the government taking over every aspect of medical care. The program is such a disaster, so terribly conceived, that it has become an albatross around the neck of the Democratic Party.

With each piece of bad news, approval of the program wanes. According to the *New York Times*/CBS survey, approval of Obamacare dropped from 47% support and 44% oppose in June of 2015 to only 40% support and 52% oppose in December, six months later. The most recent poll—at this writing—was completed by Rasmussen on March 1, 2016, and found Obamacare still underwater with support down to 43% and disapproval up to 54%.[66]

And remember, before there was Obamacare, there was Hillarycare, her 1993 version of the program. So deeply is Hillary identified with mandatory government health insurance that we can beat her on this issue alone. We don't even need the Benghazi issue. Or the e-mails. Or even the speeches-for-favors deals. Forget her and Bill raking in over $100 million for speeches. Obamacare, Hillarycare, are enough to defeat her. Who ever would have imagined that Obamacare would collapse under its own weight—that before the Republicans could take the presidency and repeal this obnoxious statute, its own inherent flaws are bringing about its demise?

Obamacare: Dying on Its Own

Obamacare is in a death spiral. The president's socialistic/bureaucratic insistence that everyone get full health care coverage for every possible service, whether they want it or not or need it or not, has driven costs so high that young, healthy people are refusing to buy policies. After all, why should a man get covered for maternity costs? Why do we all need to cover sex change surgery? Substance abuse therapy? Psychotherapy costs? By loading the insurance policies you have to get under Obamacare with all these goodies, the cost of premiums became astronomical. And when the Obama administration found the high premiums embarrassing, they got the insurance companies to hold them down by charging outrageous deductibles of $7,000 or more and by demanding onerous copayments.

Obamacare was such a bad deal that the target audience—healthy young people—spurned it. When young people rejected his program, Obama tried to force them to get covered by fining those who refused up to 2% of their income or $325 per year. But even so, 34 million Americans still have refused to buy insurance.

Obamacare has come to be only for the sick, needy, and older patients (still under 65) making the risk pool unsustainable. Of course, insurance companies passed on these high costs to the consumer, fanning their rebellion against the program. Obama's solution was to guarantee insurance company profits with federal tax money, in effect, making them public utilities.

It was the opposition of the insurance industry that killed Hillary's health care program in 1993. To sign up their support this time Obama bought their backing for his plan by inserting the "risk corridors" provision that provided for government subsidies should insurance profits fall from their projected levels. In 2014, the government paid almost $1 billion to insurance companies, making them America's newest and richest welfare recipients.

But for once, Congress acted to rein in Obama's largesse and insurance company greed. Faced with rising subsidies triggered by diminishing insurance company profits, Republicans, led by Senator Marco Rubio of Florida, capped the amount of subsidy the insurers could get, terminating the open-ended commitment to company profits Obama had made.

The result was that insurance companies pulled out of Obamacare entirely. UnitedHealth, the nation's largest health insurer, announced that it would not cover people in most Obamacare exchanges, leaving half a million without coverage. The company suspended marketing of its Obamacare exchange plans for 2016, saying, "We see no data pointing to improvement"[67] in the financial performance of public-exchange plans. Other companies are also reassessing their participation in the program. Cigna Insurance appears likely to follow UnitedHealth's lead. Soon, all the others will follow as their stockholders come to demand an end to the bleeding.

Even as the insurance companies are abandoning the shipwreck that Obamacare has become, doctors are voting with their feet to leave the discredited program as fast as they can. Already, about a quarter of all doctors in America have refused to participate. By mid-2014, 214,524 of America's 893,851 doctors won't allow Obamacare health exchanges to offer their services. Seventy percent of California's doctors have turned their backs and refused to enroll in the program[68] (only 1% of doctors refuse to participate in Medicare).

The Uninsured Say No to Obamacare

In the ultimate insult to Obamacare, one-third of the uninsured have said they have no intention of purchasing Obamacare coverage despite the fines they may face for not doing so. Treasury officials estimate that between three and six million Americans will have to pay a tax penalty for not having insurance in 2014. While the fine was modest—$95 or 1% of income, whichever is higher—it rose to $325 or 2% of income in 2015. Still tens of millions think so badly of Obamacare that they'd rather pay the fine than get covered. Another 15 million to 30 million people requested and got exemptions from having to pay the fine. These included illegal immigrants, low-income people, and those for whom insurance premiums were more than 8% of their household income.

Bankrate's latest health insurance Pulse survey found that 34% of the uninsured "have no intention of buying insurance." Forty-one percent cited cost as the reason, 17% said they oppose Obamacare, and 13% said they are healthy and don't need it.[69] To try to counter this avalanche of negative publicity, the Obama administration has called attention to the fact that a net of 16.9 million people who were uninsured have become insured since the program started.

But the stat is deceiving.

- More than half of them got insurance through employer-sponsored health plans that have nothing at all to do with

Obamacare. (Remember that the employer mandate to provide coverage has not yet kicked in).

· Another 6.5 million (20%) got their coverage through Medicaid, a welfare program that predates Obamacare by some 50 years. (Obamacare did raise the income level at which one could be eligible for Medicaid, but it's the same old program).

· And 1.2 million (3%) got individual plans that have nothing to do with Obamacare.

That leaves a net of 9.1 million people whom Obama says have gotten coverage through the Obamacare exchanges. But half of them previously had insurance that the government made them cancel.

So all told, only 4.1 million people who were previously uninsured got coverage through Obamacare's exchanges, a minuscule number in a nation of 320 million people.

Nor is the situation likely to get much better. The Department of Health and Human Services estimates that only one million new people will sign up for Obamacare during the 2015–2016 enrollment period—way short of the hopes and projections of the program's sponsors.

Premiums Are Soaring . . .

Obamacare is dying.

As fewer young and healthy people apply for coverage, the risk pool that insurers must cover becomes older and sicker, forcing premiums up. And the more premiums rise, the more young and healthy people see no reason to buy. Obamacare premiums are projected to rise by 20.3% in 2016, instead of the 7.5% the government had predicted.

Now reports are coming in that those who are currently signing up for Obamacare are sicker than those who have already signed up—which means even higher premiums for everybody. The *New York Times* reported that "people newly insured under the Affordable

Care Act were sicker, used more medical care and had higher medical costs than those who already had coverage." The paper noted that "because insurers' premiums have to cover their medical expenses, the new report helps explain why Blue Cross plans have sought, and insurance commissioners have approved, substantial rate increases in many states."[70]

Healthy and young people are being forced into the health insurance boat with older and sicker patients, driving up their cost just as they face the financial pressures of starting a family and paying off student loans. So a great many are choosing not to buy insurance at all and pay the fine instead. And the premiums were plenty high before these rate increases.

In his weekly address on January 22, 2016, President Obama said, "Most folks buying a plan on the marketplace can find an option that costs less than $75 a month."[71] $75 a month? What planet has he been living on? $840 a month is more like it. That's the average premium for a family of four. For a single person, the premiums run about $240 a month!

Hillary, too, seems not to realize how heavy the cost of insurance has become under her pet program. At a town hall meeting in Ohio, she came face-to-face with a real person—Teresa O'Donnell, an office manager—who told Hillary that her insurance premiums for her family had risen from $490 to $1,081 per month.

"I know Obama told us that we'd be paying a little more," O'Donnell said. "But doubling, over doubling, my health insurance cost has not been 'a little more.' It has been difficult to come up with that kind of payment every month. I would like to vote Democratic, but it's cost me a lot of money, and I'm just wondering if Democrats really realize how difficult it's been on working-class Americans to finance Obamacare?"[72]

Incredulous, Hillary asked O'Donnell: "So you were going to a broker and buying a health insurance policy? And in effect, it nearly tripled after you went onto the exchange and bought a policy under the Affordable Care Act? Is that right?" Clinton asked.

O'Donnell answered, "We could not do that. It was much more expensive than just purchasing private insurance from an insurance company."

"So you're still buying the private insurance directly?" Clinton said.

"Yes," O'Donnell said.

Hillary swung into her speech about how much she wanted to get the cost down and then, in a moment Marie Antoinette (who said, "Let them eat cake") would envy, Hillary recommended to O'Donnell to keep shopping. "And one thing that I would like you to do, and I'm not saying it's going to make a difference, but I would like you to just go shopping on that exchange," Clinton said.[73]

Welcome to the planet Earth, Hillary!

(Actually, Obama promised to cut premiums when he first ran for president. He said, "We will start, by reducing premiums by as much as $2,500 per family."[74])

Part of the problem is that about a quarter of those who need a federal subsidy to afford Obamacare can't get it. They fall into the cracks in between coverage. They are too rich for Medicaid and too poor for Obamacare subsidies. The gap was created when the Supreme Court ruled that states do not have to expand their Medicaid program as required by Obamacare. As a result, 21 states have taken advantage of the Court ruling and refused to do so.

Obamacare's subsidies were meant to come on top of Medicaid. Medicaid was supposed to cover people up to about $25,000 of income and the Obamacare subsidies kicked in for those with incomes above $25,000. But in the states that refused to expand their Medicaid program, Medicaid may only be available for people making less than $10,000, leaving those earning between $10,000 and $25,000 uncovered.

. . . and Deductibles Are Too

But higher premiums are only part of the story. The real kicker is the high deductibles on most plans. They are a total disaster.

The New York Times noted that "for many consumers, the sticker shock is coming not on the front end, when they purchase the plans, but on the back end when they get sick: sky-high deductibles that are leaving some newly insured feeling nearly as vulnerable as they were before they had coverage."[75]

A Commonwealth Fund study called the deductibles under Obamacare "daunting."[76] The deductible for a "Silver" level Obamacare plan, the most popular, is $2,951, according to the Commonwealth Fund study, more than twice the $1,217 deductible for the average employer-sponsored plan. More than half of the Obamacare plans have deductibles above $3,000. *The New York Times* reported that "in Miami, the median deductible is $5,000. . . . In Jackson, Miss., the comparable figure is $5,500. In Chicago, the median deductible is $3,400. In Phoenix, it is $4,000; in Houston and Des Moines, $3,000."[77]

These high deductibles are the result of a trick the Obama administration played on the American people. Determined to portray Obamacare as affordable, they encouraged insurance companies to hold down premiums and recoup their high costs through bigger deductibles. But there are no federal tax subsidies to cushion high deductibles as there are with premiums. The patient has to pay the whole thing. And deductibles discourage people from getting timely care, subjecting them to risk and leading them to avoid seeking treatment.

So Obamacare is having the exact opposite effect of that intended by its sponsors. Because of high deductibles and the millions who can't get premium subsidies, people are not getting the care they need. As people use Obamacare and face the limited choice of doctors—more limited as more doctors don't participate—and the high deductibles, the more they come to dislike it. In a Rasmussen Reports survey in December 2015, those with direct experience with the new program say, by 2 to 1, that that the law has hurt them more than it has helped.[78]

At the core of objections to Obamacare is the program's restriction of a patient's ability to choose his or her doctor. Long dead is

President Obama's famously broken promise: "If you like your doctor, you will be able to keep your doctor. If you like your insurance plan, you can keep your insurance plan."[79]

Instead, insurers are restricting patients' choice of providers by limiting the number of doctors and hospitals they cover. Insurance plans under Obamacare have, on average, 34% fewer hospitals and doctors than policies sold outside the exchanges. The only alternative a patient has—particularly if he wants to see a specialist in whom he has faith—is to go out-of-network and face huge, uncapped out-of-pocket expenses.

Obamacare: Stupidity Reigns!

Prime among Obamacare's goals was to lower the patient readmission rate. Administration officials said that there was a revolving door that drove up medical costs. The theory was to cut hospital reimbursement rates under Medicare and Obamacare if there was a high rate of readmission of patients who had been discharged.

The problem is that recent studies conclude that a quarter of all hospital readmissions are unavoidable. In fact, readmission may be indicative of a better level of care. Indeed, in studies by the Brisbane Cardiac Consortium and the Cleveland Clinic, readmission and mortality were inversely related—when the hospitals readmitted more patients, they succeeded in keeping more of them alive. The Heritage Foundation reported that when the Brisbane Consortium sought to "improve the process of care, the program was successful in reducing mortality rates, but, unexpectedly, readmission rates actually increased." The study noted that "this same paradox was further noted by Cleveland Clinic clinicians in a study that showed that while the Cleveland Clinic has lower mortality rates for heart failure than the rest of the nation, its readmission rates are higher, indicating that taking better care of more patients and preventing deaths may increase readmission."[80]

Even more ridiculous is the effort to improve the quality of patient care by monitoring each doctor and measuring his or her performance against national norms. The result is a blizzard of forms doctors must complete after each patient visit. It is driving doctors nuts!

The RAND Corporation undertook an extensive study in 2013 of how one key aspect of the program was impacting doctors: the Electronic Health Records requirement. To gather data—that the Feds say is to assess how to be more efficient and to recommend certain treatments over others—doctors have to spend hours and hours each day filling out forms on their computer for each patient they see.

A study by the Physicians Alliance of America found that 37% of doctors reported having to spend between one and two hours each day filling in the required information forms. Twenty percent said they had to spend two hours or more. Forty-five percent of doctors said that the record-keeping requirement cut into their productivity, and they complained that it reduced the time they could spend with each patient. One Connecticut doctor said he worked all weekend filling in the forms for the patients he had seen during the week. He said that he has to spend about 20 minutes on the forms for each patient he sees. So, he reported, he had to spend almost as much time filling in the reporting forms as seeing the patient.

Some doctors said that the fact that they had to sit down at the computer and look at the screen while talking to the patient undermined the patient's sense that the doctor was paying attention to them. It led, they said, to the impression that all he wanted to do was to fill in the forms.

It is also becoming clear that hospitals that serve richer, healthier patients score best on the quality measurements. The outside health care services in these communities are generally better and more available. Doctors at hospitals that serve lower income areas have to cope with more problems, which show up negatively in their quality of service score. The result is that the hospitals that serve the poor have lower ratings and get less funding as "punishment," making their care even worse. In the grand battle of Bureaucracy vs. Medicine, paperwork is winning the day!

The Issue to Defeat Hillary

The failure of Obamacare is a dagger poised to strike Hillary Clinton. Remember, before there was Obamacare, there was Hillarycare. In 1993, the newly minted First Lady sought to pass a program very similar to Obama's Affordable Care Act (ACA). Even as Obamacare is falling apart, Hillary—with predictable self-righteousness and stubbornness—is doubling down on its failures, promising to "strengthen" the program.

Her plan to solve the ills of Obamacare is to play, on a grander scale, the shell game that Obamacare has been playing with the American consumer: Hide the costs and pretend that they don't exist. Are consumer's burdened by high premiums? Hillary would "solve" the problem by empowering state insurance regulators "to block or modify unreasonable health insurance rate increases."[81] Of course, that would drive health insurers to refuse to cover Obamacare patients, just as UnitedHealth is already doing. But Hillary is still charging ahead. It is so much easier to pretend that high premiums stem from "unreasonable" charges by greedy hospitals and insurance companies than to admit that they come from the fact that only the sickest and the oldest are signing up for Obamacare and the rest of the uninsured would rather pay a fine than participate. Or that the high costs are driven by the broad and unnecessary range of medical and psychological services Obamacare insists be covered.

Are the deductibles under Obamacare stopping people from getting treatment? Simple! Hillary would just require all health plans to ignore required deductibles and give patients three doctor's visits for illnesses without charging deductibles. Fine. But doctors will still charge for the patient visits. They won't work for free. Hillary proposes to make the insurance companies eat the costs. Won't that drive insurance premiums up higher to cover the extra costs? Of course it will.

But Hillary won't let the premiums increase, she says. So won't that drive more insurance companies to refuse to participate in

Obamacare? Don't ask annoying questions! After all, the purpose of deductibles is to limit overuse of medical services so insurance companies can still afford to offer coverage. Hillary's proposal will flood providers with unnecessary patient visits and push insurance companies out of Obamacare. Then she says she would limit all out-of-pocket spending by chronically ill patients for drugs to $250 per month. Fine. Well and good. But all that does is drive up premiums to pay for the extra cost.

How is Hillary going to pull off limiting out-of-pocket drug charges and requiring doctor visits with no deductible while not allowing insurance companies to raise rates "unreasonably?" Like a person sleeping with a blanket that is too small for her, plans like Hillary's pull the blanket up to cover her neck but leave her feet uncovered. No matter how she tries, she'll never cover everything with a too-small blanket. And with excess utilization flooding the system and doctors limited in what they can charge, won't that drive doctors out of Obamacare?

Of course it will. The basic problem of Obamacare won't be solved by Hillary's plan; it will be worsened. How can you cover 10 million more people without more doctors? The only real way to lower costs is to educate and turn out more doctors. By increasing the demand without raising the supply, Obamacare is forcing costs up when it should be holding them down. Inevitably, Hillary will go to a single-payer system. Forget the insurance companies. Let them die. Go to a system where the government pays everything. Socialized medicine. That's her real objective, but she can't admit it.

But that begs the question of how you keep doctors in the system. Answer: Force them to stay. Make it illegal to go outside it. Government medicine or no medicine. If doctors want to practice their healing arts or if patients want care outside the government system, that's too bad. That would be illegal, just as it has been for years in Canada (although the Canadians are increasingly showing some needed flexibility). That's the end product of Hillary's plan to "strengthen" Obamacare, and it's where she always wanted to go in the first place. Her way or the highway.

Many will assume that Obamacare is dying a natural death. Even Hillary can't put all the pieces of this medical Humpty Dumpty together again. But she won't have to. If we make the colossal mistake of electing her, she will force us into collective socialized medicine. No choice of doctors. No choice for doctors. All decisions are made in Washington.

CHAPTER 4

Throw the Left Hook!—
Destroy the Obama/Hillary Base

W<small>E MUST GO GROUP</small> by group to weaken, undermine, and ultimately convert the elements of the Obama/Hillary coalition. We can't ignore them and focus only on increasing the turnout of our own base. African Americans, Latinos, young people, single women, and gays—we must go to each group and explain why Donald Trump is more relevant to meeting their needs than are Obama or Hillary. We won't convert them to a conservative ideology. But we can use the ways in which Obama and Hillary have failed them to harvest their votes. Throw the left hook!

Winning the White Working Class

"The Republicans are the party of the rich and the Democrats represent the poor and the middle class." This viewpoint, fundamentally ingrained in popular wisdom for over a hundred years is wrong. Just plain wrong.

On the one hand, the Republican Party has become divided between its Wall Street/establishment wing and its more populist Main Street/Tea Party elements. The fierce Republican nominating contest of 2016 and the majority that lined up behind antiestablishment candidates like Trump, Cruz, Carson, and Paul demonstrates the depth of this split. The new Republicans are set on breaking up the big banks and limiting their powers and privileges, while the establishment wing of the party is linked to Wall Street at the hip. The Republicans who won the battle for the party's soul and spirit in the 2016 primaries have more in common with the Occupy Wall Street demonstrators than with the board members of the big banks.

On the other hand, the Democratic Party has embraced Wall Street with gusto, relying increasingly on its financial largesse and protecting its interests in Congress. It's just that the old adage that Democrats are for the poor and Republicans for the rich hasn't been updated. To get the white working-class vote, we need to bring them up-to-date.

In the past, we could use the tax issue to get their votes. But Obama has outflanked us on the tax issue by differentiating between those who make more than $250,000 and the rest of us. Even as he regularly crosses the line and taxes us all, he still has managed to blunt taxation as an issue, undoing the good work of Ronald Reagan.

And Obama has succeeded brilliantly in substituting class for race among whites even as he doubles down on racial rhetoric among his black base. By getting blue-collar whites to resent rich whites more than poor blacks, he has cancelled out the policies Richard Nixon used to augment the GOP base.

We must accept what Obama has done and move on by explaining to the working class how the establishment Democratic Party, represented by Obama and Hillary Clinton, is no friend of theirs. America's working class has not seen its household income rise—adjusted for inflation—since 1985. While it briefly ticked up during the Clinton years, the Great Recession and Obama's policies have snuffed out the gains. So while the US economy, as noted, expanded by 30% since the middle of the Reagan years, net median family income has remained absolutely flat.

There are two major reasons the poor are getting poorer or at least not getting richer: trade with China and immigration. On both issues, the Democrats are taking a position against the interests of the working class and Republicans, led by Donald Trump, are lining up on the other side.

Trade: Bring the Jobs Home

Even the labor unions—as sycophantic as they always are toward the Democratic Party—can't stomach the trade deals America has been making lately.

That's why Donald Trump has attracted so much working-class support. He rightly attacks the trade agreements as bad deals, conceived by idiots and negotiated by weak bureaucrats.

"Who is our chief negotiator (in Japan)?" the Donald asked. "Essentially it is Caroline Kennedy. I mean give me a break. She doesn't even know she's alive."[1] Trump has shattered the post–World War II American political consensus that free trade is necessary and good. The governing class abused the patience of the American worker as he saw his job being exported under generous trade deals. Often bought off by the very foreign interests with whom they were negotiating, our trade representatives gave too much away and lost the confidence of the American worker.

Beginning with President Clinton's hard sell that led to the ratification of NAFTA, Democratic politicians have found it more and more difficult to get their base to accept the premise that freer trade means more prosperity. They are opting out of the consensus that has animated American foreign policy for the past hundred years. Why? Because they see that American manufacturing jobs are disappearing due to unfair trade competition from China. This rapid erosion of our blue-collar jobs is more responsible than any other factor for the income stagnation of the American working class.

Since 1979, we have lost 7,231,000 manufacturing jobs in the United States—37% of our total manufacturing employment. At the same time, the real (inflation-adjusted) median household income of Americans who have completed high school but not gone on to college, has dropped from $56,395 to $40,701—a drop of $15,694, or 27.8%.[2] No longer are our Democratic friends willing to follow their leaders to support trade deals. The idea that free trade will bring prosperity is falling flat in the face of the obvious evidence of Chinese chicanery and the equally apparent refusal of a Democratic president to confront it. Free trader or not, Adam Smith would never have found these one-sided trade deals acceptable.

CHINA CHEATS

The Economic Policy Institute puts the blame for this job loss where it belongs, on trade. The Institute reported, "The United States lost 5 million manufacturing jobs between January 2000 and December 2014. There is a widespread misperception that rapid productivity growth is the primary cause of continuing manufacturing job losses over the past 15 years. Instead, as this report shows, job losses can be traced to growing trade deficits in manufacturing products prior to the Great Recession and then the massive output collapse during the Great Recession."[3]

The biggest trade deficit is with China. Apologists in both parties say that China has a lower labor cost and naturally makes more money selling to us than buying from us. But China's edge in labor costs is more than offset by the cost of transporting goods from there to here, especially at times of high energy prices. It is not greater efficiency or lower labor costs that give China its advantage so much as its artificial currency manipulation (i.e., cheating).

China undervalues its own currency, the yuan, by about 25% so that Chinese products are 25% cheaper in US stores and American goods are 25% more expensive in China.

China's huge trade deficit, brought about by its massive cheating, increased by over half on Obama's and Hillary's watch. When they took office, China had a deficit of $229 billion with us. Now it is $367 billion.

Everyone understands that the United States has been hemorrhaging jobs to China ever since Bill Clinton let Beijing into the World Trade Organization (WTO). Clinton promised America that admitting China would be a win/win for Americans. But the opposite has been the case. It's been a great deal for China, but a terrible one for us. And yet no politician has the courage to take on China. Congress passed a law requiring the president to cite any nation that manipulates its currency to gain unfair trade advantage. Each year, he is required to make a finding on whether or not China is a currency manipulator.

And for each of the eight years, including during Hillary's tenure at the State Department, our government has refused to cite China as a currency manipulator, even though virtually all the job loss to Beijing comes about precisely because of its currency shenanigans.

The president won't crack down on China and Congress won't act either. While the Democrats say they fight for the working person, they don't utter a peep about this gigantic global fraud that is draining the good paying manufacturing jobs out of the country. Big business and the banks don't care about the job loss. China is a convenient, ready, and cheap place for American companies to outsource their production, cutting back jobs in the United States, but increasing their corporate profits. While the Democrats do nothing to stop China's games, they rant and rave about corporate outsourcing and "sending jobs overseas."

Before 2001, when we let China into the WTO, its trade with the United States was relatively small. We sold them about as much as they sold us. Back then, the main complaint of American businesses and workers was the competition of Japan. But Japan fought fair, outclassing us by making better, smaller, and cheaper products. China gets its edge by stealing our technology and manipulating its currency to make its products artificially cheaper. Look at how our trade deficit with China jumped in 2002. Since then, it has quadrupled.

US TRADE DEFICIT WITH CHINA

1994	$39 BILLION
1995	$33 BILLION
1996	$39 BILLION
1997	$50 BILLION
1998	$56 BILLION
1999	$68 BILLION
2000	$83 BILLION
2001	$83 BILLION—CHINA JOINS WTO
2002	$103 BILLION
2003	$124 BILLION
2004	$162 BILLION
2005	$202 BILLION
2006	$234 BILLION
2007	$258 BILLION
2008	$268 BILLION
2009	$229 BILLION—OBAMA STARTS
2010	$273 BILLION
2011	$295 BILLION
2012	$315 BILLION
2013	$318 BILLION
2014	$343 BILLION
2015	$367 BILLION

Once China entered the WTO in 2001, it took advantage of the lower tariffs to undercut American manufacturers all around the world, causing huge trade deficits.

Although China buys only 7% of our exports, it sells us 20% of our imports and accounts for half of our total trade deficit with the entire world.[4] The job loss to China as a result of the trade deficit has been horrific. Since China joined the WTO in 2001, we have lost 2.4 million jobs to Chinese exports.[5] Some experts have tried to belittle the loss of jobs. They say that other factors like automation, environmental regulation, fuel costs, and competition from other countries are more responsible for our manufacturing job losses. But a recent study by a group of economists who were initially skeptical of the impact of China on American jobs affirms that the total loss is, indeed, in the millions. To be exact, the study found that of the five million manufacturing jobs lost in the United States since China joined the WTO, between one and two million are attributable to Chinese imports.

While the economists participating in the study shared a bias toward free trade, the evidence soon made it apparent that the job loss to China was real. "The 'aha' moment," said Massachusetts Institute of Technology economist David Autor, "was when we traced through the industries in which China had surging exports to the local addresses of their U.S. competitors and saw the powerful correspondence between where China had surged and where U.S. manufacturing employment had collapsed."[6]

Bloomberg reported that Justin Pierce of the Federal Reserve and Peter Schott of Yale University found in April 2015 "that the biggest U.S. manufacturing employment declines and largest surges in imports were in products for which China permanently locked in the greatest reductions in tariffs as part of its entry to the WTO. Industries such as apparel, leather goods, plastic plumbing fixtures and surgical and medical equipment sustained substantial hits."[7] Schott said the changes since China entered the WTO were the "smoking gun" proving that Beijing's exports were responsible for our job loss.[8]

More than any other candidate, Donald Trump has singled out China for blame for US job loss. "We have been too afraid to protect and advance American interests and to challenge China to live up to its obligations," he said. "We need smart negotiators who will serve the interests of American workers—not Wall Street insiders that want to move U.S. manufacturing and investment offshore."

China manipulates its currency by using Chinese yuan to purchase American-dollar-denominated Treasury bills at a frantic pace. By buying dollars and paying for them in yuan, they keep the price of the dollar artificially high and the price of the yuan correspondingly low, making Chinese products less expensive in the United States and American goods more costly in China.

Chinese currency manipulation really got started in 2005 when its currency traded at 8.2 yuan to the each dollar. At the end of Bush's term, it had dropped to 7.6 to the dollar. But during Obama's first term and Hillary's tenure as secretary of state, it really crashed. It was down to 6.2 by the time Hillary left office in 2013. Since then, it has remained about the same. All told, the yuan has lost about one-quarter of its value since 2005. And that means that Chinese products in the United States cost one-quarter more than they should. If we ended Chinese currency manipulation, the effect on our economy would be huge. The Alliance for American Manufacturing, a labor-management partnership, says that a 28.3% increase in the value of the yuan would create two and a quarter million US jobs and cut the trade deficit by $190.5 billion.[9]

Why does the United States let China get away with its currency manipulation? American politicians and Treasury officials claim that they are reluctant to rein in China's purchases of American Treasury notes since, in effect, China is lending us money with each purchase, relieving our banks and citizens of the necessity of lending their own money to our government to cover its deficit. (And making it less necessary for the Fed to monetize our deficit by printing currency to cover it.) But that reason is obviously phony. If China stopped "lending us money" by ceasing to buy our Treasury bills, its currency would become stronger and its goods less attractive to American customers, causing a reversal of the jobs outflow from our country. We would prosper as a result, reducing our deficit dramatically. Even if China immediately stopped buying our Treasury bills, the effect would be minor. The Federal Reserve Board is, by far, the biggest lender to our government, lending us the money it creates to pay off our debts. Undesirable as a long-term policy, this "monetization" of the debt has not set off the feared inflation. In fact, as China has oscillated its level of purchase of US securities, the markets have scarcely noticed.

While China's trade in dollars is opaque to say the least, there is evidence that China dumped about $94 billion in US securities in August 2015, bringing its holdings down to $1.3 trillion. And the world didn't fall apart. The Fed just cranked up the old printing press once more. Nobody much noticed.[10] Why doesn't the WTO crack down on China's cheating? The rules of the World Trade Organization are biased in China's favor. The rules of the WTO do not even address currency manipulation. While the WTO holds down tariffs, it does nothing about artificially holding down the value of a nation's currency to gain competitive advantage.

A tariff, of course, is a tax imposed on imports to make them more expensive for consumers to buy. Tariffs are a no-no. The entire thrust of global economics in the years since World War II has been to hold them down and, eventually, to eliminate them because they give one country an unfair competitive edge against another. But currency manipulation does the exact same thing. Not by taxing imports from the other country to make them more expensive, but by weakening a country's currency to make their exports to other countries cheaper.

If the World Trade Organization has a blind spot where currency manipulation is concerned, the International Monetary Fund (IMF) does not. The IMF forbids currency manipulation but, unfortunately, does not have adequate enforcement power. The WTO, which has the power to stop currency juggling, won't use it. Of course, if Obama—or the next president—wanted to, he or she could force China to abandon its unfair manipulation. The first step would be for the White House to label China as a currency manipulator and then invoke sanctions on Chinese exports to the United States to force Beijing to reverse its policy. China would, doubtless, crack down on American exports to China in retaliation, but since they sell us four times as much as we sell them, that's not a sanction that is likely to bring us to our knees.

University of Maryland economist Peter Morici suggests that the United States impose a tax on Chinese imports equal to the extent of its currency manipulation, rising or falling as China pushes its currency value down or lets it float up to the market rate.

CHINA BUYS OUR POLITICIANS

The real reason our White House—and Hillary's State Department— did not and will not crack down on China is that Beijing has its tentacles deep into the Clintons. China hired Patton Boggs, a top US lobbying firm, for a fee of $35,000 per month, to fight against curbs on Chinese currency manipulation. Reuters reported that "the Chinese hire top-notch lobbying firms whose ranks are filled with well-connected former U.S. and Canadian officials [and] buy TV advertisements to buff their image."[11]

While US law bars candidates from taking campaign contributions from foreigners, a ton of money from China has found its way into the Clinton Foundation, which funds Hillary's staff and travel needs. One donor, Rilin Enterprises, pledged $2 million in 2013 to the foundation's endowment. While allegedly a private company owned by Chinese billionaire Wang Wenliang, it has strong links to the government. Jim Mann has written several books on China's relationship with the United States and points out that the company was one of the contractors that built Beijing's embassy in Washington. Mann points out that the Chinese government was especially careful in choosing Rilin to build the embassy because of its close ties to the company. "So you want to have the closest security and intelligence connections with and approval of the person or company that's going to build your embassy," Mann writes.[12] Rilin also keeps its US contacts up to date, spending $1.4 million since 2012 to lobby Congress and the State Department.[13] And remember who was secretary of state.

The Clintons began raking in money from China in 2008, a few days after Hillary was nominated to be secretary of state. Bill hosted a special meeting of the Clinton Global Initiative called CGI Asia. The keynote speaker was Chinese Foreign Minister Yang Jiechi, who is particularly famous for saying that the Chinese people do not consider the Dalai Lama to be a "religious leader." He described the Dalai Lama as, instead, "the mastermind behind [Tibet] separatist sabotage" and the "personification of evil and deception," whose efforts are "doomed to failure." Since then, the Clintons and their foundation have gotten millions from Chinese sources in donations and speaking fees.

Other top American foreign policy experts and former diplomats also find fertile soil in dealings with China. Former Secretary of State Madeleine Albright currently serves as the chair of the Albright-Stonebridge firm. The late Sandy Berger, Clinton's National Security Advisor and Hillary confidante, was her cochairman. Albright-Stonebridge offers its clients "the knowledge and on-the-ground resources to help businesses and organizations successfully navigate this often complex [Chinese] market. Our team in Beijing and Shanghai works to create allies within the Chinese system, through an approach that emphasizes systematic engagement with agencies and nongovernment stakeholders at the central, provincial, and local levels. We offer the agility, insights, and practical support to overcome challenges and a strategic approach to help you thrive for the long term."[14] In other words, the firm that includes Bill Clinton's secretary of state and a key Hillary ally promises an inside track to Beijing's wealth, a sure inducement to any politician to sell his soul to China.

As Democrats watch Hillary take money from Chinese interests to sell them out, they feel abused and spurned, betrayed by those who claim to fight for them. With friends in high places, protective lobbyists hovering over Congress, and funds flowing to the secretary of state, China has been more than able to protect itself against charges of unfair trading practices. The American worker has been less fortunate. In fact, competition from China—through lower wages and currency manipulation—has introduced a third-world wage standard into American manufacturing. No longer do US workers compete with one another or even along union/nonunion lines. Rather they are being forced to a global, third-world level of compensation entirely incommensurate with middle class life in the United States. It's time that US voters stand up and demand that their elected officials declare their independence from China and resolve to advance the needs and interests of American workers instead.

IT'S NOT JUST CHINA . . . IT'S MEXICO TOO

It is not only China that is sucking jobs out from the United States. It is Mexico too. As a result of NAFTA, our balance of trade has changed drastically from a positive $2.2 billion in 1991 to a negative $59 billion in 2015![15]

NAFTA, hailed as a job-creating agreement for American workers, has proven to be the exact opposite. Ross Perot predicted, when he ran for president against Bill Clinton and George H. W. Bush in 1992, that NAFTA would create "a giant sucking sound" as jobs fled over the border. Derided and even ridiculed at the time, Perot was right, and the statistics prove it![16]

US TRADE BALANCE WITH MEXICO

1991	+$2.2 BILLION
1992	+$5.4 BILLION
1993	+$1.7 BILLION
NAFTA TAKES EFFECT	
1994	+$1.4 BILLION
1995	−$15.8 BILLION

1996	−$17.5 BILLION
1997	−$14.5 BILLION
1998	−$15.9 BILLION
1999	−$22.8 BILLION
2000	−$24.6 BILLION
2001	−$30.1 BILLION
2002	−$37.1 BILLION
2003	−$40.8 BILLION
2004	−$45.1 BILLION
2005	−$49.9 BILLION
2006	−$64.5 BILLION
2007	−$74.6 BILLION
2008	−$64.7 BILLION
2009	−$47.8 BILLION
2010	−$66.3 BILLION
2011	−$64.6 BILLION
2012	−$81.7 BILLION
2013	−$54.5 BILLION
2014	−$53.8 BILLION
2015	−$58.6 BILLION

Ever since NAFTA was passed, our trade deficit with Mexico has soared. The blame for NAFTA falls squarely on the shoulders of Bill and Hillary Clinton. It is the centerpiece of the new Left's criticism of the Clintons and their wing of the Democratic Party. While its adoption and ratification by the Senate were heralded in the mainstream media as the signature achievements of the Clinton administration's first year, it has been a disaster for working Americans. It led to deficits, deficits, and more deficits.

In a way, the deficit with Mexico is more problematic than the one with China. American businesses are flocking to Mexico as Chinese wages increase. The *New York Times* reported that businesses are turning to Mexico for outsourcing where once they chose China:

"With labor costs rising rapidly in China, American manufacturers of all sizes are looking south to Mexico with what economists
describe as an eagerness not seen since the early years of the North
American Free Trade Agreement in the 1990s. . . . Mexican workers
are increasingly in demand."[17] US trade with Mexico has grown by
30% since 2010 and foreign direct investment is up to $35 billion.
Mexico now makes 14% of the manufactured goods imported by the
United States.

"When you have the wages in China doubling every few years, it
changes the whole calculus," said Christopher Wilson, an economics scholar at the Mexico Institute of the Woodrow Wilson International Center for Scholars in Washington. "Mexico has become the
most competitive place to manufacture goods for the North American market, for sure, and it's also become the most cost-competitive
place to manufacture some goods for all over the world."[18]

The list of fleeing US companies is long and painful: Caterpillar,
Chrysler, Stanley Black & Decker, and Callaway Golf. Americans are
hearing "that giant sucking sound" and resent it mightily. Again,
Donald Trump was first on the case saying Mexico is "killing us
on trade."[19]

Workers at the Carrier Corporation, a big air-conditioner manu-
facturer who just announced plans to move to Mexico, would agree.
Founded by Willis Carrier, who invented air conditioning, the formerly Indianapolis-based company stands to save $81 million a year
by kicking 1,400 Americans out of their jobs. The company pays its
Indiana workers $34 an hour, including benefits, but will have to
pay its new Mexican employees only $6 an hour.[20] Trump was quick
to pounce: "I would go to Carrier and say, 'You're going to lay off
1,400 people. You're going to make air conditioners in Mexico, and
you're trying to get them across our border with no tax.' I'm going
to tell them that we're going to tax you when those air conditioners
come. So stay where you are or build in the United States because we
are killing ourselves with trade pacts that are no good for us and no
good for our workers."[21]

TPP: MORE BAD TRADE DEALS

But this dismal experience with China and Mexico has not soured the Obama administration—or Hillary—on free trade deals. Obama, with Hillary's support, has approved free trade deals with Colombia, Peru, Chile, and a host of other countries. But the big player is the TPP—joining us to 11 countries on the Pacific Rim: Singapore, Brunei, New Zealand, Chile, Australia, Peru, Vietnam, Malaysia, Mexico, Canada, and Japan.

To win in 2016, we must exploit the fault lines revealed by the Democratic Primaries. None is greater than the TPP, which Bernie Sanders has denounced and Hillary helped to negotiate (although she now says she's against it). James Hoffa (the younger) spoke on behalf of the Teamsters, Steelworkers, Food and Commercial Workers, Machinists, and Communication Workers in denouncing TPP. Hoffa said, "Bum trade deals like NAFTA have killed upwards of 1 million U.S. jobs, many of which moved abroad. And that's the concern with the looming TPP. These big business handouts continue to hollow out the manufacturing base of communities and destroy middle-class jobs in their wake."[22]

The goal of the TPP goes far beyond the elimination of tariffs (we already eliminated them for Canada, Mexico, Chile, and Peru, who account for the vast majority of our trade with the 11 TPP partners). The TPP takes control of a host of issues away from Congress and the executive branch and vests the power in international courts established to police the deal. For example, regulation and labeling requirements for genetically modified foods (GM) would no longer be the subject of state or federal legislation or FDA or USDA oversight. Instead, the decisions governing what our consumers will see on the food labels will be made by the TPP administration—with no right of appeal.

We can see how this international usurpation of our sovereignty can hurt when we look at the issue of protecting dolphins. In recent years, environmentalists and naturalists have grown increasingly concerned about the dolphin death rate in the Pacific Ocean. Area nets, which catch everything within their parameters, snare large numbers of tuna, their intended target, but also a lot of dolphins are caught as collateral damage. Dolphins were becoming an endangered species as a result. Concerned activists spurred research that led to a new net design that lets dolphins escape while catching the tuna. Fishermen, particularly in Japan, were reluctant to have to replace all their nets and, at first, wouldn't do so. Activists met with US and European tuna companies and persuaded them to put "dolphin safe" labels on all tuna caught with the new nets. As a result, most fishermen switched to the new nets. Virtually every can of tuna sold in the United States now has the dolphin safe label and dolphin deaths are way down.

But in 2015, the WTO, on a complaint by Mexico, ruled that the dolphin-safe labels violated the free trade agreements and could not be used in the United States. So they will start disappearing from the shelves and the dolphins will start dying again. What is our recourse? Our courts? Federal or state regulators? Congress or state legislatures? All are neutered by the WTO agreement and none can overrule their decisions. The TPP extends this loss of our national sovereignty to international organizations.

Hillary helped to negotiate the TPP and, in her book, *Hard Choices*, endorsed it as the "gold standard" in trade agreements. She said the deal was "important for American workers, who would benefit from competing on a more level playing field." She also called it "a strategic initiative that would strengthen the position of the United States in Asia."[23] But when Hillary makes a promise, be sure to cash the check quickly. Once her polls or political objectives change, her position is also bound to change. After she announced for president in 2015 and leftist Senator Bernie Sanders (D-VT) said he'd run against her, she sensed the need to move to the left to avoid being upended in the primary. So Hillary flip-flopped and came out against the deal saying that its final text fell short of the "gold standard" she wanted to hold it to. And this about a treaty she negotiated! If she wins, we know what will happen. She will insist on some largely cosmetic changes in the treaty language, declare it fixed, and—presto—be back on board advocating it.

Trade takes a big bite out of US manufacturing. But plans are afoot to do the same with the service industry, which accounts for more than 80% of US jobs and has, so far, been largely immune to foreign competition. Obama is working hard on a new Trade in Services Agreement (TISA) that will do to the service sector what NAFTA, WTO, and TPP are doing to the manufacturing sector. Even as trade agreements like NAFTA and the currency manipulation of countries like China have more than decimated America's manufacturing sector, we have survived because our service industries have done very well. It's easy to make something somewhere else and ship it here. But it's a lot trickier to deliver services when you are not on location.

Since World War II, manufacturing employment has dropped from 33% of all jobs to 12% while the service sector has risen from 24% to 50%. As we have lost millions of manufacturing jobs, we have gained tens of millions of jobs in the service industries. A big reason for the disparity is that it has been harder to import services from abroad than it is to import products. But with the Internet and other modern communications capabilities, it may be getting easier for foreign-owned firms to compete in delivering services to American consumers.

Enter the TISA that is designed to facilitate trade in services. A key obstacle to the importation of services from abroad is the difficulty in importing workers from other countries into the United States. Our current immigration laws, while filled with loopholes, do a lot to constrain the importation of foreign workers to replace Americans. But Obama is about to try to change all that. While the TISA is still being secretly negotiated by 50 countries, leaks from Julian Assange's WikiLeaks expose some of the contents of the never-made-public draft treaty.

Assange's revelations make it obvious that the TISA is a backdoor attempt to allow unrestricted immigration into the United States and, indeed, to remove the power to regulate most immigration from Congress or the president. Under the proposed deal, foreign workers could be transferred from a foreign location to a domestic one simply as the company wishes. Immigration limits would not apply. So Sheraton International, for example, could move its kitchen or hospitality staff from hotels in Singapore to facilities in the United States and nobody could stop them.

The principle of free flow of labor is fundamental to the European Union, central to its efforts to create a common market where labor and goods can flow freely, just as they do from state to state in the United States. But applied internationally, they amount to a total override of our immigration or work-permit laws. Since virtually any company could make such a transfer, it obliterates our national boundary and permits free flow across it.

In our current political situation, where the parties are often at war with one another over immigration policy, this treaty removes the power to regulate our borders from Congress, or even the president, and makes them totally open. Since this proviso would be included in a treaty, which has the effect of the "law of the land" according to the US Constitution, it could not be abrogated or even modified by an act of Congress or by the president. Even US courts would have to apply the provisos of the treaty rather than American or state law. This override is a deliberate effort by the Obama administration to remove immigration from the control of the American people and our government. It would set up permanently open borders.

The TISA would also restrict American laws governing worker safety, environmental regulations, and consumer protections. It would treat all these rules as impediments to trade in services and subject them to being struck down—with no appeal—by an international body. TISA would also "restrict our ability to license health care facilities, power plants, waste disposal facilities and even university and school accreditation," according to Professor Jane Kelsey from the Faculty of Law at University of Auckland in New Zealand.[24]

Kelsey also points out that TISA will be "expected to lock in and extend their current levels of financial deregulation, lose the right to require data be held onshore, face pressure to authorize potentially toxic insurance products and risk legal challenge if they adopt measures to prevent or respond to another crisis."[25] Public interest groups opposing the TISA cite a litany of top corporations that are pushing the agreement including Microsoft, JP Morgan Chase, CHUBB, Deloitte, UPS, Google, Verizon, Wal-Mart, Walt Disney, and IBM.[26]

When Obama sought approval of the TPP, he asked Congress to grant him "fast track" authority over trade agreements, which limited the Senate to an up or down vote on the treaty with no amendments of filibusters permitted. He did so because he had a hope of getting the power—he got it—with the relatively mild TPP in the offing. But his real goal was to pass the TISA and to jam it through on an up or down vote. Otherwise, why put free flow of workers into a trade bill? It has nothing to do with trade. Besides, the United States already has free trade under NAFTA with Canada and Mexico and under bilateral treaties with Peru and Chile, 4 of the 11 countries in the TPP. And these 4 account for over three-quarters of our trade with the 11 countries in the deal. We didn't need a free trade treaty to have free trade with them.

But a TISA agreement, breaking entirely new ground, would change everything. Obama is putting it into a trade bill so he can take advantage of fast track to jam it through. Setting up free flow of service workers would eliminate the only advantage US workers have over foreign competition. Under TISA, workers from high tech firms to McDonald's would be subject to low wage competition from foreign workers for whom employers would not be obliged to purchase Obamacare (since they aren't Americans). This would create a built-in advantage for non-American workers of about $3,000 a year per worker (the estimated fine for not covering a worker in your employ under Obamacare).

Conservatives and establishment Republicans usually back free trade deals because of an ideological commitment to free trade,

going back to the theories of Adam Smith, so they have been reluctant to crack down on Chinese currency manipulation or to oppose
TPP or TISA. But they misunderstand the issue. We are not talking
here about free trade. We are talking about blatant cheating by currency manipulation where China is concerned and about an open-
door immigration policy masquerading as a trade deal in TISA.

Antiestablishment Republicans and Democrats can both rally
under the banner of opposing TISA and other free trade deals. Under
free trade, each country does what it does best and cheapest, creating a global free market to the benefit of all. But when one country is
only pretending to produce goods more cheaply by manipulating its
currency, the rules do not apply. But let's face it—trade is being used
to hold down the American worker to maximize profits for business
and lower prices for the consumer. Both parties are complicit in
the deal and both get campaign contributions to perpetuate it. But
this deal is a major cause of income inequality. The poor and middle
class keep getting poorer. The other half of this process of impov-
erishing the American working class is immigration, which keeps
wages low and unemployment of Americans high so as to benefit
business profits and Democratic vote getters.

Immigration

Even when we succeed in keeping jobs in the United States despite
our porous trade policy, they do not necessarily go to American
workers. Immigration will be the key issue in the 2016 election. More
and more, Americans are learning that our national safety in a world
of terrorism hinges on our immigration policies. And as Americans
realize that immigrants are taking away their jobs and stagnating
their incomes, it will be the central economic issue as well.

ILLEGAL IMMIGRANTS ARE TAKING OUR JOBS AND HOLDING DOWN OUR WAGES

Illegal immigration threatens our national cohesion and identity
and makes us vulnerable to crime and terrorism. But it also poses an

economic threat to our workers. The Democrats and liberals don't like to talk about the economic aspect of illegal immigration. They would much rather paint Republican opponents of open borders as racist of anti-Hispanic. Democrats do not want hardworking Americans to realize that illegal immigrants are taking our jobs and, by working for low wages, holding down pay for Americans.

Since 2000, virtually all the job growth in the United States has gone to immigrants with almost no increase in employment for those who were born in the USA. The Center for Immigration Studies reported that "government data show that since 2000 all of the net gain in the number of working age (16–65) people holding a job has gone to immigrants (legal and illegal)."[27] (The Census Bureau divides employment data into two categories: Native-born Americans and foreign-born Americans. The latter includes both immigrants—legal and illegal—and naturalized US citizens.)

Since 2000, there are 127,000 fewer working-age native-born Americans holding a job while the number of foreign-born Americans who have a job has risen by 5.7 million during the same period. The center reported that "immigrants have made gains across the labor market, including lower-skilled jobs such as maintenance, construction, and food service; middle-skilled jobs like office support and health care support; and higher skilled jobs, including management, computers, and health care practitioners."[28] And the trend is increasing. In August 2015, for example, while 698,000 native-born Americans lost their jobs, 204,000 foreign-born Americans gained employment, according to the Census Bureau and Bureau of Labor Statistics data.

Beyond the sheer number of jobs diverted to foreign-born people, the influx of foreign-born workers has stopped wage growth among native-born Americans. We can't get raises while millions pour over our borders who are willing to work for next to nothing. Workers cannot hold out for higher wages when legal and illegal immigrants are available to work for much less. The same incentive business owners have to outsource to low-wage countries operates within the United States to use cheap illegal labor.

The economic effect is deeply felt throughout the United States. In 2014, Americans who were born here saw their income *drop* by 2.3% while immigrants saw theirs *rise* by 4.3%. The US Census Bureau's "Income and Poverty in the United States: 2014" report reveals that, between 2013 and 2014, foreign-born households saw their median incomes go *up* by $2,031, while native-born households experienced a moderate income *decline* of $1,311.

In the United States today, naturalized citizens make much more than their American-born counterparts, earning a median household income $59,261 in 2014 while native-born households made only $54,678. In fact, the data so clearly demonstrates that immigration depresses American wages and incomes that it points to the likelihood that employers in the United States want all the immigration they can get to hold down the wages they have to pay to native-born or immigrant workers.

Democrats want illegal immigrants to vote but not to work (so as not to rile their union supporters) while some establishment Republicans want them to work (for low wages) but not to vote! Liberal Democrats, like those who support Bernie Sanders, are getting the point that the establishment backing for open borders is motivated by a wish for higher profits and lower labor costs.

When establishment politicians like George W. and Jeb Bush back amnesty for illegal immigrants, they often say they favor immigration because our country was founded by immigrants and speak of keeping an open door to the rest of the world. But the truth is that their corporate sponsors and contributors see it as a way to keep down wages for tens of millions of American families. Even worse, the establishment Left says that opposition to immigration is racist, creating a facade of tolerance behind which to hide their desire to hold down wages and incomes for their employees.

There is an eerie resemblance between today's immigration debate and the abolitionist views of Abraham Lincoln. Lincoln said there could be no upward mobility for wage-earning Americans as long as five million slaves could be forced to work for free. Now there will be none—and has been none—as long as 12 million illegal immigrants are willing to work for next to nothing. Why was Abraham Lincoln both antislavery and procapitalism? Why was he a Republican in the first place? Born to a subsistence farm family, he saw that since his father and family ate all they grew that they were locked on the farm for all their days on Earth. He left the farm as a boy and went to work on Mississippi riverboats, freed from the never-ending treadmill of subsistence farming by the miracle of cash wages. But how could he get wages when slaves could do the job for free? He realized that slavery imperiled the gains for others who wanted to follow his lead. Slavery had to go for working class Americans to be free. What was true in Lincoln's time is also true in ours. And so illegal immigration has to stop for wage-earning Americans to move up.

For all the liberal protestations of empathy for the working-class poor and their willingness to soak businesses by raising the minimum wage, it is only by cutting the flow of illegal immigrants that we can offer American workers real upward mobility. Liberals like to spread the myth that illegal immigrants take jobs Americans don't want. Like what? Landscaping? Dishwashing? Cleaning hotel rooms? Construction? Data from the Center for Immigration Studies explodes this canard. The fact is that Americans *do* want these jobs. In fact, they take them when they can.

Native-born US citizens comprise

- 55% of maids and housekeepers

- 58% of taxi drivers and chauffeurs

- 63% of butchers and meat processors.

- 65% of grounds maintenance workers

- 65% of construction workers

- 71% of porters, concierges, and bellhops

- 75% of janitors

What Americans don't want is the dirt-poor wages the illegal immigrants are willing to accept in these occupations. And the fact that illegal immigrants are willing to work for so little is just more evidence of how they depress wages and incomes for the rest of us.

H-1B VISAS: UNEMPLOYMENT FOR COLLEGE GRADUATES

Increasingly, the unemployment and stagnant wages brought by massive immigration—legal and illegal—is being visited on well educated Americans seeking well paid jobs. Obama has acted vigorously to expand immigration and its inroads into the American job market.

On New Year's Day, January 1, 2016, President Obama issued an executive order vastly increasing the number of green cards that will be issued to foreign college graduates seeking employment in the United States. *Breitbart News* reported that Obama's new "181-page rule focuses primarily on giving work-permits to foreign college-grads who will compete against Americans for white collar jobs, despite the large number of American graduates now stuck in lower-wage positions and struggling to pay off college debts. The rule will also make each foreign graduate much cheaper for U.S. employers to hire than many U.S.-born college grads."[29] Immigration lawyer John Miano predicts that Obama's action will lead to 100,000 new green cards every year.[30]

The new regulation comes on top of the 800,000 new two-year work permits that were issued to "dreamers" in 2012. ("Dreamers" are foreign migrants who were brought here by their illegal immigrant parents.) In 2013, Obama added about 2 million extra foreign workers to a US economy stagnating under persistent low wage levels. *Breitbart* explains that "roughly 650,000 foreign graduates are working in the United States for roughly 5 years each under the H-1B program. Roughly 120,000 foreign graduates of U.S. colleges are working in the United States for two years each via the OPT program, often called the 'mini-H-1B program.'" Obama's new executive order means that most of those foreign graduates will not have to "return home after several years, so American companies can continue to avoid hiring U.S. workers in their place."[31]

So up and down the wage and education scale, Obama's policies—with Hillary's support—are denying jobs to Americans while opening up new opportunities for foreigners. Of course, behind each foreign job applicant is a business eager to hire him or her to cut payroll costs. Not only can immigrants be asked to work for lower wages, but they need not be offered health insurance under Obamacare. With employers facing a fine of $3,000 per uninsured worker, what better built-in incentive to hire foreigners who need not be covered? Democrats hope that most of these businesses show their appreciation by giving money to Hillary's and the party's campaigns. But to ask these workers who are losing jobs and wages to illegal immigration to vote Democratic to allow more illegals in is the height of arrogance.

Liberals are fond of saying that conservatives are against illegal immigration because we are racist. But race and ethnicity have nothing to do with it. We will never be able to restore the American dream to reality until we stop letting our wealth drain away through illegal immigration.

There are 7 billion people in the world and most of them want to come here to live. Why wouldn't they? With the opportunity and freedom we have here, they'd be foolish not to. And with generous benefits awaiting them here, why not give it a try?

Republicans need to stand firm for:

a. Border security; a wall to keep illegal immigrants out. Walls work. Israel has kept the suicide bombers at bay for a decade with walls.

b. Deportation of all illegal immigrants. Liberals like to say that you can't go door to door and round up 12 million people. They say this would be like the Gestapo. But Obama deported 438,000 people in 2013. If we raised that total to one or two million a year, the rest would read the writing on the wall and leave.

c. An E-verify system to stop illegal immigrants from getting jobs. Cut off the jobs and the flow of immigrants will stop. Potential employers will have to hire Americans and pay them real American wages. It's about time!

Democrats need to grasp the essential reality that when they protest that the poor are getting poorer, the two key reasons are immigration and unfair foreign trade competition.

Increasing the minimum wage, the Left's standard solution to income inequality, will help only a few people at the bottom of the economic ladder. In the United States, the minimum wage is only $7.25. But the median wage is $17.09 and the mean wage (the average) is $22.71. Clearly, increasing the minimum wage, even to $15 per hour, is not going to help the majority of American wage earners.[32] Last year, only 3.3 million people worked at or below the federal minimum wage. They made up just 4% of the 76 million hourly workers in the United States.[33] Raising the minimum wage may be the right thing to do, but it's not a solution to income inequality.

The real solutions, curbing unfair trade practices and illegal immigration, are much tougher for the establishment of each party to achieve. They involve real sacrifices. The Republican candidate in 2016 must embrace policies designed to move up the incomes of the average worker—limiting immigration and fighting against unfair trade deals.

Go after Wall Street

Nothing so defined the Hillary vs. Sanders battle for the Democratic nomination as their different views of Wall Street. The class resentment against financiers/billionaires leveraging federal guarantees and special tax privileges to profit from the global economy is a key force that can cripple Hillary, whether deployed by a Republican or a Democratic challenger.

95% of the income gains of the Obama presidency have gone to the top 1% of earners in our economy (families who make more than $400,000 household income per year), a level without precedent in modern history.[34] Under Clinton, the equivalent figure was 45%, and under Bush, it was 65%. So while Bill Clinton did what he could to share the wealth, Obama has blatantly showered the ultrawealthy on Wall Street with his largesse. Our central task is not just to get voters to see the difference between Wall Street's incredible aggregation of income and Main Street's lack of progress but also to place the blame where it belongs, with the bipartisan establishment, including the Democrats to whom they are so loyal.

The concentration of wealth has escalated in recent years, but this is not due to increased earnings in the regular economy. It is almost entirely because of the rapid growth in both income and wealth of the Wall Street investor class and their Silicon Valley partners. This bicoastal accretion of wealth has left the rest of the country out in the cold, watching the money pile up in New York and California.

We Republicans must stress this point. We do so not to fan the envy of class conflict, but to focus on the unjust diversion of funds from the average American family to the very wealthy. This transfer occurs, not because of hard work or even shrewd investments, but because of wholesale subsidies, special privileges, immunities, guarantees, and tax advantages both parties have showered upon the wealthy in America. We must demonstrate that it is the establishment of both parties that benefits from this process and guarantees its perpetuation. Democrats are as responsible for it as are Republicans. And you can quote Bernie Sanders, Elizabeth Warren . . . and Donald Trump on it.

Donald Trump has taken the lead on the Republican side in denouncing Wall Street and its denizens. "The hedge fund guys didn't build this country," he says "These are guys that shift paper around and they get lucky."[35]

This concentration of wealth is largely due to the runaway incomes in the financial sector that now account for one-third of all corporate profits in the United States (double the figure of 30 years ago). It hasn't always been so. Throughout the 20th century until the 1980s, the average income of people in the financial sector was approximately the same as those in other businesses. But now it has ballooned to twice as much. The odyssey of the top 1% is a strange one.

They suffered more during the Great Recession of 2007–2008 than the rest of us did because they had more income from capital investments that crashed with the market. But then they came roaring back, gobbling up an obscene portion of national income.

During the Great Recession, the top 1% lost a third of its income, three times as much as the rest of the country. They bottomed out in 2009 when their share of the national income fell to only 13.4% (two years earlier, it had been 18.7%). As Gershwin says in *Porgy and Bess*, "A depression is when white folks are poor too." Then, when the so-called recovery took hold, the very rich recouped their losses and soon went on a tear, piling up income faster than anyone had ever done before in our history.

The fiscal policies of the Obama administration, in particular those of the Federal Reserve Board, kindled a growth in income for the top 1% unrivaled in history.

By 2012, the top 1% was back, making 23% of the national income. Now, in the election of 2016, we must make the Democrats eat these Wall Street gains. We must make it clear that it was they, not we, who made Wall Street rich.

Obama, Hillary, and the rest of the Democratic establishment cannot pretend that increasing the minimum wage will be the answer to preventing this kind of rampant inequality. As noted, this increase will bring more income to 3.4 million working Americans. But the real answer is to redistribute income by eliminating the unfair advantages that have been given, largely by Obama and Hillary, to the richest people in our country.

We must not call for income redistribution, just power redistribution. The rapid appreciation in the income of the richest is not due to industriousness, risk taking, wise investments, or frugality, but comes almost exclusively from massive subsidies from the Federal Reserve, protected by tax shelters and accounting gimmicks.

HOW WALL STREET GOT RICHER

The first thing a foreigner learns about American politics is that the rich are Republican and the poor are Democrats. But that was before the politics of the Clintons and Obama built a passageway from the White House to Wall Street and then on to the Silicon Valley. Through this passage went massive campaign contributions to the Democrats and, in return, many special favors to the Manhattan bankers and the northern California entrepreneurs.

It is the greatest myth in our politics that Republican policies created and catalyzed income inequality. In fact, the responsibility resides mainly at the doorstep of the Federal Reserve Board, whose chairmen and a majority of whose members are appointed by the president.

Since the recession officially ended in June of 2009, the Federal Reserve Board has operated as, in the words of former budget director David Stockman, "a cash machine in the Wall Street casino,"[36] letting its top operators help themselves to mountains of newly minted money with little accountability over how they spend it. The policy of quantitative easing (QE) deluged Wall Street banks with cash, supposedly to get them to lend it out to small businesses to create jobs. At least that's what the Fed said.

But the reality—and the result—were quite different. The loans never got made. Of the $3.7 trillion in cash the Federal Reserve Board gave to the banks under Obama, almost $3 trillion of it is still sitting right where it's always been—in the bank vaults, particularly in the Fed's vault where it is helpfully storing the money for the banks. There, it earns a quarter of 1% interest each year, a windfall of about $10 billion that goes to the big banks every year, courtesy of the Fed.

Former Federal Reserve chairman Alan Greenspan said that as of 2012 he could discern "very little impact on the economy" from all that cash flooding Wall Street. Welfare for Wall Street.[37] Economists, including Dhaval Joshi of BCA Research, agree that the rewards of QE have done little to help the real economy. He wrote, "QE cash ends up overwhelmingly in profits, thereby exacerbating already extreme income inequality and the consequent social tensions that arise from it."[38] And the president of the Federal Reserve Bank of Dallas, Richard Fisher, who sits on the Federal Reserve Board, admitted that that cheap money has made rich people richer, but has not done quite as much for working Americans.[39]

Why didn't the banks lend out the money they got from the Fed? Part of the reason is that they couldn't find credit-worthy borrowers who wanted and needed the money. Ever since the recession got started, Obama has followed the doctrines of British economist John Maynard Keynes and pumped money into the economy in the hopes of stimulating demand. But you can't push a string.

Major companies and small businesses alike had so little confidence in the future of the US economy that they didn't want to spend the money they had piled up over the years. After many months of accumulating cash, America's businesses have $1.7 trillion of cash on hand. So why borrow more? Even at rock-bottom interest rates, they would rather stick the cash under the mattress than invest it in the economy. That's how much confidence they have in Obama's economic wisdom.

The other reason the banks won't lend is that Obama's bank regulations made it very, very dangerous to make loans to businesses, especially those that are left as possible borrowers after the big corporations have said "no more." Even as his administration was shoveling money into the upper echelons of Wall Street, it was enacting bureaucratic regulations that made it virtually impossible for the banks to use the funds to create jobs. Under Obama, bank regulation, aimed largely at midsize and small community banks, has become tight and strict. Even though these institutions were not responsible for the crash of 2007 and 2008, they are bearing the brunt of the regulatory retaliation.

Between 2009 and 2015, Obama has closed 500 community banks, with a collective $75 billion in assets. Counting these closures along with other bank failures, the total number of banks in the United States has dropped to the lowest level since the Great Depression. We are shedding hundreds of banks per year and now are down to 6,270 commercial banks and savings institutions.[40] This policy of closing community banks makes it almost impossible for local banks to take advantage of the quantitative easing funds to lend to local business. Banks are scared to death of making loans that could be seen as risky by nit-picking federal regulators. Each audit kindles a morbid fear of being closed down, wiping out the salaries, bonuses, stockholdings, and in some cases, even the pensions of their executives. Who would lend money in that kind of regulatory environment? And what incentive was there to lend out the money? The Fed was, after all, paying banks interest not to lend it out, but to keep it in its vaults.

As Trump put it: "Under Dodd-Frank, the regulators are running the banks. The bankers are petrified of the regulators. And the problem is that the banks aren't loaning money to people who will create jobs."[41]

And the regulatory excesses were totally unnecessary. It wasn't the small community banks that had caused the 2007–2008 crash. They didn't buy subprime mortgages. They didn't need TARP federal bailout funds. They lent to their own communities and were largely solvent. But Obama came down on them like a ton of bricks. Why would he do that? To help the big banks. Obama wants to get rid of the thousands of small banks throughout the country. By forcing small banks out of business, he increases the market share of the giant banks. And they give a lot of money to Democratic candidates.

Between 2006 and 2014, Wall Street gave $348 million to Democratic candidates and committees. They gave comparable amounts to Republicans. Both parties are part of the Capitol gang that fixes things for Wall Street and screws the average American.

Besides, helping big banks gobble up small ones is part of Obama's economic philosophy. Myriad small banks would be hard to control; their whims would make a mockery of the central planning that underscores Obama's socialist worldview. But concentrate power in a handful of banks, a few big unions, and big government regulators, and you can control the economy. Just like they do it in Europe. No more of this messy and wasteful free enterprise.

So while Obama was hell on wheels on the small banks, he coddled the big ones, giving them $3.7 trillion in QE money. The money was given to these big banks largely in exchange for worthless mortgage-backed securities that were lying fallow in their vaults. These securities were backed by mortgages on bankrupt properties that had long since stopped making payments and that could not be sold on any open market. But the Fed was a willing purchaser. Not only didn't the Fed get any real consideration for this avalanche of money, but it actually paid interest to the banks in return for storing the money it had paid them. The big banks were supposed to lend out the money to help the economy, but they held onto the money. They didn't lend it out. They kept it in the vault. They didn't earn it. They don't lend it. They don't do anything for it. And the $10 billion interest the Fed pays these banks just rolls in year after year.

If the big banks don't share their largesse with job-creating American businesses, they are very generous with their employees, their stockholders, and, most of all, with their executives, driving up the incomes of the richest 1% beyond all comprehension. While they don't lend out the money the Fed gave them to businesses, they do use it to buy stocks and push up the Dow Jones to new heights. They buy their own company stock and give it to employees as a stock option bonus. They pay lavish salaries to top executives and a lot to everyone else.

In 2014, the average income of a Wall Street employee was over half a million a year—$355,900 in base income and $172,860 more in bonuses. This income level is more than 10 times higher than the median family income in the United States. Total Wall Street bonuses in 2014 came to $29 billion.

And when the income goes to hedge fund managers, they pay only the capital gains tax rate rather than the ordinary income tax the rest of us have to pay. Usually, you can get capital gains treatment on that portion of your income that is a return on an investment. The idea is that you already paid taxes on the money you invested so you get a lower tax rate on the profits the investment returns to you. The larger economic purpose of separate capital gains taxation is to encourage investment through lower tax rates. Wages and salaries are not capital gains—except for hedge fund managers.

They get a special tax break—called "carried interest"—even though they are not risking their own money but are simply managing money for others, yet they get to treat their income as a capital gain. But even though they are like all other wage earners, they only pay a 20% capital gains tax, not the almost 40% they would pay if their checks were treated as ordinary income. The carried interest loophole is a $13 billion annual subsidy to hedge fund managers.

Donald Trump will end it. He said "the hedge fund guys are getting away with murder." Pledging to end the carried interest loophole, Trump said "the hedge fund guys won't like me as much as they like me right now—I know 'em all, but they'll pay more."[42]

As the playing field has been tilted sharply in favor of big banks and their employees and against small banks, the top six banks—JP Morgan Chase, Bank of America, Citigroup, Wells Fargo, Goldman Sachs, and Morgan Stanley—have assets equal to 67% of the total assets of all US banks combined. Six banks out of 6,000 (one-tenth of 1%) have two-thirds of the bank assets. Over the past five years, these six biggest banks have grown by 37% in their assets while the total assets of the other banks have risen by only 8% over the same time period. These top six banks now have almost $10 trillion in assets.

Obama famously denounces "trickle down" economics when the rich get tax cuts that they fail to pass on down the line. Yet, there is no form of trickle down as blatant as the fiscal policy of the Fed under Barack Obama's management. But as president, Obama exploits resentment against the massive Wall Street wealth in order to keep the loyalty of his Democratic, blue-collar legions. His rhetoric soaks the rich while they flood him with campaign contributions and he drenches them in cash in return. With such income inequality created by the Fed giving the richest banks extra money year after year, any Republican attempt to win back alienated voters has got to start with a full frontal attack on Wall Street.

But the attack must do more than simply give middle-income voters a chance to vent their anger at Wall Street. We must make clear that the massive money paid out by Obama to Wall Street was money that was supposedly for job creation in middle America. But it never reached us. Obama gave it to the richest people in America instead. The Fed swore that making Wall Street richer was just an unintended consequence of a policy designed to create jobs. Baloney. It was the Federal Reserve Board governors and staff feathering the nests of the banks from which they came and to which they planned to return once their government careers ended.

Obama's policies have concentrated wealth and growth at the upper end of the banking spectrum. These banks are not about to lend much money to Joe's Corner Grocery or the local manufacturing plant. They do business on Wall Street and prosper, not by lending to create jobs, but by the free interest they get from the Federal Reserve Board.

WALL STREET AND THE CLINTONS: A LONG-TERM ROMANCE

Is there a connection between the huge donations Wall Street gives to Hillary and the Democrats and the Fed's largesse? You bet there is.

Hillary Clinton is uniquely a beneficiary of Wall Street and its corrupt money. Since they left the White House in 2001, the Clintons have raked in more than $100 million from Wall Street in personal speaking fees (income to them), donations to the Clinton Foundation (which they control), and campaign contributions.

In fact, a few months after Hillary left the State Department, she gave two speeches to Goldman-Sachs for a quarter of a million dollars each. This cool half a million was not paid out in campaign contributions that go only to political purposes nor to the Clinton Foundation, but went directly into Hillary's and Bill's personal bank account. Cash income for Hillary and Bill. Her record makes her the poster girl for Wall Street and running against Wall Street is the key to defeating her.

According to a May 2106 *New York Times* report, between them, Bill and Hillary Clinton have made "at least $30 million over the last 16 months, mainly from giving paid speeches to corporations, banks and other organizations, according to financial disclosure forms filed with federal elections officials."[43]

Remember that it was Bill Clinton who opened the door to the massive giveaway to Wall Street by signing a bill to repeal the Glass–Steagall Act in 1999 and by approving legislation to bar federal regulation of derivatives (highly risky Wall Street bets with big returns if you win).

Wall Street's current rampage started with the repeal of the Glass–Steagall Act that had reined in its investment opportunities for 65 years. Reinstating the Glass–Steagall Act, over Wall Street's and Hillary's strenuous objections, must be the centerpiece of the Republican campaign to win back alienated voters who resent the rich getting richer while their incomes stagnate. We must make Glass–Steagall not merely an issue, but a rallying cry. Reinstating it is the only way to stop Wall Street from the excesses that leave the taxpayer holding the bag.

Glass–Steagall was passed during the Great Depression as bank failures gripped the nation. Millions stood on line only to have their bank's window shut in their face as they tried to take out their savings deposits. (Dick recalls that his own mother, as a 15-year-old girl, was sent by her illiterate Hungarian mother to run to their bank to take out their money as the market crashed. She came away empty handed—a story that has a sacrosanct place in family lore.)

The banks, which usually keep only a fraction of the money deposited in their vaults on hand while they lend out the rest, could not honor the demands when everybody tried to pull out their money at once. Banks coast to coast closed down and millions lost everything. On taking office in 1933, FDR declared a bank holiday to stop the panic and gradually reopened the banks, one by one, as they were certified to be financial solvent.

For a longer-term solution, New Deal liberals called for federal deposit insurance so that ordinary Americans would not face the loss of all they had during depressions and bank panics. But Virginia's crusty, conservative senator Carter Glass, chairman of the Senate Finance Committee, stood in the way. Glass, who was FDR's original choice for Treasury Secretary, said he was only going to let deposit insurance out of his committee if legislation accompanied it to control how banks invested their money. Glass's point was that he was not prepared to give depositors a taxpayer guarantee if the banks could use the federally guaranteed money to gamble on the stock market. He insisted on rigid controls over banks barring them from investing in securities and other risky assets. And so the Glass–Steagall Act passed as a companion measure to federal deposit insurance.

For decades, the banks have chaffed under the restraints of Glass–Steagall and lobbied hard for its repeal. Of course, the banks wanted to get rid of the Glass–Steagall restrictions but were very happy to continue to accept federal deposit guarantees. (During the crash of 2007–2008, a new de facto layer of federal guarantees of bank capital emerged when the "too big to fail" doctrine made its way into national policy. Now not only would depositors' money be protected, but the risky investments and wagers of the bank, its managers, and its owners would, in effect, be guaranteed as well.)

The big task before the GOP in 2016 is to make it clear that Hillary is the candidate of the big banks while Donald Trump is their opponent.

Bernie Sanders has done all he can to make people understand the connection between the Hillary and Bill Clinton wing of the Democratic Party and the Wall Street speculators. We have only to quote him to prove that part of our case. In the first Democratic debate,

Sanders opened up on Hillary over the issue: "Here's the story," the Vermont senator said. "I mean let's not be naive about it. Over her political career, why has Wall Street been a major, the major, campaign contributor to Hillary Clinton? Now, maybe they're dumb and they don't know what they're gonna get, but I don't think so."[44]

Sanders was appropriately dismissive of Hillary's claims that she would not be influenced by swimming in Wall Street money. "I have never heard a candidate," he said, "—never—who's received huge amounts of money from oil, from coal, from Wall Street, from the military-industrial complex, not one candidate, who doesn't say, 'Oh, these contributions will not influence me, I'm going to be independent.' But why do they make millions of dollars of campaign contributions? They expect to get something. Everybody knows that."[45]

Hillary replied by claiming that she had "hundreds of thousands of donors—most of them small—and I'm proud that for the very first time, a majority of my donors are women—60 percent."[46] Of course most of one's donors are small contributors. But even though the Wall Street money comes from only a few donors, the total of the donations constitutes a huge part of her total campaign treasury.

Then Hillary tried to say that the Wall Street money she got was given as a gesture of gratitude for her help to the downtown New York City area after 9/11. She said this of her support from Wall Street: "I represented New York on 9/11 when we were attacked. Where were we attacked? We were attacked in downtown Manhattan where Wall Street is. I did spend a whole lot of time effort helping them rebuild. That was good for New York, it was good for the economy, and it was a way to rebuke the terrorists who had attacked our country."[47]

Who does she think she is kidding? The contributions she got were in gratitude for relief measures for downtown New York after 9/11? No, they were payoffs for her past support of Wall Street and down payment for future favors.

The most important of those favors came in 1999 when President Bill Clinton abandoned the traditional Democratic position against repeal and signed legislation to wipe Glass–Steagall from the books. (Was it any coincidence that Clinton must have known that his law license was in jeopardy in the Paula Jones case—he was, in fact, stripped of it as he left office. How would he earn a living? In fact, he raked in massive fees for paid speeches, much of it from the very banks he had helped by signing the repeal legislation. Were they paying him back for signing the bill?)

The repeal of Glass–Steagall catalyzed the huge returns Wall Street has reaped since. Goldman-Sachs launched an initial public offering (IPO), taking 12% of the company public in 1999, just as the ink was drying on the repeal of Glass–Steagall. That year, now that Glass–Steagall no longer bound its hands, Goldman acquired Hull Trading Corporation, one of the world's top market-making firms for $531 million, and bought Speer, Leeds & Kellogg, one of the largest firms specializing in the New York Stock Exchange, for $6.3 billion in 2000. And when the banks crashed in the subprime crisis of 2007–2008 and the feds stepped in to give them TARP money to bail them out, the concept of depositor insurance was, de facto, extended to the banks and their executives. Everyone but the taxpayers.

The Wall Street Casino was open for business.

REINSTATE GLASS–STEAGALL

Reinstating Glass–Steagall is a crucial first step in reining in Wall Street and ending the gross wage inequality it has caused. Democrats, led by Hillary Clinton, have opposed reinstatement (to do so would be to condemn her husband's position) while many good Republicans have embraced reinstatement. Old Senator Carter Glass had a good point. If we let Wall Street do as it pleases while we protect their depositors money through the FDIC and safeguard the bank's profits through the "too big to fail" policy, we had better restrict banks to conservative investments.

The rich get richer because the Federal Reserve Board sees to it that they do. That wasn't their original mandate. The Fed was established in 1913 to strengthen the banking system after a series of catastrophic failures during financial panics. Over the years, the Fed has expanded its job to include fighting inflation and protecting the currency. In 1947, the Congress added the goal of promoting full employment to the Fed's mission. Now, in theory, the Federal Reserve Board has three purposes:

- Maximize employment
- Stabilize prices
- Moderate long-term interest rates

But these days, its formal mandate has been eclipsed by its desire to keep Wall Street wealthy and growing. The Fed has become a personal piggy bank for the richest bankers in America to use to play the stock market and drive up prices. The Fed's former focus on creating jobs and stabilizing prices has fallen back in its priorities. Now—with the strong support of Obama's Treasury Department—this mission has been eclipsed by their personal financial interests, and those of their friends, to keep stock prices soaring even in a tepid and largely stagnant economy.

Even as the personal income of the average American stayed flat and the American economy (GDP) grew by only 20% during the four-year period between 2009 and 2014 (unadjusted for inflation) while the Dow Jones Industrial Average rose by 143%! Wall Street doesn't make its money from a growing economy. It makes it from the rise in stock prices reflected in the Dow Jones index. And the policies of the Fed—by pumping in money the banks can use to buy stocks and take risks—have made the phenomenal income increases on Wall Street over the past five years possible. Indeed, it makes them inevitable.

Why is the Fed so solicitous of Wall Street and its top executives? Two reasons:

- The Fed staff and board members came from there.
- They will return to Wall Street when they leave.

There is a revolving door between the Federal Reserve Board and the banks it is supposed to regulate. A study by the New York Federal Reserve Banks found that 10% of all Federal bank regulators left the Fed just in 2014 alone to take jobs with the banks they used to regulate. There is an especially active exchange between the major banks and the Treasury Department. Jack Lew, the current secretary, came from Citigroup. Timothy Geithner, his predecessor, went to the private equity firm Warburg Pincus after leaving Treasury. And his predecessor, Henry Paulson, was the CEO of Goldman Sachs before becoming Secretary of the Treasury.

This revolving door creates an identity of interests between the regulators of the Fed and the Treasury Department on the one hand and the big banks on the other. The regulators who are working for the government want to protect their future earnings for when they return to Wall Street. And if they are now on Wall Street, they can keep reminding the bureaucrats of their shared interests whenever the need for special favors or bailouts arises.

HILLARY'S PATHETIC WALL STREET "REFORM" PLAN

Under pressure from her supporters like Massachusetts Senator Elizabeth Warren and opponents like Vermont Senator Bernie Sanders, Hillary released her own Wall Street regulatory plan in a December 7, 2015, Op-Ed in the *New York Times*. The key part of the plan was what was not in it: She opposed reinstatement of Glass–Steagall.

We Republicans must make reinstatement of Glass–Steagall our rallying cry in 2016. This one law, albeit with some updating, is the key to stopping the kind of federally insured Wall Street gambling that has put the taxpayers on the hook and created historic income inequality. Instead, Hillary proposed to "impose a new risk fee on . . . banks with more than $50 billion in assets . . . to discourage the kind of hazardous behavior that could induce another crisis."[48]

The idea of fining or taxing banks is popular with the Obama administration and their allies on Wall Street because, while the fines seem high and sound like a harsh punishment, they really matter little to the big banks who are the offenders. They know full well that the feds will never fine them so much that it risks their business—because they are, after all, too big to fail. They treat the fines as a cost of doing business. In fact, it is a kind of fee splitting with the federal government as the fines are paid to Washington to use as it pleases rather than to provide any relief to the ordinary Americans Wall Street's corrupt practices have defrauded.

Indeed, Obama uses the revenue from fines like these to support community action groups that are allied with him politically. He has broad discretion in the use of these monies and uses it to his advantage. You will never discipline Wall Street with fines. The bankers will just laugh.

Hillary dismisses the Glass–Steagall Act as a "depression-era rule" and laments that it wouldn't have stopped Lehman Brothers or AIG from their conduct in the financial scandal. She attributes her opposition to Glass–Steagall to the need to regulate such nonbank institutions. But obviously, any reinstatement of Glass–Steagall will include updating it to cover these growing nonbank firms. The principle behind Glass–Steagall is what is key: Federally insured deposits must not be used for insecure, speculative investments.

Hillary has left herself very vulnerable on the Glass–Steagall issue and we must hammer her over it. Remember that five of the top six organizations that have given campaign money to Hillary Clinton since her current political career began in 1999 are all big banks:

BIG BANK DONATIONS TO HILLARY SINCE 1999[*]

CITIGROUP INC.	$891,501
DLA PIPER	$852,873
GOLDMAN SACHS	$831,523
JPMORGAN CHASE & CO	$801,380
MORGAN STANLEY	$765,242

---

[*] Figures current as of the time this book went to press.

And this total of over $3.5 million does not include speaking fees paid directly to the Clintons nor does it include donations to either the Clinton Foundation or the Clinton Global Initiative. Never has a candidate gotten more money from a single source than the Clintons have received from Wall Street.

Wall Street will loom large in the election of 2016. Exposing Obama's failure to control it, and his record in allowing it to grow at the expense of the rest of us, will be key to winning.

TURNING CLASS WARFARE AGAINST THE DEMOCRATS

But most important, the Wall Street issue can turn the whole class warfare shtick of Obama's around to work against Hillary. Mrs. Clinton's prodigious involvement with Wall Street, her husband's approval of the law repealing Glass–Steagall, and her own refusal to support reinstating the law, make her very vulnerable on the issue.

But we will have some educating to do. We need to explain to blue-collar Democrats how Hillary's and Obama's infatuation with Wall Street is causing the income inequality about which they complain. We need to show how stopping these abuses and the reckless trading in government-guaranteed funds are essential to avoiding another crash.

The Democrats will push proposals to raise the minimum wage. But only a small part of the labor force gets the minimum wage, and most of them are not the primary wage earners in the family. They are sons and daughters who deliver groceries or work in Wendy's to supplement the family income. The wage should be raised, but it won't do much about income inequality.

We must expose the corrupt, insider relationship between Wall Street and Hillary and make the young people in the Occupy Wall Street group who oppose the bloated incomes of the top one percent to understand that Hillary is their enemy.

Every issue in American politics comes to be equated with one or the other of the parties. Decades of experience have taught voters that holding down taxes, cutting spending, and strengthening the military are Republican issues. Meanwhile, they agree that

Democrats, in general, are better at helping education, protecting the environment, and giving aid to the elderly.

Now the Democrats and the liberals have staked their claim to the new issues of income inequality and of Wall Street's abuses. Capitalizing on the GOP's long identification with the more wealthy in our society, the Democrats are working to make income inequality and big bank abuses work against the Republicans.

But the record is quite different. It was Obama's policies that swelled the incomes of the wealthy and allowed Wall Street to get away with the most predatory of practices.

Trump must tie Wall Street around the neck of the Democrats, using the facts to dispel the myth that it was Republicans who allowed the rich to get so much richer.

Trump must take strong positions on the issue by committing to:

1. reinstating Glass–Steagall,

2. mandating criminal penalties and jail time for those who create financial crises by irresponsible investments,

3. imposing a fiduciary duty on Wall Street not to lie to investors and to act in their best interest, and

4. refusing to bail out big banks if they face failure; paying off the depositors through the FDIC, but for the bank executives and stockholders, it's YOYO—You're On Your Own.

CHAPTER **5**

Peel Away Hillary's Base Constituencies

A FRICAN AMERICANS, LATINOS, SINGLE women, and young people cast 40% of the general election vote. Obama was elected
by winning disproportionately within each of these groups. He
carried blacks 93%–7%,[1] carried single women 67%–33%.[2] Under-30
voters backed him 60%–40%,[3] and Latinos voted for Obama
71%–29%.[4] Obama carried these four groups by a combined margin of almost 3:1. So before anybody outside the Democratic Party
base voted, Obama already had locked up between a quarter and a
third of the total vote.

In 2016, we must take bold action to shatter the Obama coalition
of women, blacks, Latinos, and young people. We can't let the Democrats win in 2016 by harvesting a disproportionately large vote
from these groups. We must shatter their base.

Winning Women

Many assume that Hillary Clinton, by virtue of being female, can win much more of the women's vote than a typical male Democratic candidate. That's just not true. In 2012, women voted Democratic by 10 points. Donald Trump's challenge is to better that performance.

Whether or not he can will be the central test of his candidacy. Hillary will use his past put-downs of certain specific women—such as Rosie O'Donnell and Megan Kelly—to try to paint him as a misogynist, generalizing from his often too candid remarks about particular women to paint a false picture of his general attitude.

Donald Trump is no misogynist as the women who have known him well—wives, employees, daughters, friends—can attest. He does strike back when he feels he's been attacked unfairly, but he is a gender-neutral combatant.

But Trump's reputation is out there for all to see. A FoxNews poll in April, 2016 found him losing women by 55%–33% even as he carries men by 51%–40%.

Nobody can win if they lose women by twenty-two points. Romney lost in 2012 when he only lost women by ten.

Trump must close the gap. Those who watch Donald's interaction with his family—particularly with his daughters—do not doubt that he is no misogynist. His history of hiring women executives substantiates his fairness and gender-neutral ability to spot talent.

Trump is likely considering whether to select a woman as his vice presidential running mate. If he did find a qualified woman to run with, it would go a long way toward offering proof of his essential feminism. As he campaigns with her, listens to her opinions, takes her advice, and advances her in public, the ticket will be a public demonstration of his lack of sexism.

Hillary will try to paint Trump as a vicious sexist. Particularly as she seeks to parry his attacks on her lack of integrity, she will try to hide behind her gender and say he is attacking all women. A female running mate, who echoes his critique of Hillary, will do much to overcome her strategy.

Trump can also select his issues carefully to show his feminist impulses.

Ever since the 1970s, when Roe v. Wade made abortion a key federal issue, a major gender gap has divided America's voters, with men tending to vote Republican while women vote mainly Democrat. More sophisticated analyses have identified single women as the most pro-Democrat group. While married men, married women, and single men vote more or less the same, single women vote substantially more Democratic than the other three groups. With half of all American women unwed, single white women have become more and more the base of the Democratic Party. And as the ranks of the unmarried have grown, so has the gender gap.

But abortion has gradually receded in the public consciousness as a key dividing issue. More and more Americans are reporting their feelings as ambivalent on the issue.

Gallup reported that, while Americans are pro-choice by 50%–44%, only half of those who are pro-choice approve of it in all circumstances while only 37% of the pro-life voters want it banned entirely.[5]

Despite its polarizing role in so many elections, most voters do not see abortion as a crucial issue. Gallup reported that only 19% say a candidate "must share their views" on the issue to win their votes, 28% say it is not a major issue at all, while 49% say that it is just one of several important issues.[6]

Education is a much more important issue, particularly to America's women voters.

Education: The Key to Women Voters

Donald Trump is the only candidate running for president who believes that parents should have the right to decide where their children should go to school. "Competition is why I'm very much in favor of school choice," he declared. "Let schools compete for kids," Trump writes. "For two decades I've been urging politicians to open the schoolhouse doors and let parents decide which schools are best for their children."[7]

While Hillary would chain students and parents to the failing public school system, Donald Trump would open school choice to private or charter schools as well. Even though Hillary and Bill chose a private school for Chelsea, they would deny the same option to poor families.

By a margin of 54% to 45%, voters report that they are dissatisfied with the quality of education in America.[8] This dissatisfaction opens a political opportunity for Trump.

The Democratic Party has become increasingly dependent on the teachers' union for campaign money and political support. But more and more, the interests of the union and children diverge—and Democrats stand with the union that donates hundreds of millions a year to their campaigns. Educational quality lags far behind in the party's calculations. Democrats increasingly echo the famous comment of the first teachers' union leader Albert Shanker, who said, "When children start paying union dues then I'll start representing the interests of children."[9]

The battle to improve schools used to be a quantitative contest between advocates of more spending and conservatives who insisted on holding it down. But increasingly, voters—particularly mothers—are coming to realize that more money is not the whole answer. It is becoming apparent that freeing schools from the clutches of the teachers' unions and permitting competition and parental choice is at least as important as extra money. Politically, this means forcing Democrats like Hillary to choose between parents and teachers' unions, between children and union campaign donations.

The gap between the political priorities of the Democratic Party and those of America's public school parents is wide enough to drive a truck through. And in 2011 and 2012, that truck was named Scott Walker, the Republican governor of Wisconsin.

Scott Walker Showed the Way

Walker was the first Republican to use the division between the needs of unions and the interests of parents to flip votes from Democrat to Republican. Walker attempted to go where no other governor of a blue state has ever gone before: He backed major education reform, dramatically curbing the power and financial clout of teachers' unions and restoring school governance to local boards.

The unions, threatened as never before, pulled out all stops to defeat him and his proposals. And they lost each time, even though Wisconsin is a decidedly blue state. These election results demonstrated dramatically the power of the education reform issue to flip votes from left to right. After four years of unending controversy, a statewide recall election, and massive teacher demonstrations and sit-ins, Republican Scott Walker was reelected by a margin of 57% to 43% in this state that last went Republican in a presidential election in 1984.

Walker was first elected Wisconsin's governor in 2010 by a 52%–48% margin. Facing a huge budget deficit, he introduced a "budget repair bill" on February 11, 2011. Rather than the usual mix of spending cuts and tax hikes, Walker decided to zero in on the school system and demand major changes. He required additional contributions by state and local government workers to their health care plans and pensions, cutting their take home pay by an average of 8%. More importantly, he proposed to eliminate, for most state workers except police, many collective bargaining rights they had enjoyed for decades. No longer could they bargain over work rules, teacher tenure, class size, and school policy. They could not require the state to contract with the insurance firms controlled by the union (that typically added about 20% to the cost, money that went to the union coffers). Public employee pay could not be raised above the rate of inflation unless the increase was approved by a popular referendum. Public employee unions would have to win yearly votes of their members to continue representing them. Dues could no longer be deducted automatically from paychecks.

The unions went berserk. Led by the teachers, they conducted massive sit-ins at the state capitol building in Madison, effectively locking state officials out of their offices. With Republican majorities in both Houses, the unions had little prospect of blocking the bill, so they induced 14 Democratic state senators to walk out of the Senate chamber to deny the quorum needed to pass the bill. When the sergeant-at-arms was ordered to round them up, the fugitive senators crossed the state line to hide out in Illinois. Eventually the bill passed and the union immediately launched a campaign first to recall the key state senators whose votes had passed it and then to unseat Governor Walker himself.

The recall effort, sponsored by all the state's unions, became a ballot test of the power of the education reform movement. With tens of millions of dollars pouring into Wisconsin from both sides of the political spectrum, it became a key battleground for both sides.

Walker won the tests decisively. On June 12, 2012, he defeated his Democratic rival in the recall election by a 53%–47% margin. And he went on to be reelected governor in 2014 by a 57%–43% margin, an astounding defeat for the teachers' unions.

In the years following the passage of Walker's bill, teachers' union membership in Wisconsin dropped from 187,000 in 2011 to 124,000 in 2014. Taking advantage of the legal requirement that public unions hold elections to continue to represent the teachers, educators in 70 of the 408 school districts voted to throw the union out![10]

Education Reform: Democrats and Unions vs. Parents and Kids

Even as voters in Wisconsin were registering their discontent with teachers' unions and their negative impact on education, people throughout America felt we were getting shortchanged by the amount we spend on schools. The Rasmussen Reports poll of May 17, 2015, told voters that our school budgets spent an average of $11,000 per year per student and asked if we were getting our money's worth, 63% answered that we were not.[11]

Teacher tenure and restrictions on merit pay plans do more than anything else to hobble our public schools.

Tenure protects bad teachers and restrictions on merit pay stop us from rewarding good ones. In New York City, for example, 4,000 teachers are so bad that the chancellor of the public school system will not permit them to be in the classroom with students. They have such bad histories of abusing the children that they cannot be trusted. But New York City cannot fire them. They have tenure and are protected, in their union contract, against dismissal. Even if grounds exist to fire them, the costs of years of litigation over each case would be prohibitive. So these tenured teachers show up each morning in what are called "rubber rooms" where they sit and read the paper or books all day while continuing to draw full pay and benefits.

Indeed, when New York had to lay off thousands of teachers in one of its budget crises during the '08–'09 recession, the Board of Education asked the union's permission to lay off the rubber room teachers. The union refused. It insisted that the board hew rigidly to the "last in, first out" policy meaning that thousands of new, young, idealistic teachers, including hundreds from the special Teach for America program, were fired. But the rubber room remained full. Even beyond the rubber room, teacher tenure lets burned out, unqualified, and even partially senile teachers remain on the job, advancing children who have learned very little.

By contrast, merit pay permits local school boards to stray outside salary guidelines to reward exceptional teachers based on their classroom performance and the improvements in student test scores. While the American Federation of Teachers (AFT), the union for teachers in the bigger cities, has permitted merit pay under certain conditions, the larger teachers' union, the National Education Association (NEA), is dead set against it. The NEA will brook no deviation from teacher pay based strictly on seniority and advanced degrees. It worries that teachers will "teach to the test" to inflate their students' test scores artificially and that principals and other teacher evaluators will vent their prejudices on those they dislike.

So every teacher is rigidly circumscribed within the pay guidelines based on seniority and advanced degrees.

Partially because they are frustrated at the lack of upward mobility, one-third of all new teachers leave after two years, and one-half check out after five. The unions, which govern in the interests of the older, senior, tenured teachers, do nothing to keep younger talented staff on the job. But if pay and tenure are conditioned and based on student performance on standardized tests, teachers will lean on their unions to allow incentives for better teaching and new ways to stimulate student performance.

But even tenure reform and merit pay will only accomplish so much. Many parents want to escape the work rules and teacher qualification requirements in traditional public schools that keep the quality of education low. Many opt to send their children to charter schools in areas where they are available. Charter schools can be public, private, or parochial, and are sometimes sponsored by private businesses, churches, parent groups, local government, or even teachers' unions. While not all charters are equal in quality, as a whole, they consistently outperform traditional public schools. As a result, there are usually long waiting lists to get in.

The most important educational reform is to allow school choice, to permit parents to decide to which public, private, or church school they wish to send their children. Most school choice plans include variants of the "voucher system," where the money the state spends on education follows the child to the school of the parents' choice. In Indiana, the state with the most fully developed statewide school choice plan, the state spends $7,000 per student with an additional $4,000 coming from local sources. The voucher plan sends that $7,000 of state money to whichever public or nonpublic school the parents choose.

The resulting competition is intense, and schools have to measure up to get the money. In some states, parents can choose to which public school they send their child rather than have him or her assigned to a school based on where they live.

Hillary Clinton has endorsed public school choice, but has drawn the line against allowing state funds to go to nonpublic schools. She recently said, "I want parents to be able to exercise choice within the public school system—not outside of it." She attacked charter schools, parroting the teachers' union line that "they don't take the hardest-to-teach kids, or, if they do, they don't keep them. And so the public schools are often in a no-win situation, because they do, thankfully, take everybody, and then they don't get the resources or the help and support that they need to be able to take care of every child's situation."[12]

Hillary is wrong. The differences between the proportion of students in traditional public schools and charter schools who receive special education funding is very small. In traditional public schools, 12.5% of the students are in special education programs while in charter schools it is 10.4%, hardly a huge difference. And when it comes to the most disabled, those who get services under the Individuals with Disabilities Education Act, or Section 504 of the Rehabilitation Act of 1973, there is virtually no difference at all: 1.53% in traditional public schools and 1.52% in charter schools.

Hillary's refusal to consider subsidizing parents who choose to send their children to nonpublic schools stands in glaring contrast to the decision she and Bill made about their daughter's education. When time came to enroll Chelsea in a DC public school, they sent her to the private Sidwell Friends School rather than to a public one. Of course, she, like President Obama, was able to afford private school tuition. Those who aren't so endowed financially have to leave their children in bad schools and settle for a bad education. Hillary will have a hard time explaining to young parents why they should be bound—shackled really—to the poorly performing public schools.

About one-fifth of charter school students are nonwhite. All over America, parents are voting with their feet to send their children to charter schools both in and outside of the public system. In Philadelphia, for example, 30% of all students go to charter schools and the system has a waiting list of tens of thousands more.[13] Nationally, 6.2% of all students in America are in charter schools, up from 1.7 percent in 2000. In all, about 2.8 million children attend them.[14] Another 12% of students are in private or church schools—a total of 5.3 million children.[15] And 3%, or 1.5 million, were home schooled. So even though parents pay taxes to support public schools, about one child in five goes to some other kind of school (even though some of the charter schools are public).

If white parents will object fiercely to Hillary's refusal to allow school choice, minority parents will react even more strongly. As a result of decades of housing discrimination, school choice has become the integration issue of our time. Faced with low performing schools in poor neighborhoods, parents have banded together to establish charter schools outside of the control of the teachers' union. Some charter schools are still public, owned by the government and subsidized by state spending, while others are private schools, which may or may not receive state funding.

By insisting that parents send their children only to the public school designated for their zip code, the Democrats are consigning minority students to terrible, failing schools. We must attack Hillary's refusal to support nonpublic charter schools by saying that she is extending housing discrimination—which leads to all-white neighborhoods—into the school system to produce all-minority schools.

How Hillary Sold Out to the Unions

Hillary wasn't always owned lock, stock, and barrel by the teachers' union. Indeed, she began her political career by dramatically defying teachers' unions. After Bill lost his first bid for reelection as Arkansas governor (after serving only two years), he and Hillary fought a determined campaign to get back in office. After they succeeded, the Arkansas Supreme Court dealt the former and now future governor a severe blow: It declared Arkansas's system of financing public education discriminated against poor school districts. The Court ordered the state to give richer districts less money, because their more wealthy homeowners could afford higher property taxes to fund schools, and give poorer districts more funding to make up for their lack of a viable property tax base.

Governor Clinton, who had been defeated for a second term because, in part, of his decision to raise taxes, now faced the need to increase them again. To meet the demands of the Supreme Court, Arkansas would have to raise its sales tax by one-half of 1%—the first such increase in many years. It was Hillary who boldly proposed that Bill reject half measures and raise taxes by a full point and reform education in the state.

She toured the state holding hearings on the quality of education and was appalled by what she uncovered. Teachers who had themselves been educated in low-quality black segregated schools were now being called upon to teach new students. Many did not master even the subject matter they were called on to teach. (One teacher was found to be teaching her class about "world war eleven"—World War II.)

Hillary demanded that all teachers in the state be tested for overall competency and knowledge in their specific area of teaching. Many states required new teachers to be tested, but Hillary was unique in calling for existing teachers to be tested. She insisted on legislation that provided that those who failed the test would be put on probationary status and have another chance to pass the test. If they failed again, they would be discharged. (And in fact, about 10% of Arkansas teachers were fired—although evidence indicated that a larger percentage should have failed.)

The teachers' union went crazy! They battled Hillary's proposal tooth and nail, showering the state legislature with letters, petitions, telegrams, and demonstrations. But Hillary and Bill stood firm. It was their finest hour. The teachers' union, the bedrock of the state's Democratic Party, refused to endorse Clinton for governor for the rest of the 1980s, each time backing his primary opponent and then sitting out the general election against the Republican—highly unusual in a Southern state.

But when Hillary moved to the national stage, she morphed into a compliant tool of the teachers' unions. There was no daylight between them in their opposition to tenure reform, merit pay, and school choice. She went from a crusading battler for students to a tool of the unions.

Hillary's weakness on the education issue will sit especially badly with minorities. African Americans are desperate to get their children into charter schools. A recent poll conducted by the Black Alliance for Educational Options, shows 60% of African Americans support school choice. Matt Frendewey of the American Federation for Children, the organization that sponsored the survey, says, "Too often urban families have children assigned to some of the worst schools in America. Especially those who live in an inner-city environment— where some of the worst and lowest-performing schools are found— recognize that their best option to get their child to a better school is private choice."[16]

Frendewey is quick to point out the political salience of the issue to black voters. "Really," he says, "among African American voters, education is a driving issue. It is an issue they care deeply about, that they want to know their representatives and the politicians who represent them care deeply about, and [they want to know] that they're aligned with their views. And I think that means candidates should be aligned with school choice."[17]

The school choice issue is also especially important for Latino parents. Harvard professor Caroline Hoxby found that Florida's Hispanic public-school students underperform their white, non-Hispanic peers by 21 points in math and 22 points in reading. But fortunately, Florida has been a leader in adopting school choice. Hoxby has determined charter school students in predominantly Latino communities outperform their peers in neighboring public schools, with 7.6% more students meeting state reading standards and 4.1% more meeting mathematics standards.

Trump can make huge inroads in the Latino vote by pushing the school choice agenda. To adhere to the dictates of the teachers' union and confine students to the bad public schools is to imprison them in a poor education and deny them a future.

Those who claim that more money for public schools is the way to solve the problem aren't looking at the evidence. Public schools in Washington, DC, for example, spend the highest amount per student in the nation—$18,000, 50% higher than the national average—but rank last in the percentage who graduate or go on to college. Pouring more money after bad won't work as a strategy to improve public education.

School choice creates competition and lets parents "vote" on the results of their child's education by deciding where to send their children. If the public schools don't measure up and parents send their children to other schools, teachers and administrators in failing schools will lose the state funding that they would normally get for each child. This trend could lead to them losing their jobs, creating a wonderful incentive to do better.

But the issue of school choice begs the ultimate question: What are Hillary's priorities? Do they lie with parents and students or with teachers and their unions? The dilemma this poses for Democrats is well-nigh unsolvable. They need the votes of the parents and the campaign money and organization of the unions. Hillary's entire public persona is based on her claim that she represents the needs of women and children. Yet, here, on the most fundamental issue facing our children, she sides with the providers of service—the teachers—not the consumers of the service—children. She follows the money, not the needs of our kids.

School Choice: A Winning Issue

Is this issue of school choice and education reform a voting issue? Is it strong enough to alter how people vote? Again, look at Wisconsin. A historically blue state that narrowly elected a Republican governor in the national GOP sweep of 2010, Wisconsin tested how effective the issue is at the ballot box.

Scott Walker was elected in a squeaker—just 52%–48%—amid the national GOP sweep of 2010, an election in which the Republicans picked up over 60 new House seats and narrowly missed taking control of the Senate. His victory was widely dismissed by pundits as a fluke in a landslide year.

But as opposition to his bold education reforms intensified and he faced new electoral tests, he rose in each one. As voters began to learn about the details of his education plan, they rallied around and gave him increasing margins of victory. In the 2012 recall election, he picked up a point, winning by 53–47. Then, when Walker ran for a second term, he triumphed by a hefty 57–43. Battling against the unions on education, Walker and the Republicans were able to make decisive inroads among Latino, black, and female voters. Among women, Walker picked up six points from 2010 to 2014. Among blacks, he picked up three. Among voters aged 18–44—mostly parents—Walker gained four points.[18]

Can a Republican win on the education issue? The George W. Bush campaign of 2000 proves that the answer is yes. During the Clinton presidency, voters rated the Democratic Party as best in addressing education issues. But Bush and the Republicans devoted their entire 2000 National Convention to the education issue, touting Bush's record as governor of Texas to show his commitment to better schools. And when he took office, Bush's first important piece of legislation—passed with overwhelming bipartisan majorities—was his No Child Left Behind Law that established national standards for America's schools. For the first time, Republicans passed Democrats as the party most trusted on the education issue.

We can do so again as long as we switch the debate from a bidding war to see who can spend more money to an issue-based discussion of reform and choice. With parents, especially minority families, clamoring for more school choice, and Democratic politicians trying to force them into regular public schools regardless of their preference, there is a huge opening for Republicans to show that they put children ahead of the unions.

We permit people to choose their own kind of car, appliances, houses, and all manner of consumer goods. But the most important decision of all—where to educate their children—is taken out of their hands and given to bureaucrats based on a zip code. Democrats cannot decry housing discrimination on the one hand and insist that the results of that bias determine which schools one's children should attend.

In desperation, some parents are flouting the laws that require them to send their children to failing public schools rather than quality ones nearby. They are today's civil rights protesters as they risk jail and heavy fines by camouflaging their real residences to get into better school districts.

Kyle Spencer of the Hechinger Report describes how Philadelphia resident Hamlet Garcia and his wife, Olesia, an insurance agent, were arrested for "theft of services," a charge usually reserved for those who skip out on restaurant checks or steal cable TV. Their crime was stealing an education for their eight-year-old daughter, Fiorella, a crime that carries a maximum sentence of seven years.[19]

In the 2011–2012 school year, Garcia's wife and daughter spent nine months during a marital separation living in his wife's father's house in Lower Moreland, a township in Montgomery County, Pennsylvania. That year, Fiorella attended Lower Moreland's much-sought-after elementary school, where, Spencer writes, "She read picture books, learned the alphabet and made friends."[20]

The Moreland County prosecutor charges that the separation was a sham designed to get Fiorella into a better school in Lower Moreland. Arrested in August 2012, they had to pay more than $10,000 in restitution to the school district.[21]

Unfortunately, there are many other examples of prosecutors persecuting parents whose only goal is to give their child a quality education—a right rich people have no problem securing by writing a check to a private school.

- Kelley Williams-Bolar, a special education aide in Akron, Ohio, actually had to spend nine days in jail for sending her two daughters to a better school where her father lived.[22]

- Tanya McDowell, a homeless mother in Bridgeport, Connecticut, was arrested for sending her five-year-old son to a Norwalk, Connecticut, school.[23]

- In 2009, Yolanda Hill, a Rochester, New York, mom, was charged with two felonies for enrolling her children in a better suburban school district where she didn't really live.[24]

- The school district in Orinda, California, a rich suburb of San Francisco, actually hired a private investigator to spy on a seven-year-old suspected of living in another town.[25]

- A New Jersey detective firm, VerifyResidence.com, says it works with more than 200 districts on enrollment issues and residency fraud.

Do they deserve these fines? Remember that most of these parents are already paying property taxes to support their local schools. Now, in addition, they are being asked to pay restitution to the school outside their district to which they sent their children—a form of double taxation.

It is just outrageous that parents have to lie and falsify their addresses in order to send their children to good schools just because they can't afford private school tuition. The reason for such laws—and the prosecution that enforces them—is simply that teachers' unions know that if they let parents choose where to educate their children, the bad public schools would lose their children.

Once Dick was speaking at a pro–education choice rally in Orlando, Florida, when a teachers' union heckler yelled out, "Which of our public schools do you want to close?" He shouted back, "The empty ones!"

Ryan Smith, executive director of The Education Trust, made the point that "the real issue is how do we provide quality schools for all children so parents don't have to make decisions that ultimately break the law."[26] If Trump can frame this issue properly, he can make it clear that Hillary spurns parents and children as she embraces the unions.

In addition to holding down Hillary's margin among women, we must do the same in the Latino community.

Go for Hispanics

If Trump has a problem with female voters, pundits believe that is nothing compared to the difficulty they expect him to have among Latinos. Because Donald has threatened to deport all illegal immigrants in the United States—indeed, because he dares to call them "illegal" not "undocumented"—he is thought to be on the verge of being wiped out by Hillary among Hispanics.

The insiders feel that Trump's advocacy of building a wall along the Mexican border is sure to turn off Latinos and lead them to vote for Hillary in numbers that will dwarf even Obama's 2012 triumph among Latinos by 73-27.

Go beyond Immigration

Just as the mainstream media and political pundits have convinced America that abortion is the most important issue among American women, so they have sold us that immigration reform is the key to Latino attitudes in 2016.

Immigration is key for some Latinos. But polling suggests that there is a big divide between the one-quarter of Latino voters who were born abroad and the three-quarters who were born here. While immigration remains the key issue for those Latino voters who are foreign born, it has receded in importance for those who were born in the 50 states.

Since media coverage of Latino attitudes is largely shaped by the statements of ethnic group leaders who tend to represent the immigrant population more heavily, the importance of other issues among Hispanics is often obscured.

In a 2011 survey by the McLaughlin Group, the sharp divisions between Latinos based on their place of birth became evident. Asked if they supported President Obama's decision to grant amnesty to many of the immigrants who arrived here illegally, 83% among foreign-born Latinos supported the president's decision. But among those born in the United States, support fell to 50%, with 40% opposing the president's position. Asked which issues were the most important to them, American-born Latinos put immigration reform last while foreign-born Hispanic voters put immigration first.

WHAT IS THE MOST IMPORTANT ISSUE? AMONG US-BORN LATINOS

ECONOMY	40
HEALTH	25
EDUCATION	23
IMMIGRATION	10

. . . AND AMONG NON-US-BORN?

IMMIGRATION	34
HEALTH	26
ECONOMY	23
EDUCATION	14

Source: 2013 Survey by McLaughlin and Associates, http://www.mclaughlinonline.com/lib/sitefiles/National_Hispanic_Presentation_06-21-13_-_FOR_RELEASE.pdf

Indeed, with many Latinos thrown into competition with recent arrivals for jobs and wages, a certain reserve about opening our borders further would be easy to understand.

But just as the quality of life here in the United States is important to American-born Latinos, McLaughlin's survey found that they are very concerned that Obama is leading America to make the same mistakes as the leaders in their former countries did.

When their ancestors came to America, they felt they left behind a culture of government dependence, large debts, and irresponsible giveaways by politicians seeking votes. But now they report seeing these things right here in America. These American-born Latinos worry that the experiences their forebears had in Mexico, Guatemala, Honduras, and other countries from which they fled in search of a better life is being replicated here in the USA.

Indeed, a survey by Rafael Giménez, former Public Opinion coordinator for the office of the Presidency in Mexico, tends to confirm the idea that Latinos in the United States are deeply concerned about the welfare-state orientation of the Democratic Party. Giménez interviewed a national sample of 1,100 US citizens of Latino origin using telephone, cell phone, and many in-person interviews between January 15 and February 15, 2013. Giménez elicited broad support when he asked participants if they agreed or disagreed with the following statement:

> Democrats are closer to the leaders we had in Latin America, always giving handouts to get votes. If we let them have their way, we will end up being like the countries our families came from, not like the America of great opportunities we all came to.

The results were as follows: agree: 59%; disagree: 34%. These fears—that America is going the way of the mismanaged countries they left—will make Latinos increasingly look to Donald Trump and away from Hillary Clinton.

By 78%–16%, US Latinos agreed that "Latino immigrants must not go the way some have gone into high unemployment, crime, drugs, and welfare. They must be more like the hard working immigrants who came here and worked their way up without depending on the government."

When Giménez asked his Latino sample which party most shares this sentiment, they chose the Republicans, by a margin of 45%–29%. The survey also found that US Latino voters feel Republicans are more likely than Democrats

- to "work hard to reduce the incidence of teen pregnancy" (45% 31%)

- to agree that "the family fabric in America is being ripped apart. Parents are too permissive. There is too much divorce, too many unwed mothers, and too many children who don't listen to their parents" (49%–32%)

- to avoid "ruining the United States" with too much debt (39%–37%)

- to "strengthen churches so they can help the poor and teach values of faith and family" (52%–31%)

Latino voters agree that "too many people depend on the government and its handouts. That way of thinking is very bad and leads to lifetimes of unemployment, poverty, and crime" (89%–7%). And by 45–37, they believe the Republican Party is more likely to share their view than Democrats are.[27]

McLaughlin's survey found that Latino voters in the United States described themselves as pro-life by 67%–25%, about 30 points to the right of Americans generally.

Donald Trump must seek to rekindle in the United States the same debate that polarizes people in Mexico: Whether to create a welfare state or one that is governed by traditional values. After all, the ancestors of America's Latinos voted with their feet to leave nations organized around giveaways and handouts. They are sure to be vigilant in avoiding the same pitfalls here that ruined their native countries.

Polling shows that social problems, particularly those that concern their families and child-rearing have especial salience among Latino voters. Latina mothers are especially worried about the collapse of authority and discipline among their children and the declining importance of religion in their lives. Trump must address these issues and refuse to confine the debate among Latinos to the immigration issue.

YOUNG VOTERS DON'T LIKE HILLARY

Young voters are Hillary's single biggest problem.

The vote of people under 35 was a key element in Obama's victories in 2008 and 2012. In 2012, Obama lost among voters over the age of 40 by five points. 52% voted for Romney and only 47% backed Obama. His victory was entirely due to his gigantic margin among younger voters, whom he carried by 20 points, 58%–38%.

But it is young voters who animated Bernie Sanders' challenge to Hillary's nomination. A FoxNews poll in April of 2016 found that voters under 45 backed Sanders by 65%–30%.[28] The younger they were, the more these Democrats voted for Sanders and against Hillary in the primary. The *Washington Post* reported that "in Iowa and Nevada, voters under 30 went 6 to 1 for Sanders. In New Hampshire, 5 to 1."[29]

Hillary is not unique in her problems with young voters. Between 2014 and 2015, Obama's job approval has dropped from 52% to 41% according to a survey by the Harvard Institute of Politics. Of the young voters Harvard surveyed, 55% said they voted for Obama in 2012, but only 46% said they would vote for him again.[30]

Among young white and Hispanic voters, Obama and the Democrats are in even worse shape. The Harvard Poll found that "though Obama maintains a 78% approval rating among young African Americans, his favorability among young Hispanics has plummeted. Obama commanded an 81% approval rating in the young Hispanic demographic in 2009. Today, that number is 49%. His approval is also down among young white Americans. In 2006 and 2008, a majority of young white millennials supported Democrats. Now the percentage of young white Americans who support President Obama is only 31%."[31]

Obama isn't on the 2016 ballot, but his Party is, and younger voters are taking out their disapproval of him on Hillary.

Part of what is driving younger voters in their growing disapproval of Democrats is a rapid drop in the popularity of Obamacare. The Harvard Poll found that 57% of young voters disapproved of Obamacare, with 40% saying it will worsen the quality of their care, and a majority believing it will drive up costs.[32] Since Obamacare is a program designed to tax young people to subsidize the medical care of their elders, its unpopularity is likely to remain and even grow.

Obamacare negatives are Hillary negatives because of her record of having proposed a similar program in 1993. The Republicans need to run a targeted campaign against Hillary among younger voters.

In a curious sense, this task is easier among people who have only limited experience with Mrs. Clinton. Voters over 35 are a bit jaded when it comes to Hillary. They have watched scandal after scandal reaching back all the way to Whitewater, each sapping whatever residual credibility she had with them. But to those under 35, all the Hillary scandals are new. These voters, after all, were under 15 years of age when the Lewinsky scandal unfolded and were way too young to have followed Hillary's misadventures over the years.

Trump must slam Hillary on the credibility issue. Her lies and distortions are so well documented and extensively filmed that they will make excellent fodder for negative campaign ads. Whether it is Hillary erroneously saying that she was under fire in Bosnia (she was greeted by a child bearing flowers on a red carpet) or that she was named after Sir Edmund Hillary (who climbed Mt. Everest four years after her birth) or that she was instrumental in the Irish peace process (a memory nobody else confirms) or that she left the White House "dead broke" (despite an $11 million book deal) or that she used a private e-mail server for convenience, all these stories make great ammunition.

Time has always been Hillary's biggest ally. People forget scandals and they fade from the front pages as the news cycle moves on. But now time is her enemy since these scandals are all new, exciting, and interesting to young voters who have never heard them before.

GO AFTER THE BLACK VOTE: HILLARY IS NOT OBAMA

Woody Allen famously said, "Eighty percent of success is showing up."[33]

But will black voters show up for Hillary in the same recordsetting numbers as they did for Obama?

Barack Obama, running as the first African American to seek the presidency as the nominee of a major party, carried the black vote by 95%–4% in 2008 and by 93%–6% in 2012. In each contest, blacks cast a record 13% of the total vote.

This huge African-American turnout is not typical of American elections. In 2000 blacks cast 10% of the vote and in 2004, they accounted for 11%. Since African-Americans have not increased their share of the nation's population in the last two censuses, there is no reason why black turnout should continue at record levels.

If African American turnout dropped from 13% to 11%, Hillary would lose about two points in her race against Trump—about half of Obama's margin against Romney.

The handoff between Barack Obama and Hillary Clinton need not be seamless. The Trump campaign affords us an opportunity to show how Democrats will always side with the municipal unions against the black community. Whether the issue is school choice, sanitation services, health care, or law enforcement, city government officials depend on unions to get elected and take the black vote for granted. On each of these issues, Democrats have had to choose between the consumers of the city services (such as children in school or patients in city clinics and hospitals) and the providers of the service (the teachers and health care unions). Since these politicians have always been able to count on a bloc vote from African Americans, they have little incentive to cater to them and, since their campaigns are financed by municipal unions, a great deal of incentive to side with the service providers.

Republicans need to make it clear that we seek and want the black vote and, now that Obama is not on the ballot, do not believe that they will vote for Hillary as a knee jerk reaction. The African American community is particularly unhappy with how white liberals govern their cities. Their resentment usually spills over in mayoral elections that pit a white liberal (e.g., Emanuel in Chicago, de Blasio in New York) against an African American candidate. The black urban voter resents being taken for granted by his white liberal elected official. These Democratic office holders treat blacks as if they were a golf handicap, a lead with which they start the race and which they never have to earn.

Trump should select key issues (like school choice) where he can side with the black community against City Hall.

As noted, there is strong African American support for school choice. In Philadelphia, 58,000 children attend charter schools and another 40,000 are said to be on waiting lists. The majority of these children are nonwhite. The charter school space is so limited in Philadelphia that the city runs a lottery each year to decide who gets in. Tens of thousands of families are turned away and are disappointed. The teachers' union does all it can to limit and cut the charter school program. By decisively siding with parents and backing expansion of charter schools, Trump can show that he puts the people ahead of those who are supposed to serve them.

Even on the issue of police brutality, there is running room for Donald Trump.

Big city mayors—Democrats all—are wont to sweep reports of police brutality under the rug, particularly at election time. Chicago Mayor Rahm Emanuel actually refused to release a video showing a Chicago officer shooting a 17-year-old who was obviously posing no threat. Emanuel, locked in a tight runoff race with an African American candidate, held onto the video to avoid embarrassment—and to hang onto his share of the black vote.

Knowing that her popularity among African Americans, while broad, is still thin, Hillary will try to get a large turnout in the community by portraying Trump as their enemy and trying to draw racial issues against him. Trump must avoid this characterization and show how he is fighting for the community against City Hall, where necessary, it is unlikely that Hillary can raise the fear level to the point where it generates a large black turnout.

It isn't that Trump needs to carry the black vote. He just has to stop Hillary from scaring African-Americans to death over the prospect of his victory so they do not come out to vote.

CHAPTER 6

Can Donald Trump Win?

Can He Win the Popular Vote?

YOU BET HE CAN. To see how, lets reverse engineer Obama's victory over Romney. Obama beat Romney by 5 million votes in 2012.

White Voters

Trump increased turnout in Republican primaries by a projected total of 14 million votes. How many of those are people who did not vote in 2012 but participated in the 2016 primary? Exit polls didn't ask.

But we know that turnout among white registered voters fell by 3.1% (or 6.3 million voters) from a high in 2004 to 2012. With Trump's drawing power, it is not unreasonable to posit that the white vote will rise by ten million from 2012 to 2016. If Trump carries it by the same margin Romney did (61-39) it will give him 1.2 million more votes than Romney got in 2012.

Trump up 1.2 million

Black Voters

There is no reason to suppose that black turnout for Hillary will equal that for Obama. In 2004, African-Americans cast 11% of the national vote. In 2012, with no increase in their share of the national population, blacks cast 13% of the vote. If they fell back to their historic level of 11%, it would deny Hillary 2.5 million votes that Obama got.

Hillary down 2.5 million

Young Voters

Those under 30 voted for Obama by a margin of 8 million total votes, backing the Democrats 60-37. Hillary has shown great weakness among young voters, losing them to Bernie Sanders in the primaries by huge margins. If we assume that among white under 30s, Obama won by 5 million votes, Hillary's unpopularity among younger voters should show up by cutting her margin by at least two million.

Hillary down 2 million

When we combine a Hillary loss of 2 million young voters and 2.5 million blacks with a Trump gain of 1.2 million white voters, we see a reversal of the 2012 verdict. While Obama beat Romney by 5 million votes, Trump would defeat Hillary by 700,000.

And in the Electoral College?

Some say that the electoral map is so tilted in favor of the Democratic Party that a Republican cannot win. While this statement is not true, a Republican does have a difficult task ahead to climb to a majority of the electoral vote.

The key to winning the Electoral College is a Virginia-plus strategy. Here's the math: Romney won 206 electoral votes in 2012, short of the 270 votes needed to win. To get the remaining 64 votes, the Republicans would first need to carry the two states where Obama's margin of victory over Romney was the smallest—where the election was closest—Ohio (18 electoral votes) and Florida (29). Obama beat Romney in the national popular vote by 51.1–47.2, a margin of 4.1%. Of all the states Obama carried, he had the smallest margin in Florida (0.9%) and in Ohio (3.0%).

If we lose the popular vote by anything like Romney's 4.1%, we will lose both states—and the election. But if we can tie or pass Obama's 2012 vote share, we should have no problem carrying them. That would give us 47 of the 64 electoral votes we needs to win. To pick up the remaining 17 votes is more complicated. A Republican would need to carry some of the following states:

SWING STATES

STATE	ELECTORAL VOTE	OBAMA MARGIN (%)
VA	13	3.9
CO	8	5.4
PA	20	5.4
NH	4	5.6
IA	6	5.8
NV	6	6.7
WI	10	6.9

Of these states, Virginia seems the closest within reach. And that's the key. If we can win Ohio, Florida, and Virginia, we will have 266 electoral votes, just four short of victory. We could pick those votes by winning any one of the remaining six toss-up states (Pennsylvania, Colorado, New Hampshire, Iowa, Nevada, and Wisconsin).

And we probably can do it. Ed Gillespie, Republican, came within less than one point of winning the Virginia senate seat in 2014.

Colorado and Iowa are also moving our way. Both elected new Republican senators in 2014, and in Colorado, we even overthrew a Democratic incumbent. Pennsylvania and New Hampshire already have Republican senators, and in Pennsylvania, the GOP controls both houses of the legislature. Any one of them would suffice to win.

The 2016 election will, of course, revolve around not just the issues but the candidates as well. In Hillary Rodham Clinton, the Democrats have nominated one of the most unpopular, compromised candidates in recent years. The list of her negatives is so long as to be daunting and her record is so filled with evidence of corruption, incompetence, deceit, prevarication, inconsistency, self-dealing, and cover-ups as to make her practically unelectable.

Conclusion

To defeat Hillary, we need to use every weapon in our arsenal. We need to use the right jab—to animate our base and get them out to vote. Then we must throw the left hook—to attract the Bernie Sanders voters by appealing to their essential populism. And throughout, we must keep Hillary under pressure and on the defensive by revisiting the various scandals, lies, flip-flops, and failures in her record.

We know that Hillary makes mistakes under pressure. We've seen it. Confronted with her past, she resorts to lies, evasions, and distortions. When she gets caught in these misstatements, she lies again and again and again. Keep pressing her and she will keep making mistakes. So we need to keep pressing her. And isn't Donald Trump just the man to do it? By constantly calling her "corrupt Hillary," he hammers away at her scandals and her lies, evasions, and misstatements.

Won't Hillary's handlers prepare her for these attacks, scripting her replies? They won't. Hillary's handlers are usually terrified of their candidate. They can't sit down with her and discuss how she handled Bill's sexually predatory conduct. Nor can they ask her about e-mails, or Benghazi, or her theft of the White House china, or the pardons her brothers secured in return for fees, or the quid pro quo she dished out to those who paid Bill for speeches. If they dared to ask—or even raise these topics—she'd take their heads off (and they would never be seen in her campaign again).

In handling and protecting a candidate, consultants have to know the truth—the full truth. Unless they do, the truth will come back to bite them and their candidate. You can't defend a scandal if you don't know what really happened. But Hillary will never ever tell her advisors the truth. It is likely she never admits the truth to herself. Denial is her way of life. It's how she keeps going every day. She will not breech that wall of denial unless she is forced to do so. And no advisor, consultant, or handler has the clout or security to make her tell the truth.

So when we challenge Hillary, it will be like peeling an onion: Each time we disprove one layer of denial, another will take its place. Hillary's denial strategy will blow up in her face. On the campaign trail, she will hang herself by lying and covering up. The key is to keep her under pressure.

Bernie Sanders's basic mistake was not to raise any of these important issues. He based his campaign on his ideology and condemned Hillary for her dependence on special interest and Wall Street money. But Hillary's scandals played no role in his effort. He never discussed them and famously dismissed her e-mails, saying that "nobody gives a damn about your e-mails." In the Democratic primary, perhaps not. But in the general election, her blatant breach of the law and of national security ranks high on her list of negatives. Throughout the primary campaign, Hillary's supporters and the entire Democratic establishment warned Bernie about his "tone" in attacking Hillary. And like the good liberal he is, Sanders did not go for the jugular.

But Donald Trump will. He won't ignore the idiocy of her excuses. We've listened to her talking points about why she won't release the transcripts of the paid speeches she's made. We've heard her say she'll do it when everyone else does and not before then. We've heard her say that everyone did it—other secretaries of state like Colin Powell and Madeline Albright and Henry Kissinger gave paid speeches. But Donald Trump will point out the flaw in her silly argument—that none of them were running for president and could do favors down the line.

That's why people paid Hillary such exorbitant speaking fees—not because they wanted to hear her view of the world, but because they wanted to create an IOU. Donald will flatten her arguments and repeatedly point out why she is a flawed candidate.

Keep up the pressure. Make her make mistakes. Force her to dig herself deeper and deeper into lies and cover-ups. That's how we keep Hillary out of the White House. And put Donald Trump in.

Notes

Preface

1 http://www.realclearpolitics.com/video/2015/06/18/trump_on
_trade_we_dont_have_our_best_and_brightest_negotiating
_for_us_were_getting_ripped_off_major_league.html

Introduction

1 Trump warns Hillary To Tread Carefully On Demeaning Women,
CNN, January 18, 2016; http://www.cnn.com/2016/01/18/politics/
donald-trump-bill-clinton-past/

2 Alana Goodman, Audio: *Bill Clinton Privately Mocked Paula Jones as an
Attention-Seeking "Floozy,"* WND, January 6, 2016; http://freebeacon
.com/politics/audio-bill-clinton-privately-mocked-paula-jones-as
-an-attention-seeking-floozy/

3 Lenzner, Terry, *The Investigator,* Kindle Edition, p. 202; https://
read.amazon.com/?asin=B00DMCV24G

4 Maxwekk Tani, *Bernie Sanders Is Continuing To Escalate His Attacks
On Hillary Clinton,* Business Insider, May 2, 2016; http://www

.businessinsider.com/bernie-sanders-hillary-clinton-indiana
-polls-attacks-2016-5

5   $153 Million In Clintons Speaking Fees Documented. http://
www.cnn.com/2016/02/05/politics/hillary-clinton-bill-clinton
-paid-speeches/

Chapter 1   A Dozen Reasons Hillary Clinton Shouldn't be President

1   https://sharylattkisson.com/8-major-warnings-before-benghazi
-terrorist-attacks/
2   Ibid.
3   Ibid.
4   Ibid.
5   http://www.cnsnews.com/news/article/melanie-hunter/more-600
-benghazi-security-requests-never-reached-clintons-desk-reports
6   http://www.foxnews.com/world/2015/12/08/spinning-up-as-speak
-email-shows-pentagon-was-ready-to-roll-as-benghazi-attack.html
7   http://dailycaller.com/2015/12/08/new-clinton-email-shows
-pentagon-had-forces-ready-during-benghazi-attack/
8   http://www.realclearpolitics.com/video/2015/10/22/rep_jim
_jordan_vs_hillary_clinton_why_did_you_tell_egyptians
_benghazi_was_a_terrorist_attack_but_not_the_american
_people.html
9   Ibid.
10   http://www.breitbart.com/video/2015/12/06/hillary-i-didnt-lie-to
-benghazi-families-it-was-the-fog-of-war/
11   http://www.breitbart.com/big-government/2015/08/27/poll-liar
-tops-list-of-50-words-americans-used-to-describe-hillary-clinton/
12   http://www.newsmax.com/t/newsmax/article/323326
13   http://www.starpulse.com/news/index.php/2015/10/04/hillary
-clinton-dislikes-military-in-u
14   http://www.nytimes.com/1994/06/15/us/hillary-clinton-says-she
-once-tried-to-be-marine.html
15   http://www.telegraph.co.uk/news/worldnews/1581606/Hillary
-Clinton-I-was-instrumental-in-Northern-Ireland-peace-process
.html
16   http://www.telegraph.co.uk/news/worldnews/1581150/Nobel
-winner-Hillary-Clintons-silly-Irish-peace-claims.html
17   See George Mitchell, *Making Peace* (New York: Penguin, 2012).

18 http://www.nytimes.com/2008/03/22/us/politics/22irish.html

19 http://www.politifact.com/truth-o-meter/statements/2008/mar/
25/hillary-clinton/video-shows-tarmac-welcome-no-snipers/

20 http://arkansasgopwing.blogspot.com/2016/02/hillary-lies-about
-lying.html

21 https://www.washingtonpost.com/news/post-politics/wp/2014/
06/05/hillary-clinton-on-iraq-vote-i-still-got-it-wrong-plain-and
-simple/

22 http://www.washingtontimes.com/news/2015/may/15/guess-who
-voted-iraq-war-she-opposed-it-hillary-cl/

23 http://thehill.com/policy/defense/194673-hillary-opposed-iraq
-surge-for-political-reasons-gates-says

24 https://newrepublic.com/article/121879/hillary-clinton-should
-take-blame-disastrous-libyan-intervention

25 Ibid.

26 Ibid.

27 Ibid.

28 http://www.theguardian.com/world/2014/jun/06/hillary-clinton
-arming-syrian-rebels-memoir

29 http://www.mediaite.com/online/donald-trump-bashes-libya
-intervention-which-he-strongly-advocated-for-in-2011/

30 http://www.ibtimes.com/us-strategy-arm-syrian-moderate
-opposition-has-failed-experts-say-1725801

31 Ibid.

32 Ibid.

33 http://freebeacon.com/blog/hillary-clinton-huma-abedin/

34 http://www.frontpagemag.com/fpm/259805/huma-abedin
-security-breach-hillary-still-hiding-frontpagemagcom

35 Ibid.

36 http://www.politico.com/story/2015/08/donald-trump-anthony
-weiner-pervert-2016-election-213158

37 http://www.standwithus.com/news/article.asp?id=1757

38 http://www.nationalreview.com/article/312211/huma-abedins
-muslim-brotherhood-ties-andrew-c-mccarthy

39 http://www.nbcnews.com/id/41337168/ns/world_news-mideast
_n_africa/t/clinton-urges-transition-democratic-regime-egypt/#
.VpGTis4-DVo

40 http://www.nytimes.com/2013/04/10/world/middleeast/coptic
-christian-leader-criticizes-morsi-government.html?_r=0

41 http://www.breitbart.com/video/2013/07/04/flashback-clinton
    -pledges-support-for-morsi/

42 Ibid.

43 http://www.jihadwatch.org/wp-content/uploads/2014/04/clinton
    -morsi.jpg

44 http://beforeitsnews.com/politics/2015/03/hillary-clinton-and-her
    -long-friendship-with-egypts-morsis-wife-2694332.html

45 http://www.politifact.com/truth-o-meter/statements/2015/jun/
    17/hillary-clinton/hillary-clinton-change-position-same-sex
    -marriage/

46 Ibid.

47 Ibid.

48 Ibid.

49 http://www.politifact.com/truth-o-meter/statements/2008/feb/25/
    barack-obama/clinton-has-changed-on-nafta/

50 Ibid.

51 http://www.politifact.com/truth-o-meter/statements/2015/oct/13/
    hillary-clinton/what-hillary-clinton-really-said-about-tpp-and-gol/

52 Ibid.

53 http://www.opensecrets.org/news/2015/05/hillary-clinton-morgan
    -stanley-and-tpp-a-free-trade-triumvirate/

54 Ibid.

55 http://www.theguardian.com/us-news/2015/oct/13/hillary-clinton
    -trans-pacific-partnership-debate

56 Ibid.

57 http://thehill.com/policy/healthcare/257234-clinton-brings-in
    -most-big-pharma-money-of-2016-field

58 https://www.youtube.com/watch?v=bzQxFtM9cfk

59 http://www.washingtontimes.com/news/2015/oct/12/hillary
    -clinton-flip-flops-from-2008-positions-in-/?page=all

60 http://dailycaller.com/2015/04/16/hillary-clinton-flip-flops-on
    -drivers-licenses-for-illegal-immigrants/

61 Ibid.

62 http://dailycaller.com/2014/06/17/hillary-clinton-deport-the
    -illegal-children-back-to-central-america/

63 http://dailycaller.com/2015/12/26/in-apparent-flip-flop-hillary
    -now-says-shes-concerned-with-plan-to-deport-central-american
    -families-video/

64 Taming the Beast: Wall Street's Imperfect Answers to Making Money

65 http://www.youbemom.com/forum/permalink/8154917/despite-31
    -trillion-to-1-odds-hillary-turned-1k-into-100k-trading-futu
66 http://www.wsj.com/articles/SB91266144592420000
67 http://www.nytimes.com/1996/01/05/us/memo-places-hillary
    -clinton-at-core-of-travel-office-case.html
68 http://www.washingtonpost.com/wp-srv/politics/special/clinton/
    stories/thomason012998.htm
69 www.pbs.org/wgbh/pages/frontline/shows/arkansas/castle/
70 http://nypost.com/2015/04/26/charity-watchdog-clinton
    -foundation-a-slush-fund/
71 Ibid.
72 Ibid.
73 Ibid.
74 https://www.washingtonpost.com/news/post-politics/wp/2015/12/
    22/charity-watchdog-removes-clinton-foundation-from-its-watch-list/
75 Ibid.
76 http://www.breitbart.com/big-government/2015/04/25/timeline
    -timeline-bill-clintons-trip-to-kazakhstan-followed-by-windfall-for
    -clinton-foundation/
77 http://www.brainyquote.com/quotes/quotes/h/henryakis115118
    .html
78 https://www.youtube.com/watch?v=CQuSzFJGv3o
79 http://www.chicagotribune.com/news/nationworld/ct-hillary
    -clinton-emails-20150731-story.html
80 Maureen Dowd, Liberties; Hillary's Stocking Stuffer, *The New York
    Times,* December 24, 2000. http://www.nytimes.com/2000/12/24/
    opinion/liberties-hillary-s-stocking-stuffer.html
81 Thomas B. Edsall, *The Clintons Take Away $190.000 In Gifts. The
    Washington Post,* January 21, 2001. https://www.washingtonpost
    .com/archive/politics/2001/01/21/clintons-take-away-190000-in
    -gifts/36773cf2-8120-4d58-b903-d76d39a6cc3f/
82 https://www.washingtonpost.com/posteverything/wp/2014/06/
    27/chelsea-clinton-perfectly-explains-how-millennials-feel-about
    -money/
83 http://www.jewishworldreview.com/0615/morris060115.php3
84 http://rense.com/general31/surf.htm
85 http://www.nytimes.com/2015/07/07/us/politics/clinton-first
    -brother-is-wary-chatty-and-still-occasionally-attracting-attention
    .html

86 https://lorrab.wordpress.com/2015/04/03/roger-clinton-told-fbi
-that-he-accepted-foreign-cash-for-president-bill-clinton/

87 http://articles.latimes.com/2002/mar/13/news/mn-32562

88 http://thehill.com/blogs/ballot-box/presidential-races/251759
-omalley-gop-raise-legitimate-clinton-email-questions

89 Christopher Marquis with Michael Moss, *A Clinton In-Law Receives
$400,000 For Two Pardons, The New York Times,* February 21, 2001.

90 *Justice Undone: Clemency Decisions in The Clinton White House,* Second
Report, of The House of Representatives Committee on Government
Reform, Volume 1, 739-42, 765-773; https://www.gpo.gov/fdsys/
pkg/CRPT-107hrpt454/html/CRPT-107hrpt454-vol1.htm

Chapter 2   How to Beat Hillary

1 http://www.washingtonsblog.com/2015/11/new-poll-shows-60-of
-americans-think-hillary-clinton-is-untrustworthy-and-dishonest
.html

2 https://www.youtube.com/watch?v=2OznoFCZdS8

3 http://www.brookings.edu/research/papers/2013/05/10-election
-2012-minority-voter-turnout-frey

4 http://www.cbsnews.com/elections/2016/primaries/republican/
michigan/exit/

5 http://www.bls.gov/opub/ted/2015/median-weekly-earnings-by
-education-gender-race-and-ethnicity-in-2014.htm

6 http://www.cnsnews.com/commentary/curtis-dubay/1-percenters
-pay-24-percent-and-top-10-percent-pay-533-percent-all-federal

7 Ibid.

8 https://www.whitehouse.gov/photos-and-video/video/2012/04/11/
president-obama-speaks-buffett-rule

9 https://jackrasmus.com/2016/03/01/bill-clintons-dubious
-economic-legacies/

10 https://ourfuture.org/fact_sheet/ten-years-bush-tax-cuts
-benefiting-rich

11 https://eml.berkeley.edu/~saez/saez-UStopincomes-2014.pdf

12 https://www.census.gov/prod/2012pubs/acsbr10-19.pdf

Chapter 3   Use the Right Jab to Bring Out Our Base

1 https://www.youtube.com/watch?v=208t80uceSg

2 http://www.mediaite.com/tv/giuliani-hillary-could-be-considered
-founding-member-of-isis/

3 http://www.cnn.com/2016/03/24/politics/rudy-giuliani-hillary
   -clinton-isis/

4 http://www.cnn.com/2008/POLITICS/02/14/mccain.king/

5 Ibid.

6 Ibid.

7 http://www.aei.org/publication/brennan-admits-isis-was
   -decimated-under-bush-but-has-grown-under-obama-by-as-much
   -as-4400-percent/

8 http://www.nhregister.com/article/NH/20151117/NEWS/151119588

9 http://www.barenakedislam.com/2016/03/29/has-the-cia-director
   -been-fired-by-obama-look-what-he-said/

10 http://www.politifact.com/truth-o-meter/statements/2014/sep/07/
   barack-obama/what-obama-said-about-islamic-state-jv-team/

11 http://politics.blog.ajc.com/2015/12/20/parsing-hillary-clintons
   -we-now-finally-are-where-we-need-to-be-comment-on-isis/

12 http://www.nationalreview.com/article/427219/obama-still
   -convinced-his-isis-strategy-events-what-events-jonah-goldberg

13 http://www.theguardian.com/us-news/2015/oct/13/donald-trump
   -foreign-policy-doctrine-nation-building

14 http://www.jihadwatch.org/2014/08/morsis-wife-threatens-to
   -publish-letters-from-hillary-clinton-exposing-special-relationship
   -between-muslim-brotherhood-and-obama-administration

15 http://thehill.com/blogs/blog-briefing-room/261283-ex-cia-chief
   -fear-for-environment-stays-us-hand-on-isis-oil-wells

16 http://www.ibtimes.com/hillary-clinton-flip-flopping-ground
   -troops-fight-isis-us-sends-troops-iraq-clinton-2206261

17 http://www.washingtontimes.com/news/2015/jul/9/donald
   -trump-id-bomb-hell-out-oil-fields/

18 http://www.breitbart.com/big-government/2015/12/19/
   hillary-clinton-blames-donald-trump-video-for-next-terror
   -attack/

19 https://en.wikipedia.org/wiki/International_aid_to_Palestinians
   #Major_donors

20 http://content.usatoday.com/communities/theoval/post/2011/
   05/obama-rebuffed-by-netanyahu-on-land-for-peace-deal/1#
   .Vwab7M4-DVo

21 https://books.google.com/books?id=RlB1CAAAQBAJ&pg=
   PA263&lpg=PA263&dq=For+the+Israelis,+we+requested+that
   +they+freeze+all+settlement&source=bl&ots=FBj2WcbxlB&

sig=NTy06FWyCBOW0tbgUUf7xTd8XPw&hl=en&sa=X&ved
=0ahUKEwjs6pyYmeTLAhXCwxQKHbcOA7cQ6AEIHTAA#v
=onepage&q=For%20the%20Israelis%2C%20we%20requested
%20that%20they%20freeze%20all%20settlement&f=false

22 http://www.jns.org/latest-articles/2014/7/9/on-israeli-palestinian
-conflict-hillary-clintons-hard-choices-offers-the-same-choices#
.Vx7qGz-IQSA=

23 http://www.breitbart.com/national-security/2015/03/20/a
-complete-timeline-of-obamas-anti-israel-hatred/

24 http://www.nytimes.com/2015/07/25/world/middleeast/kerry-says
-israel-may-deepen-its-isolation-by-opposing-iran-nuclear-accord
.html?_r=0

25 http://www.funtrivia.com/playquiz/quiz88097a18480.html

26 http://www.cnsnews.com/news/article/michael-w-chapman/
pew-144000-us-muslims-say-suicide-bombings-civilian-targets
-often-or

27 http://dailycaller.com/2016/03/28/poll-majority-now-support
-trumps-muslim-travel-ban/

28 http://www.state.gov/j/ct/list/c14151.htm

29 http://www.wnd.com/2015/11/big-list-all-these-terror-attacks-in-u
-s-covered-up-by-feds/

30 http://www.breitbart.com/big-government/2015/11/16/since-911-u
-s-accepted-2-million-migrants-majority-muslim-nations/

31 http://www.washingtonexaminer.com/byron-york-trump-and
-muslims-by-the-numbers/article/2577962

32 http://www.breitbart.com/video/2015/12/27/former-dhs-secretary
-tom-ridge-middle-eastern-refugee-pause-appropriate-at-this-time/

33 http://pamelageller.com/2015/10/fbi-no-way-to-screen-refugees
-coming-to-u-s.html/

34 http://lastresistance.com/poll-70-of-american-muslims-vote
-democrat-only-11-vote-republican/

35 http://www.rasmussenreports.com/public_content/politics/
current_events/iran/most_think_iran_unlikely_to_honor_nuclear
_weapons_deal

36 http://thehill.com/blogs/ballot-box/presidential-races/253027
-clinton-backing-iran-deal-as-part-of-larger-strategy

37 http://www.un.org/en/sc/2231/restrictions-ballistic.shtml

38 https://www.armscontrol.org/factsheets/Security-Council
-Resolutions-on-Iran

39 http://www.politifact.com/truth-o-meter/statements/2016/mar/17/
    donald-trump/no-donald-trump-we-are-not-giving-iran-150-b
40 Ibid.
41 Ibid.
42 Ibid.
43 http://www.thedailybeast.com/articles/2014/05/15/hillary-clinton
    -celebrates-the-iran-sanctions-that-her-state-department-tried-to
    -stop.html
44 http://www.quotationspage.com/quote/3235.html
45 http://www.thedailybeast.com/articles/2014/05/15/hillary-clinton
    -celebrates-the-iran-sanctions-that-her-state-department-tried-to
    -stop.html
46 Ibid.
47 Ibid.
48 Ibid.
49 Ibid.
50 Ibid.
51 https://www.facebook.com/IsraeliPM/posts/759021880779226
52 http://www.iar-gwu.org/node/428
53 http://www.npr.org/sections/parallels/2015/07/16/423562391/
    lifting-sanctions-will-release-100-billion-to-iran-then-what
54 Ibid.
55 http://www.breitbart.com/big-government/2015/07/27/iran-deal
    -worth-more-than-all-u-s-aid-to-israel-since-1948/
56 http://www.centredaily.com/news/business/article69159007.html
57 http://www.cbsnews.com/news/new-us-sanctions-concession-to
    -iran-may-be-in-works-ap/
58 https://www.washingtonpost.com/world/national-security/nuclear
    -deal-with-iran-scrutinized-by-experts/2015/07/17/8a53aaae-2c92
    -11e5-bd33-395c05608059_story.html
59 Ibid.
60 http://english.aawsat.com/2015/08/article55344933/opinion
    -kennedy-nixon-reagan-and-obamas-illusions
61 http://www.npr.org/2015/07/20/424571368/if-iran-violates-nuke
    -deal-a-look-at-how-sanctions-would-snap-back
62 http://www.nytimes.com/2015/07/23/world/middleeast/
    provision-in-iran-accord-is-challenged-by-some-nuclear
    -experts.html
63 Ibid.

64 http://thehill.com/blogs/ballot-box/gop-primaries/264598-trump
    -iran-deal-was-so-bad-its-suspicious

65 http://www.nationalreview.com/article/424039/ted-cruz-iran-deal
    -politifact-nuclear-weapons

66 http://www.realclearpolitics.com/epolls/other/obama_and
    _democrats_health_care_plan-1130.html

67 https://twitter.com/dcexaminer/status/667432207481466880

68 http://www.washingtonexaminer.com/doctors-boycotting
    -californias-obamacare-exchange/article/2540272/doctors
    -boycotting-californias-obamacare-exchange/article/2540272

69 http://www.newsmax.com/Newsfront/americans-refuse-buy
    -obamacare/2014/03/17/id/560102/

70 http://www.nytimes.com/2016/03/30/us/politics/newest
    -policyholders-under-health-law-are-sicker-and-costlier-to-insurers
    .html

71 http://thehill.com/policy/healthcare/266776-president-pushes
    -obamacare-as-enrollment-deadline-nears

72 http://freebeacon.com/politics/clinton-stumped-health-care-cost
    -question-tells-voter-keep-shopping/

73 http://freebeacon.com/politics/clinton-stumped-health-care-cost
    -question-tells-voter-keep-shopping/

74 http://www.zerohedge.com/news/2015-09-25/obama-promised
    -healthcare-premiums-would-fall-2500-family-they-have-climbed-4865

75 http://www.nytimes.com/2015/11/15/us/politics/many-say-high
    -deductibles-make-their-health-law-insurance-all-but-useless.html

76 http://thehill.com/policy/healthcare/264530-stronger-obamacare
    -faces-new-fights-in-2016

77 http://www.nytimes.com/2015/11/15/us/politics/many-say-high
    -deductibles-make-their-health-law-insurance-all-but-useless.html

78 http://usc.247sports.com/Board/59419/Contents/ACA-approval
    -climbing-30062679

79 http://www.politifact.com/obama-like-health-care-keep/

80 http://www.heritage.org/research/reports/2013/11/what-obamacares
    -pay-for-performance-programs-mean-for-health-care-quality

81 https://www.hillaryclinton.com/briefing/factsheets/2015/09/23/
    clinton-plan-to-lower-out-of-pocket-health-care-costs/

Chapter 4   Throw the Left Hook!—Destroy the Obama/Hillary Base

1   http://www.nydailynews.com/news/politics/trump-u-s-race
-relations-bad-article-1.2351264

2   http://www.cnsnews.com/news/article/terence-p-jeffrey/7231000
-lost-jobs-manufacturing-employment-down-37-1979-peak

3   http://www.epi.org/publication/manufacturing-job-loss-trade-not
-productivity-is-the-culprit/

4   https://www.census.gov/foreign-trade/balance/c5700.html

5   http://www.reliableplant.com/Read/23597/US-job-loss-China

6   http://www.bloomberg.com/politics/articles/2015-06-18/after
-doubting-economists-find-china-killing-u-s-factory-jobs

7   Ibid.

8   Ibid.

9   http://www.uscc.gov/sites/default/files/3.30.11Scott.pdf

10   http://money.cnn.com/2015/09/10/investing/china-dumping-us
-debt/

11   http://www.reuters.com/article/us-china-northamerica-lobbying
-idUSBRE87L15N20120823

12   http://www.cbsnews.com/news/chinese-company-pledged-2
-million-to-clinton-foundation-in-2013/

13   Ibid.

14   http://www.albrightstonebridge.com/regions/china-east-asia
-oceania

15   https://www.census.gov/foreign-trade/balance/c2010.html

16   https://www.youtube.com/watch?v=Rkgx1C_S6ls

17   http://www.nytimes.com/2014/06/01/world/americas/as-ties-with
-china-unravel-us-companies-head-to-mexico.html?_r=0

18   Ibid.

19   http://www.ontheissues.org/2016/Donald_Trump_Free_Trade
.htm

20   http://www.theindychannel.com/news/local-news/how-much
-might-carrier-save-by-moving-to-mexico

21   http://www.ontheissues.org/2016/Donald_Trump_Free_Trade
.htm

22   https://talkingunion.wordpress.com/2015/10/05/five-union
-presidents-oppose-tpp-treaty/

23   https://www.americarisingpac.org/in-hard-choices-hillary-clinton
-praised-tpp/

24 http://www.altersummit.eu/accueil/article/tisa-or-the-secret
    -agreement
25 Ibid.
26 Ibid.
27 http://cis.org/all-employment-growth-since-2000-went-to
    -immigrants
28 Ibid.
29 http://www.breitbart.com/big-hollywood/2015/12/30/obamas-agency
    -reveals-plan-give-work-permits-myriad-foreign-college-graduates/
30 Ibid.
31 Ibid.
32 http://www.bls.gov/oes/current/oes_nat.htm
33 http://www.bls.gov/opub/reports/cps/characteristics-of-minimum
    -wage-workers-2014.pdf
34 http://money.cnn.com/2013/09/15/news/economy/income
    -inequality-obama/
35 http://money.cnn.com/2015/09/02/investing/donald-trump-wall
    -street/
36 http://davidstockmanscontracorner.com
37 http://www.cnbc.com/id/43598606
38 http://www.cnbc.com/id/49031991
39 http://www.cnbc.com/id/49031991
40 http://seekingalpha.com/article/3756796-number-of-banks-in-the
    -banking-system-continues-to-decline-in-the-third-quarter
41 http://thehill.com/homenews/campaign/256851-trump-economic
    -bubble-about-to-burst
42 http://www.nytimes.com/2015/09/18/business/with-trump-as-foe
    -carried-interest-tax-loophole-is-vulnerable.html?_r=0
43 http://www.nytimes.com/interactive/2015/05/16/us/politics/
    document-hillary-clintons-financial-disclosure-form.html?_r=1
44 http://www.motherjones.com/politics/2015/11/watch-bernie
    -sanders-hillary-clinton-wall-street
45 Ibid.
46 Ibid.
47 Ibid.
48 http://www.commondreams.org/views/2015/12/09/what-clinton
    -gets-right-and-wrong-about-wall-street-reform

Chapter 5   Peel Away Hillary's Base Constituencies

1   http://elections.nytimes.com/2012/results/president/exit-polls
2   http://www.theguardian.com/world/2012/nov/09/single-women
    -voted-favour-obama
3   http://elections.nytimes.com/2012/results/president/exit-polls
4   Ibid.
5   http://www.gallup.com/poll/183434/americans-choose-pro-choice
    -first-time-seven-years.aspx
6   Ibid.
7   https://books.google.com/books?id=K7eUCgAAQBAJ&pg=PT
    53&lpg=PT53&dq=For+two+decades+I've+been+urging
    +politicians+to+open+the+schoolhouse+doors&source=bl&ots
    =W_xw8Iuo5w&sig=_0vDn_hTxtlpSzTl28Joa9GdHhQ&hl
    =en&sa=X&ved=0ahUKEwi1kPCAxsHMAhWFB5oKHXJqB30
    Q6AEIJTAB#v=onepage&q=For%20two%20decades%20I've%20
    been%20urging%20politicians%20to%20open%20the%20
    schoolhouse%20doors&f=false
8   http://www.gallup.com/poll/1612/education.aspx
9   https://en.wikipedia.org/wiki/Albert_Shanker
10 http://www.maciverinstitute.com/2013/12/workers-shoot-down
    -unions-in-wisconsin/
11 http://www.rasmussenreports.com/public_content/lifestyle/
    questions/may_2015/questions_education_update_may_17_18
    _2015
12 http://www.politico.com/story/2015/12/hillary-clinton-errors
    -campaign-217185#ixzz3vjcIMvY0
13 http://articles.philly.com/2015-02-17/news/59200784_1_charter
    -enrollment-low-performing-charter-schools-charter-seats
14 http://nces.ed.gov/programs/coe/indicator_cgb.asp
15 Ibid.
16 http://www.onenewsnow.com/education/2015/12/10/school-choice
    -a-priority-for-black-voters
17 Ibid.
18 http://www.cnn.com/ELECTION/2010/results/polls/#val
    =WIG00p1
19 http://hechingerreport.org/can-you-steal-an-education/
20 Ibid.
21 http://www.timesherald.com/article/JR/20140128/NEWS/
    140129636

22 http://hechingerreport.org/can-you-steal-an-education/
23 Ibid.
24 Ibid.
25 Ibid.
26 Ibid.
27 http://thehill.com/opinion/columnists/dick-morris/287767
    -latinos-could-be-gop-allies
28 http://www.foxnews.com/politics/interactive/2016/04/14/fox-news
    -poll-national-release-april-14-2016/
29 https://www.washingtonpost.com/news/the-fix/wp/2016/02/22/
    younger-votes-didnt-come-through-for-bernie-sanders-because
    -they-almost-never-do/
30 http://www.nationaljournal.com/politics/2013/12/04/millennials
    -abandon-obama-obamacare
31 Ibid.
32 Ibid.
33 http://www.brainyquote.com/quotes/quotes/w/woodyallen145883
    .html

 # Simple **Heart Test**

Take the Test Now . . .

FACT: Nearly half of those who die from heart attacks each year never showed prior symptoms of heart disease.

Right now, millions of people over age 40 are suffering from heart disease and do not even know it!

FACT: If you suffer cardiac arrest outside of a hospital, you have just a 7% chance of survival.

Don't be caught off guard. Know your risk now.

Renowned cardiologist **Dr. Chauncey Crandall** has partnered with **Newsmaxhealth.com** to create a simple, easy-to-complete, online test that will help you understand your heart attack risk factors. Dr. Crandall is the author of the #1 best-seller *The Simple Heart Cure: The 90-Day Program to Stop and Reverse Heart Disease.*

Take Dr. Crandall's Simple Heart Test — it takes just 2 minutes or less to complete — it could save your life!

YOU'LL DISCOVER:

- **Where you score on our unique heart disease risk scale**
- Which of your lifestyle habits really protect your heart
- **The true role your height and weight play in heart attack risk**
- Little-known conditions that impact heart health
- Plus much more!

Discover your risk for heart disease now.

Go To: SimpleHeartTest.com/2016